ST. PAUL'S

EPISTLES TO THE CORINTHIANS:

AN

ATTEMPT TO CONVEY THEIR SPIRIT
AND SIGNIFICANCE.

By JOHN HAMILTON THOM.

REPRINTED FROM THE ENGLISH EDITION.

BOSTON:
CROSBY, NICHOLS, AND COMPANY,
111 Washington Street.
NEW YORK:
CHARLES S. FRANCIS AND COMPANY.
1852.

CAMBRIDGE:
METCALF AND COMPANY,
PRINTERS TO THE UNIVERSITY.

TO

THE REVEREND JAMES MARTINEAU.

My Dear Friend,—

Had I the hope of producing a Work more worthy your acceptance, I might postpone the gratification of joining your name with mine upon this page. As it is, I at least take the first opportunity of offering you this expression of grătitude and friendship ; and in making even this book my tribute to you, I try to feel that there is some fitness,—perhaps I should rather say that I am enabled to do so with the more courage,—inasmuch as, among living men, I know no one who will receive with readier welcome, or view with more generous indulgence, the humblest Work that aims to exhibit spiritual Christianity, as God's provision for the deep and glorifying Wants, that arise out of the inherent *religiousness* of Human Nature.

JOHN HAMILTON THOM.

Oakfield, Liverpool, *April 14th,* 1851.

PREFACE.

I WARN off scholars, and deep students of the Scriptures, from these pages. They are designed for the unlearned; for those whose only qualification for the reception of religious Truth is in the desire, that spiritual Things may by them be spiritually discerned; and who seek and worship Truth, as they worship and seek after God, with a hunger and thirst for Realities, and with a Love that casts out Fear. For such I think something, indeed much, needs yet to be done, to bring them into any actual communion with the mind and spirit of St. Paul.

This work will not serve for all the purposes of a Commentary. It does not attempt to solve every difficulty of expression; nor even to notice all the accidental views, the investiture of circumstance and tradition, which were clearly not inherent in the soul of Paul, nor essential to his conception of the spirit of Life in Christ Jesus. I have not indeed avoided these matters when they lay in my way;

much less have I tried to conceal that such things are; or sought to make St. Paul think like a modern, and write to the Corinthians, in the first century of Christianity, as one sometimes, with longing, conceives of a Prophet and Apostle speaking to England and Englishmen in the nineteenth. But I have not gone far, nor frequently, out of my direct way for the sake of matters of mere antiquarian interest, that have no permanent relation to the human Soul, or to Christian Truth. What I undertake to exhibit is the strong, clear current of spiritual Thought in the Apostle's mind, not all the immaterial elements it may have held in solution, or mechanically carried in its course.

And in these days of so much negative and destructive inquiry into the foundations and history of Religion, whilst I recognize the Holiness of such labors, and, whatever be their conclusions, honor all *reverential* laborers, as heartily as I revolt from the indecent bravado which sets aside all that, in all Ages, the human Soul has proclaimed and trusted of the God who inspires it, as nothing worth in the view of a flippant Dogmatism that, with heartless levity, throws down sacred things to make a pile for self-display; whilst in this age of idolatry, and of unspiritual gods, of bondage to the letter and to forms, I admit the indispensable necessity of showing plainly that we have the heavenly treasure only in earthen vessels, — I think there is at least equal need, just at present, of showing, lovingly and reverently, the imperishable Truth which these earthly vessels convey, — that it is at least as important, just now, for the best interests of religious Man, to save the kernel, as to withdraw the husk. For all those who have free souls, and are willing to be taught, the destructive work has been sufficiently done: the more difficult task remains. I believe that in these Epistles St. Paul proclaims some views of Religion, not yet recognized as his, "the excellency of whose power" is still of God, inasmuch as, through the divine attraction of spiritual *Realities*, of a living Word, a human Impersonation of His own moral glory, they transcend the perishing letter of Form and Speculation, and draw the Soul into direct communion with God Himself.

The several Sections of this work are so closely founded on the Scripture they embrace, in many cases are so interwoven with the Apostle's own language, that they will not be fully intelligible in themselves, nor in their transitions of topic, and much less as an elucidation of St. Paul, unless the reader is freshly familiar with his expressions and order of thought, in the portions of the Epistles to which they relate. These Chapters, or portions of Chapters, I have prefixed to each Section; and I would say here, that those who will not *first* carefully read these Chapters, had better lay down the book at once. It will not aid them; and they will do it injustice: they will not be in a position to estimate it aright. A mechanical imperfection in the execution of the Book, not discovered till too late, — the want of minute marginal references to the passages of St. Paul from which each paragraph is derived, — has perhaps this advantage, that it renders indispensable a previous and independent study of the whole Scriptural Text of each Section. I found it unavoidable to introduce some revisions of the Authorized Version. In this difficult task I have consulted with much benefit the Translations of the late Mr. Edgar Taylor, and of Mr. Sharpe.

As some of the elucidations I have attempted of the spirit and purport of St. Paul, through examples of their permanent application and significance, may seem to place me in the position of a Censor and Reprover in relation to some existing controversies, and some immediate, but passing, interests, I wish to state that the work was written nine years ago, in the service of my Congregation, and is now published, unchanged.

CONTENTS.

First Epistle.

PART I. (Chaps. I. - IV.)

THE DISSENSIONS OF THE CORINTHIAN CHURCH.

PART II. (Chaps. V. - XI.)

THE IMMORALITIES AND PERPLEXITIES OF THE CORINTHIAN CHURCH.

Second Epistle.

PART I. (Chaps. I. - VII.)

ADMONITIONS, AND EXPLANATIONS OF SPIRITUAL CHRISTIANITY, ADDRESSED CHIEFLY TO THAT PORTION OF THE CORINTHIAN CHURCH WHOSE AFFECTIONS, BY HIS FIRST EPISTLE, WERE REGAINED TO PAUL.

THE FIRST EPISTLE OF ST. PAUL TO THE CORINTHIANS.

PART I.

(CHAPS. I.–IV.)

THE DISSENSIONS OF THE CORINTHIAN CHURCH.

ST. PAUL'S FIRST EPISTLE TO THE CORINTHIANS.

PART I.

(CHAPTERS I.–IV.)

SECTION I.*

INTRODUCTION. — DIVISIONS IN THE CHURCH, — NO LEGITIMATE PLACE FOR THEM IN A RELIGION WHICH WAS NEITHER A PHILOSOPHY, NOR A SYSTEM OF DOCTRINES, NOR A LAW, BUT A SPIRIT OF LIFE, — OF WHICH GOD ALONE WAS THE GIVER, AND CHRIST ALONE THE CHANNEL OF THE GIFT.

CHAP. I. 1–31.

1 PAUL, called by the will of God to be an Apostle of
2 Jesus Christ, and Sosthenes† our brother, — To the
Church of God that is at Corinth, to them that are
sanctified in Christ Jesus, called to be saints, with all

* St. Paul first visited Corinth about 51 A. D., and wrote the First Epistle to the Corinthians from Ephesus, about 56 A. D. — Acts xviii.; 1 Cor. xvi. 8.

† Acts xviii. 17.

in every place that call upon the name of Jesus Christ
3 our Lord, their Lord and ours, — Grace be unto you,
and peace from God our Father, and from the Lord
Jesus Christ.
4 I thank my God always on your behalf for the grace
5 of God given to you in Jesus Christ, — that in every
thing you are enriched in him, in all utterance and
6 knowledge, — so that the testimony [evidence] of Christ
7 has been confirmed among you, — and you come behind
in no gift, waiting to receive the revealing of our Lord
8 Jesus Christ; who will also confirm you until the end,
9 blameless in the day of our Lord Jesus Christ. God
is faithful, by whom ye were called into the fellowship
of his Son, Jesus Christ our Lord.
10 I beseech you, brethren, by virtue of the name of
our Lord Jesus Christ, that ye all speak the same thing,
that there be no divisions among you, and that ye be
perfectly joined together in the same mind and in the
11 same sentiment. For it hath been declared unto me of
you, my brethren, by those of the house of Chloe,* that
12 there are contentions among you. This I mean, that you
say severally, "I am of Paul," and, "I am of Apollos,"
13 and, "I of Cephas," and, "I of Christ." Is Christ divided? Was Paul crucified for you? Or, were you
14 baptized into the name of Paul? I thank God that I bap-
15 tized none of you, but Crispus † and Gaius,‡ — so that no
16 one can say I baptized into my own name. I baptized,
too, the household of Stephanas: § besides, I know not
whether I baptized any other.

---

* Conjectured to be the mother of Fortunatus and Achaicus, who, with Stephanas, are supposed to be the bearers of a letter from the church at Corinth to St. Paul, to which this Epistle (chap. vii. 1) is in part a reply. — See ch. xvi. 17.

† Acts xviii. 3. ‡ Rom. xvi. 23. § 1 Cor. xvi. 15.

17 For Christ sent me not to baptize, but to preach
the Gospel: not in the wisdom of words [Argument],
18 lest the cross of Christ be made of none effect. For
the doctrine of the cross is foolishness to those who
are yielding themselves to ruin, but the power of God
19 to those of us who are willing to be saved. For it is
written, "I will destroy the wisdom of the wise, and
bring to nothing the understanding of the prudent." *
20 Where is the Wise? where is the Scribe? where is the
Disputer of this world? Hath not God proved foolish
21 the wisdom of this world? For when, in the wisdom
of God, the world through wisdom knew not God, it
pleased God by the foolishness of preaching to save
22 those who have faith. The Jews indeed require Signs,
23 and the Greeks seek after Wisdom: but we preach
Christ crucified, to the Jews an offence, and to the
24 Gentiles foolishness; but to the called, both Jews and
Greeks, Christ the power of God and the wisdom of
25 God. Because this foolishness of God is wiser than
men: and this weakness of God is stronger than men.
26 For you see your calling [class], brethren, that there
are not many wise after the flesh, not many mighty,
27 not many noble: but God hath chosen the foolish things
of the world to shame the wise; and God hath chosen
the weak things of the world to put to shame the mighty;
28 and the ignoble and despised things of the world hath
God chosen, and things that are not, to bring to naught
29 things that are; that no flesh should glory in the pres-
30 ence of God. But of him are ye in Christ Jesus, who
hath been made unto us wisdom from God, and right-
31 eousness, and sanctification, and redemption; so that, as
it is written, "Let him that glorieth glory in the Lord." †

---

* Isaiah xxix. 14. † Jeremiah ix. 24.

1 *

It is no easy matter for a modern European to conceive, with any truth, the state of things that presented itself to a Christian Apostle entering, for the first time, one of the great cities of Greece or Asia Minor. The materials for such a conception exist only in the indirect and evanescent reflections of ancient life and manners which a fragmentary literature presents; and much easier is it, from the remains that are left to us, to reconstruct one of the *Cities* of classic antiquity, to bring back the exact image of Athens or Pompeii, than to people its streets with veritable copies from the antique, — to picture with any reality the living throngs of Corinth, that Venice of the ancient world,* or to penetrate to the varied heart and inner spirit of that motley society, where Greek and Asiatic, Roman and Jew, trader and philosopher, Egyptian magician, sophist, and travelling impostor of every description, passed and repassed between the commercial capital of the West, that point of conflux, and the scattered cities of the East. Corinth itself was but a new city, raised from its ruins and rebuilt by Julius Cæsar. From its central situation on the Isthmus, as the gates of Greece, through which passed all communication between the Eastern and the Western Worlds, it had sprung at once into magnificence. Every thing in it was young, fresh, restless, unsettled. It was a state of society in which there were no conservative influences, no venerable usages, — where even the temples and the gods had no great

* Milman's History of Christianity, Vol II. p. 20.

antiquity to boast of, and where accordingly every variety of man, every new theory and speculation, might meet on nearly equal ground, and have a fair struggle for predominance. Now let us venture to enter this Corinth along with the Apostle, and witness his reception.

Gentile and idolatrous cities were, it is true, to him no novelties. He was himself Paul of Tarsus, a city of Cilicia, and since his conversion he had witnessed to the Truth amid the splendid temples of Asia, and stood upon Mars' Hill in Athens. It was with no unprepared spirit, with no narrow, local, and unfurnished mind, with no incompetent experience, or exclusive development of his own religious nature, that the missionary of Christ appeared among these struggling individualities to announce a universal and all-reconciling Faith. With no surprise or flurry of spirit, but with a calm and understanding eye, as a man who knew what he had to expect, would he pass along through temples, and sacred groves, and theatres, and processions, until he came to the obscurer quarters where his countrymen lived apart, and endeavored, as far as might be, to shut out idolatrous spectacles. To these expectants of Israel's Messiah, he would announce the Gospel of the *Saviour of the World;* and the Jew of Palestine, who cared nothing for the World, but only for the Israel of God, would denounce the supposed apostate from Judaism as the most accursed of blasphemers,—whilst the Jew of Alexandria, who had been brought into contact with the philosophies of Plato and the East, and had worn off the rigid nationality of the

Palestinian, would seize, with more avidity than fidelity, on the new ideas of Christianity, as a means of reconciling his old faith with his later and foreign speculations. And if, as a mean between these two, a Jew of the old school should be found to give a more favorable reception to the "testimony respecting Jesus," it would be only as to the long expected consummation of Judaism; and without accepting its more spiritual and universal elements, he would take it to be the completion of the National Religion in the subjugation of the other religions of the earth.

Expelled from the Synagogue, yet with such of its members as might have some points of affinity with the more generous faith (and at Corinth it happened that even the chief ruler was one of those),* St. Paul, in the expressive figure of the times, would "shake his raiment" before the Jews; and casting off upon themselves all responsibility for their decision, betake himself to the Gentiles. With them he would meet, if not a very earnest or respectful, yet an easy and a willing reception, so long at least as he had the power to keep their curiosity alive,— for Paganism was not deficient in toleration, except towards a religion that aimed at its destruction. Polytheism indeed could not, with any consistency, denounce the claim to notice of any new worship, nor was such exclusiveness the genius of the Greek. Paul at Athens was supposed to be only desirous of introducing some new divinity into the already full

* Acts xviii. 8.

Pantheon; and not immediately would Christianity come to be apprehended in its character of destructiveness, not as claiming a share for itself, but as the total subverter of Polytheistic worship, — making the universe and the soul the only fit temples of the One Everlasting and Omnipresent. With such minds the difficulty would be to obtain a reception for the new religion, not as a Philosophy, but as *a Life;* not as a source of intellectual or speculative interest, but as a moral spirit, breathing tender and purifying influences into the affections, developing the force of conscience, withdrawing the soul from the outer shrine to the voice of the eternal Spirit within the breast, and conforming the entire man to that divine harmony, that holy will of God, of which conscience is the faint announcer in each soul, and Christ the perfect image. The Grecian mind was extravagantly addicted to fanciful, and speculative, philosophizing; and largely used its religion as a means of sanctifying its vices, of elevating its vilest desires into the worship of some patron God presiding over the earthly and passionate elements of our mixed nature, — converting deeds of darkness into the mysteries of a sacred service; and if Christianity, through native force and the vigor of its great Apostle, made its way into such minds, there could be little hope that it should take no taint or bias from such souls, that it should all at once maintain an absolute independence on their past practices, and not be drawn into the vortex of the prevailing intellectual and practical habits. We often ask, Why does not Christianity work greater and more instant effects?

We forget that Christianity can get into a man's soul only through the existing sympathies and affinities he may happen to have with it; and that it exercises a moral power only through the love, and free will, of every heart. Now the Corinthian, though drawn to the Gospel by some secret and powerful sympathy, would not on the instant cease to be the man he had been; — he was not prepared to forget in a moment his favorite philosophy, or to renounce at once his former indulgences; and the tendency would rather be to engraft, as far as possible, his old ideas and usages on the new and healthy stock of Christianity, than to find for it immediately a clear admission into an empty bosom.

Such, then, were some of the elements of contention that divided the unity of every Gentile Church. They all had their origin in previous habits, or attachment to system, which prevented the reception of Christianity simply as a moral influence, as a spirit of Life penetrating and remodelling the heart, and breathing its purity and beneficence into the character. Putting aside the unbelieving Jews, there were the *Palestinians*, some of whom recognized Jesus only as the Messiah of the Jews, and these waited for his second coming and his Messianic reign; whilst others of them would accept the idea of his being the Saviour of the World, only by compelling the World to take upon it the yoke of Moses, as well as the spiritual rule of Christ: these two divisions, the most exclusively Jewish, ranged themselves in Corinth under the name of Peter (Cephas in the Aramean dialect), as the Apostle of the Circumcision. Then there were the *Alexandrians*, who connected both Judaism and Christianity with Orientalism, whose grand philosophical problem was the speculation on Evil, and who believed that God, retiring from all communication with matter, conducted the creation and government of the world through mediatorial Emanations from himself, of which emanations Christ was the chief. This is the party known in the Church by the name of Gnostics, and at Corinth Apollos was their reputed leader: whilst among the *Grecians* there was the philosophic party, who, like the orthodox of the present day, identified Christianity with some speculative tenets; — and what we may call the Antinomian party, who were either the insincere and unworthy disciples of all ages, disciplined by their own passions, not by the spirit of the Son of God, — or the prototypes of those fanatics of later times (and this is the *tendency* of all doctrines that teach the native corruption of man), who have maintained that the body was so radically and incurably worthless, that it might be given over to corruption without imparting contamination to the associated soul, that had no common essence with it, and was of another element.

It was to maintain the unity of the Church Universal against these unspiritual strifes, that St. Paul wrote the First Epistle to the Corinthians; and the great principle unfolded in it is the practical spirit, the *moral* force of Christianity, — that it is neither a philosophy, nor a system of doctrines, nor a ritual, nor a law; — that any of these may combine with it, or refuse to combine with it, without affecting its essence or its efficacy,—for that it is itself a baptism of the heart and of the moral affections into the spirit of the life of Christ,—a baptism not by Paul, nor Cephas, nor Apollos, but by the Holy Ghost,—a devotion of the whole man, not to any theories or speculations whatsoever, but to the mercy, the self-denial, the trust in God even to death, of the cross of Christ. Here have we from an Apostle, and he the most speculative and theoretical of them all, an exposition of the sources of Christian unity;—and putting aside the superficial differences of the intellect, he penetrates to the deep, unchanging heart of man, and declares that all are of the Body of Christ in whom his spirit of love and consecration lives and works,—and that this is the fellowship of the Son of God, to be so united to him by inward bonds, that through the imitation and the obedience of love he is made unto us wisdom, and righteousness, and sanctification, and entire redemption.* We must bear in mind, then, the sectarian state of the Corinthian Church in the examination, to which we now proceed, of the first chapter of this Epistle.

It might be possible to present in a few words the train of ideas in this introductory chapter, but it is the duty of an expositor, not to give the bare thought, but if possible to let us into the spirit of the living writer, and to clothe the exposition with *his* individuality. I shall therefore aim chiefly to throw emphasis, as it were, on those passages that

* 1 Cor. i. 30.

are most characteristic of St. Paul, and are in his peculiar manner. And I shall often have to ask your attention to two of these characteristics, — the closeness with which he adheres to his object in writing; and the rapidity and effect with which he draws conclusions, and makes applications, without any formal approach or statement of the preliminary grounds, — leaving it to the reader to discover the suppressed premises. He is at once the most discursive, and the most condensed of writers, — discursive in allowing his thoughts and heart free play, — condensed, in the quantity of argument and emotion he concentrates on every subject which he touches on his rapid way.

In the very salutation, occupying the first three verses, he lifts a warring and distracted Church out of the hot and close atmosphere of local contentions, into the loftiness and serenity of catholic sentiment. He presents them to God as part of the Church Universal. He associates them with the communion of saints. Place and circumstance disappear, — for throughout the world, and in the world beyond the grave, the people of God, those who have fellowship with Christ, have one heart, and breathe one spirit. Inasmuch as each has some resemblance to *him*, all must have that common resemblance to one another. Here, in the very first sentence, we have the essence of the Epistle: — "Paul, an Apostle of Jesus Christ, and Sosthenes *our brother*, unto the Church of God which is at Corinth, called to be saints, with all, in every place, who are disciples of Jesus Christ our

2

Lord, who is *both their Lord and ours*, grace be unto you, and peace from God our Father, and from the Lord Jesus Christ." — "Though this Epistle," says Chrysostom,* "was written only to the Corinthians, yet he makes mention of all the faithful in the whole world, showing that as the universal Church should be *one*, though separated by many places, so much more ought that in the same city, — for if *place* separates, yet a common Lord unites."

From the 4th to the end of the 9th verse, St. Paul presents to the Corinthians the obligations and thankfulness of spirit they owed to God for a participation in the Gospel of his Son, suggesting that they should not by unchristian hearts show themselves unworthy of that grace which caused "the testimony concerning Christ to take root amongst them," — and that the same God who had called them into the fellowship of his Son, must desire to keep them in the same fellowship for ever.

In the 10th verse we have another instance of the closeness with which St. Paul keeps his aim before him, even in his forms of address: — "*In the name of the Lord Jesus Christ*," into whose fellowship you are called, how comes it that *other* names are mentioned among you, — or that you break the unity of that discipleship which you all have to Christ, by taking the names of fellow-disciples? "*You* are of Paul, and *you* of Apollos, and *you* of Cephas, and *you* of Christ. Is Christ *divided?* Was Paul crucified for you? were you baptized

* Quoted by Billroth, *Biblical Cabinet.*

into the name of Paul? I thank my God that I baptized none of you, with some trifling exceptions, — so that none of you can say I baptized into mine own name." It has been much questioned whether, by the clause "*and I of Christ,*" we are to understand that there was a *Christ party* in the Corinthian Church, by a monstrous abuse of words taking that name to designate some class peculiarity, — or whether by that clause St. Paul meant to signify that there were an exceptional number who refused discipleship to others, and took the name only of their great Master. There is nothing in the construction to indicate that those who called themselves "of Christ" were less sectarian than the others, — and as there evidently had sprung up in the Corinthian Church a strong opposition to the apostolical authority of Paul, a vehement Jewish party who deemed his Christian doctrine of freedom from the law, and of the spirituality of the Gospel, to be a scandalous innovation, it may be that in the name of the *Christ* party there is a covert attack on the *apostolic* character of St. Paul, intimating that he was not, like Peter, a personal disciple and companion of the Lord; — and we shall afterwards find, that against such a party St. Paul had expressly to defend the authenticity of his Apostolic commission.

The two verses from the 14th, in which he disowns all leadership amongst them, are in the most characteristic manner of St. Paul. The dash of indifference with which he treats the whole subject of Baptism, when he finds that the converts were taking class names from those who had baptized them, breathes at once his genuineness, and the scornfulness with which his natural temper sets aside all comparisons between spiritual realities and outward forms: "I thank God that I baptized none of you, except Crispus and Gaius";—and then, as if the matter had been too trivial to live distinctly in the memory, he adds, "and I baptized the family of Stephanas,—and whether I baptized any other of you I know not."

From the 17th verse to the end of the chapter, the preaching of *the Gospel* St. Paul declares to be his only business;—that Gospel, "the glad tidings" from God, which could in no way be made a source of separation, for that it had no connection whatever with that speculative philosophy about which men may differ, nor with that glory of individuals which bands men under leaders,—and had only to do with God, and sonship unto Him after the likeness of Christ,—with the free grace of the universal Father, and our obedience as loving children after the pattern of the faith and self-devotion of Christ upon the cross. All the *glory* of this belongs to the God who gave it,—and all the *leadership* to Christ crucified, the author and finisher of this Faith. And who, besides these, in the matter of Christianity, shall presume to put in a claim for an individuality of his own? Will the Gentile, whose Philosophy could not teach him the true God, nor save the world from polytheism? Will the Jewish Scribe, whose outward Law could not keep him in spiritual and saving connections with the God whom it revealed? Will the Sceptic and Disputer, whose highest Wisdom is to doubt, and who has arrived at no sound faith on any rock of the soul? St. Paul branches his declaration of the indestructible character of Christian unity against the Jew, who would identify the Gospel with a ritual law; and against the Gentile, who would identify it with some speculative system: "Christ sent me not to baptize, but to preach the Gospel,—and not with the word-power of philosophy, but with the heart-power of the cross. The Messianic Jew—sensual, earthly, and millennial in his conceptions of Messiah—takes offence at 'the word made flesh,' the meek Son of God, the Galilean and the crucified; and to the Greek, conversant only with airy speculations, the establishment of a divine kingdom through a suffering Son of God, sounds strange foolishness, and not worthy of the notice of philosophy.* But who can escape exposure under the practical test, 'By their fruits ye shall know them'? Where is the Philosopher? What eminence has he attained, what *fruits* has he gathered, as a teacher of religion and a revealer of God? Where is the Jewish Scribe or Rabbi? Did he ever discover for the world the reconciling Gospel of God? Where is the Disputer, Critic, and Sceptic? Has he been able by cavils and dialectics to bring his own soul into the light divine? If not, then let them all give way, and, instead of dismembering Christ by pretensions of their own, accept with united hearts the salvation of his incarnate Truth. When all these had failed to reveal religious truth, and to sanctify the

* Verses 17, 18.

soul, then God sent his Son. When the world in its own wisdom knew not God with any approach to *his* wisdom, then it pleased him, by the preaching of this which the scribe and the sophist deem foolishness, to save them that believe. The Jew requires an overwhelming exhibition of *outward* power,—and the Greek seeks an intellectual display of subtle wisdom,—but we preach a *moral* power and a *moral* wisdom; even Christ the Lord, who by his doctrine and his life hath given to his true disciples the spiritual *knowledge* of his Father, and practical *power* to become the sons of God."* And since the Gospel is the gift of God to a world that knew it not, how can Greek or Jew presume now to fasten his own individuality on that universal spirit, or to make a party within the bosom of that heavenly Truth to which neither the cold speculations of the one, nor the law-wisdom and outward righteousness of the other, was able to attain,—but which God by his Son revealed to the poor in spirit, and opened as a spring of living water in the hearts of the meek? Who can claim as his own, or find a source of divisions in the Gospel of God, the Gospel of repentance and forgiveness, and the new life after the image of the obedience of Christ? The glory is God's,—for the gift is his, and *all* are his children, who by union with his Christ are formed into one spiritual family, sanctified in heart and life. This is St. Paul's idea of Christian unity; this the inward bond of the Church Universal. To partake of the spirit of

* Verses 19-24.

Christ is to be of the communion of the saints:* and to set up any other pretensions, to speak of any other qualifications, is the only heresy.†

I need not point out how healing would be the application of these catholic principles to our own times and our own hearts. How unavailingly has Paul written and preached! His writings are turned against himself; — his purposes frustrated by perversions of his own words. He is quoted in support of principles which he would have deemed destructive of the universality of the Gospel, — for he knew but of one Gospel, the union of the soul with God through the love of Christ. How can men read this chapter, and break the Christian unity by demanding other terms of Church-fellowship than some love and reverence in each heart for one common Lord, — some reflections on each spirit from him, the image of God! But we must be willing to include those in the Church Universal who would exclude us. In whatever soul we see breathings of the goodness of God, of the love of Christ, we must recognize the closest bond of Christian brotherhood, and see one of the spiritual family of the invisible Father, of the Church of God in heaven; — for there can be no eternal separation between souls that love a common master, — that revere a common image of the Father of spirits, — and whose desires, affections, and moral longings are the same.

---

* "In the strictest sense of essential, this alone is essential in Christianity, that the same spirit should be growing in us, which was in the fulness of all perfection in Christ Jesus." — *Coleridge.*

† "Schism and Separation."

SECTION II.

DISSENSIONS FROM SPECULATIVE SOURCES. — UNITY CANNOT BE BROKEN IN THINGS THAT ARE ONLY SPIRITUALLY DISCERNED, — WITH WHICH THE SPECULATIVE FACULTIES ARE NOT VITALLY CONCERNED.

CHAP. II. 1-16.

1 So I, brethren, when I came to you, came not in the
prominency of speech [Argument] or wisdom, declar-
2 ing unto you the testimony of God. For I determined
not to regard any thing among you, except Jesus Christ,
3 even him crucified. And I was with you in weakness,
4 and in fear, and in much trembling. And my doctrine,
and my preaching, was not in persuasive words of wisdom, but in demonstration of the spirit and of power;
5 that your faith may not be in the wisdom of men, but in
the power of God.
6 Yet we speak wisdom in the estimation of those
who are perfect, but not the wisdom of this world nor
7 of the rulers of this world, that come to naught: but
we speak the wisdom of God in his mystery, that
hidden wisdom which God ordained before the ages
8 unto our glory; which none of the rulers of this world
knew, for had they known it, they would not have
9 crucified the Lord of Glory, — but, as it is written,
" Eye did not see, and ear did not hear, neither entered
into the heart of man, the things which God prepared for

10 them that love Him." * But God has revealed them
to us through his † spirit; for the Spirit searcheth all
11 things, even the deeps of God. For what man knoweth
the things of a man, save the spirit of the man which is
in him? even so the things of God none knoweth, save
12 the spirit of God. Now we have received not the spirit
of the world, but the spirit that is of God, that we might
know the things that have been graciously given to us by
13 God: which things we publish, not in words [discourse]
taught by human wisdom, but in words [discourse] taught
by the spirit, explaining the spiritual by the spiritual.‡
14 But the animal man receiveth not the things of the
spirit of God, for they are foolishness to him, and he is
not able to know them, because spiritually are they dis-
15 cerned. But he who is spiritual discerneth all things,
yet himself is discerned by no one. For, "Who hath
known the mind of the Lord, that he may instruct
16 Him?" ‖ But we have the mind of Christ.

WHAT is Christianity? It is a practical power, a living energy, for the purpose of drawing the soul of man into connection with the spirit of God. And this it does, by awakening the spiritual affections of the mind through the impulse of sympathy with that heavenly model of humanity, who exhibited all the mixed elements of our nature in a state of harmony with the will of God. Whenever it is the medium of this divine attraction, whenever it brings

---

* Isaiah lxiv. 4.

† Or more probably, "through the spirit." — *Griesbach.*

‡ Or, "to those who are spiritual."

‖ Isaiah xl. 13, 14.

a soul into practical communion with the fountain of love and holiness, Christianity has accomplished its highest object; it has drawn a new member into the Church of God, a new subject into the kingdom of Heaven. And if it has really connected a soul with God, it matters not what was the particular feature of the full and perfect Christ that found a point of sympathy in the human heart, through which it was enabled to introduce itself into the affections, and imprint a divine image on the moral nature. Christ is a mediator between man and God, when, by some feeling of union with himself, some recognition communicated from him of that Heavenly Father of whom he is the image, he leads any heart, through this excitement of its spiritual nature, to unite itself in its inward life to the Father of spirits. This attraction to God through the power of his Christ is the essential spirit of Christianity,—what St. Paul calls "the energy of God in the Gospel." * Christianity is an instrument for effecting this purpose. Christ is the means that the wisdom of God, and the power of God, devised for this end. The infinite Father, removed by their sins, and outward superstitions, and speculative philosophies, from all spiritual communion with the hearts of his children, prepared a practical method for reuniting with himself these broken bonds of the human soul. He manifested *himself* in Christ, —he showed in his Son the image of his own love and holiness, that all his other children, drawn by

* Rom. i. 16.

this living appeal to that divine spirit which is in us all, might recognize in Christ the perfection of their nature, and through him be led upwards to the common source of goodness, — to *his* Father and our Father, to his God and our God: "This is life eternal, to know thee the only true God, and Jesus Christ whom thou hast sent." All those whom this love of Christ led to the love of God were the partakers of a common spirit; — a divine principle of life operated within their souls, in virtue of which they were the Church Universal — the family of the Heavenly Father, — the branches in connection with the living vine, the body of Christ.

There are but two ways, not ways of sin, in which this Christian unity can be broken. This inward communication of the heart with God, through the spiritual attraction of Christ, may be represented as so intimately connected with certain outward forms of devotion, or with certain systems of thought, that independently of them it can have no effective existence. The inward reality, the state of the affections in regard to God and Christ, may be represented as absolutely dependent on the outward methods which certain men have found effectual in their own cases, or through some intellectual peculiarities have imagined to be necessary. This is to violate the unity of the Christian spirit, — this is, in the language of St. Paul, "*to preach another Gospel*," to set aside as insufficient God's instrument of salvation. God has set forth his Christ as the means of drawing souls to himself, through moral sympathy with his Image; and all who are so attracted become his spiritual children, and through that principle in their souls which unites them with Christ they are endowed with power to become sons of God, after the likeness of him who attracted them, of the Lord who moved and won the better spirit in their hearts. But there have always been two classes of men who have not been contented with the moral power of God's Christ, as the medium of divine attraction and the instrument of salvation. These are, — first, the superstitious, whose states of soul are excited only by states of sense, and who cannot conceive the Divine Spirit communicating itself to man except through the observances with which in their own case they have exclusively associated the operations of His grace; — and, secondly, that class of minds in whom the speculative is the predominating element, and who, from some cold bias, or stern enthusiasm, of the speculative reason, connect the saving agencies of God, not with the spiritual affections of the believer's heart, but with the theological system that recommends itself to his states of thought. The Roman Catholic, and the members of the Anglican Church, the sacerdotal part of the Church of England, are, amongst us, the representatives of the superstitious Christian, — of the Jewish Christians of the days of St Paul. They say that a soul cannot be led into communion with God through the love of Christ alone. They say that though Christ is the only mediator, or means of attraction, between man and God, yet that there is a necessity for other mediators between man and Christ, — and that there is no true sympathy with

Jesus, except in those who have received the rite of baptism from a consecrated Priest in the direct line of the Apostolical succession, and who have partaken of the Lord's Supper from legitimate hands. These are the counterparts of those Corinthian opponents of St. Paul, the Jewish Christians, who maintained that Christ drew to God only the circumcised, and that the Holy Spirit disregarded the state of the affections and their moral oneness with Jesus, unless they were found keeping the Jewish law. The dogmatical Christians of this day, under all their varieties, are the counterparts of the speculative Christianity that prevailed among the Gentile converts of Corinth. They deny that Christ touches a soul with the spirit of God through the power of his character, and the overflowing fulness of that spirit in himself. They deny this direct spiritual attraction. They affirm that Christ touches a soul with the love of God, and sanctifies it by a divine affection, only when it adopts certain views of the metaphysical essence of the Deity, — only when it receives a certain theory of the nature of Evil, and of God's connection with it, and, in the spirit of the Gnostic Emanations, breaks the unity of God into three personalities, — the Father absolute and self-existent, — the Son, the first Emanation, eternally proceeding from the Father, — and the Holy Spirit, the second Emanation, eternally proceeding from the Father and the Son. Of these dogmatical Christians of our day, who make Salvation depend on an orthodoxy, and moral sympathy with God and with his Christ inseparable from certain speculative tenets, the philosophic, or theosophic, Christians of St. Paul's day, whether of the Grecian or of the Oriental school, were the counterparts. It gratifies me to be able to present, in the words of Blanco White, a lively and accurate picture of that state of philosophical orthodoxy (or theosophy, a pretended insight into the mysteries of God's nature and of the modes of his operation in the world), of that speculative dogmatism at Corinth, against the influence of which St. Paul contended as destructive of the catholic spirit of Christianity: —

"Christianity had been published only a very few years, when all the mystic and speculative sects commenced a series of efforts to incorporate the Gospel with their own tenets, and to graft their peculiar notions on the young and vigorous stock, whose branches, they could not but perceive, were about to spread far and wide. Although the writers of the New Testament do not mention the name of any philosophical sect except the Pharisees and Sadducees, it is clear to those acquainted with the doctrines of Eastern philosophy, that the notions from which Paul especially apprehended a danger to the simplicity of the Gospel belonged to those mystic systems, which, in some instances combined with Judaism, in others directly opposing it, were widely diffused soon after, under the name of Gnosis.

"But no warnings were sufficient to prevent a rapid growth of the evil which that Apostle feared and opposed. Men whose resources for wealth and distinction lay in the admiration of the multitude, saw a most favorable opportunity of rising in the world by availing themselves of the ardor with which the primitive converts had embraced the Gospel. Vain babblers, pretending to a deep and extensive knowledge of the invisible world, flocked to the infant Christian communities; and, such was their power over the ignorant and simple minds which made up the great majorities of those societies, that the founders of them found it difficult to maintain their own authority against them. Paul's distressing difficulties at Corinth are too vividly and feelingly described, in his two Epistles to the Church of that great city, to require assistance from another pen. But no tolerably well instructed reader of the New Testament can doubt that Paul's rivals belonged to the class of Judæo-philosophical speculatists. Paul's express determination to lay down all claims to that kind of knowledge which our version denominates '*wisdom*,' — to confine his teaching to the doctrine 'of Jesus Christ and him crucified,' — clearly points out by contrast what kind of preaching had seduced the minds of his converts. It is true, the Apostle mentions the names of James, Cephas, and Apollos, men who seem to have been guiltless of the spirit of party which made use of their names to oppose the authority of Paul. That the persons thus named were not really leaders of those divisions, is proved by the appearance of Paul's own name as the watchword of a party. Even the name of Christ was, we find, used for a similar purpose. The fact seems to have been, that, when various intruders undertook to reduce the Gospel to a philosophic system, each of them pretended to build his own speculations on the peculiar views — sometimes real, sometimes supposed — of the persons whose names they adopted as a party distinction.

"Besides the many remarkable passages of the two Epistles to the Corinthians, in which Paul's renunciation of all scientific teaching pointedly marks, in his rivals, a dangerous affectation of deep philosophy, there is a circumstance in the notices preserved concerning Apollos which is strongly confirmatory of the view, that the attempts of various teachers to *theorize* on Christianity was the chief source of Paul's anxiety. It is on record that Apollos was a native of Alexandria, the great seat of speculative philosophy at that period. This fact alone would be a fair ground for conjecturing that he belonged to the numerous class of Alexandrian Jews who, like Philo, united the study of the Old Testament with the idealistic and mystic system which was taught in the schools of that great city. But this conjecture will grow almost into certainty when the word which in the English version is translated *eloquent* shall be expressed by *learned*, which gives the true sense in that passage. In the public disputations with the Jews, Apollos must have found it necessary to employ all the subtlety of the Alexandrian school in defence of Christianity. He may at a subsequent period have been checked by Paul in the use of weapons which, though of service in dialectic contests, would be eventually injurious to the simplicity of the Christian system. But vain and light-minded Christians would naturally be allured by the public triumph of the Alexandrian, to imitate, and (as second-rate minds will always do) to exaggerate Apollos's manner and method. As we have the most powerful reasons to believe that Apollos himself was not actually at the head of an anti-Paulistic party, but remained in close friendship with the Apostle, we may safely conclude that his name was adopted for the purpose of expressing the nature of the system which his imitators professed to follow. In a similar manner we must conceive that the names of James * (who, as the local president of the congregation at Jerusalem, could not reside at Corinth) and of Cephas (who, as the Apostle of the Circumcision, is not likely to have ever been in Greece) were taken by other portions of the Corinthian Church, under the guidance of teachers who respectively pretended to follow the views which they described as peculiar to each of those distinguished Apostles." †

In contrast to such teachers, St. Paul, in our present chapter, refers both to *the matter* and *the manner* of his own ministration of the Gospel. He did not teach it as a *Rhetorician*, to attract admiration to himself, and give more lively impressions of Paul the Orator than of Christ the Redeemer from sin,— nor as a *Philosopher*, to raise doubtful questions on metaphysical subjects, and become the leader of a speculative School; but as the Apostle of Jesus Christ he proclaimed to the hearts of men the practical and life-giving Gospel, that "God was in

* This is a mistake: James is not mentioned in this connection.

† "Heresy and Orthodoxy."

Christ reconciling the world unto himself"; that by the universal Saviour all distinctions were for ever destroyed, and the whole family of God to grow into the common likeness of that well-beloved Son, — for that now neither circumcision availeth any thing, nor uncircumcision, but the renewal of the affections after the image of the Lord. Where could an entrance be found for party divisions in a Doctrine that professed nothing, that aimed at nothing, except to awaken the consciousness of sin within the heart, and, through trust in the God of holiness and love revealed in Jesus, to lead it to repentance and to life? All who felt this love of Christ constraining them, cleansing their souls through the divine image that had taken possession of their affections, and, through the Mercy it proclaimed, encouraging their penitence to look for pardon from their God, must of necessity be of one communion; — for this Gospel sentiment and hope could create no divisions amongst those who had it, — and those who had it not were outside the Christian pale, and, so far, could make no schisms within it. Now whence comes this Gospel sentiment, this new principle of life? Were there any who had the exclusive power of communicating it? Were there any who had power of withholding it? Did it require to be introduced by any intricate reasonings, by any subtle dialectics, which only the Masters in philosophy had at their command? Not so, says St. Paul: — it is a spiritual feeling, excited by moral sympathy, as soon as Christ is offered to the hearts that are susceptible of the sentiment; — and in whatever bosom there is not enough of the spirit of God to cause that moral attraction to take place, neither philosophy, nor outward forms, nor aught else but the divine image of goodness kept before the heart, can awaken the slumbering sensibilities which are the very faculties of spiritual apprehension, and which, as soon as they are alive, behold in Christ the solution of their own struggling and imperfect existence, their ideal and their rest. In regard to a sentiment so spiritual, a sympathy with the Image of God, where is the possibility of introducing party divisions, and violating Christian unity? There can be but two parties, — those that *have* the sentiment, and those that have it not. All Christians constitute the one, — and as for the other, in relation to Christian unity they are not in question. Such is the argument of St. Paul in this second chapter. Let us follow him through it.

(Verse 1.) " And I, brethren, came to you not in the pretensions of a Rhetorician or of a Philosopher to preach the Gospel of God; for I determined to profess no knowledge amongst you, except the knowledge of Jesus Christ, even him the crucified." I refused, says St. Paul, to connect the practical Gospel, the divine principle that showed itself in the life and death of Christ, with any speculative tenets whatsoever. " Christ crucified " was to every disciple the symbol of Christian faith and practice, the image of a life passed and sustained by a spirit in communion with God. This symbol is powerfully expressive; and the Scriptural references to it leave no doubt that it is a practical, not a doctrinal emblem,—that it is *a Sign*, not of speculative tenets, but of moral power, with which should be associated in the soul the filial trust, the unconquered love, the self-devotion of our Lord. The Scriptural usage, we say, leaves it in no doubt that *these* were the ideas intended to be awakened by the symbol "Christ crucified." "If any man will be my disciple," says our Lord himself, "*let him take up his cross*, and follow me." And what is the power that, in the very spirit of this chapter, St. Paul elsewhere ascribes to the cross of Christ?* A power to crucify worldly affections, and for God and the Truth's sake to rise superior to earthly sufferings. He boasts not of *knowledge*,—he pretends to no revelation of hidden things,—he possesses only a practical power derived from Christ to *conquer Evil:*—"I glory only in the cross of our Lord Jesus Christ, by whom the world is crucified unto me, and I unto the world."

And it cannot but strike us as very extraordinary, that these words, intended by St. Paul to express that he attached no importance to any thing but moral sympathy with the Christ of God, should now be cited in evidence that he attached no importance to any thing but certain doctrinal conceptions,—that, in fact, these words should now be quoted in support of a speculative conception of Christianity, which was the very conception of it that St. Paul used them to disclaim:—"We know nothing but Jesus Christ, and him crucified," say a certain class of preachers. But is this true? Do they not

* Gal. vi. 14.

pretend to know a vast deal more?—do they not connect this practical power and victory of the Christ, this life and death divine, after the very manner of St Paul's Gnostics, with doubtful speculations into the nature and origin of Evil,—with peculiar views of the metaphysical essence of the Deity,—with philosophical theories as to how God can operate on a human mind and pardon Sin?—and do they not, out of all these speculative elements, construct a System in which they find a place for Christ crucified,—a system which, whether true or false, is nowhere constructed in the Scriptures, and which is totally foreign to the genius of the practical Gospel? St. Paul, to avoid divisions on merely intellectual topics, declared, "I will know nothing, as affecting Christians, but the moral spirit that was in the life and death of Christ." And the Preachers of this day, in direct opposition, declare that "*only* to know this is to know *nothing*"; for that "*Christ crucified*" is only *one* part of a vast system,—which system arose in this way:—that there is an Evil Being in eternal conflict with God, a Dualism in the universe; that this Evil Being tempted Adam to sin; that this sin impregnated the whole of his race successively with the spirit of the Evil One, so that the Devil, and not God, is henceforth the Father of their moral natures; that God was willing to regenerate fallen man with a new spirit from himself, and to expel the Evil One, but that he *could* not do so in consistency with his Attributes, for his Authority had its claims as well as his Mercy, until some expiation had been offered to him, commensurate with the indignity he had suffered in the rebellion of his children; that, to meet this moral necessity of God's nature, there were in his essence three Infinite Persons, and that one of these Persons was willing to suffer in the place of men; that an infinite indemnity being thus provided for the immeasurable insult of sin, the Austerity of God no longer restrained his Love, and his sanctifying Spirit might now operate upon those who, by thankfully recognizing the substituted expiation, paid this tribute to his violated Authority. And, Is this *to know nothing* but Christ the crucified? Is not this to leave practical religion, and the moral spirit of the Gospel, for the sake of that very speculative theosophy, those theories about God and the origin of Evil, against which St. Paul so earnestly contends as destructive of the simplicity of the Gospel sentiment, "the renewed union of the heart with God through the moral attraction of his Christ"? And mark how, in the third and in the following verses to the sixth, St. Paul indicates that it was a moral conviction, a *spiritual* sentiment, which he had labored to implant in the deeper heart of this speculative and light-minded people. Philosophy has no moral anxiety about its reception in the world,—it produces its favorite system, or supposed demonstration, with undisturbed complacency. The Rhetorician has no tremors of the heart, no moral solicitude as to whether he shall touch the springs of life in the soul,—for his address is to the fancy and to the passions. But St. Paul, with something of the agony of his Master in Gethsemane, speaks of the solicitudes of a ministry addressed to the hearts and moral affections of men: — "And I was with you with none of the confident pretensions of a party leader, but in the consciousness of weakness, in holy fear and trembling, and my preaching was not directed towards speculative wisdom, but to excite within you the workings of that better spirit which is akin to the spirit of God, that your moral acceptance of the Christ — your faith — might not depend on the wisdom or rhetorical power of man, but, proceeding from the divine affections of your nature, should be founded on the persuasive power of God's spirit within you."

The remainder of the chapter, from the sixth verse, is a demonstration that Christianity, as a purely spiritual sentiment, is addressed only to the spiritual affections of man, — is understood only by that man who has in him some portion of God's spirit, — and that, being thus addressed to the divinest element of the soul, to that spiritual conscience which knows *no reasonings*, but is the *immediate* voice of God, it can be made a source of Divisions only when it is seized upon, as it were, from without, by the faculties that are not spiritual, — by the speculative ones that lead to System-building, or by the imaginative and sensuous ones that lead to the exaltation of outward Forms. I will attempt to convey the meaning that is contained in the passage from the sixth to the end of the tenth verse. "Although Christianity is not of the nature of speculative knowledge, yet to those who are spiritual it is the divinest wisdom, — not, indeed, the wisdom of men of the world, nor of the intellectual Leaders of the world, whose rule will be swept away before its power, — but a wisdom hitherto unknown to the world, and now, in the fulness of time, revealed by God to those who are of a spiritual mind, — a divine wisdom which the Leaders of the world had no perception of, for had they anticipated or sympathized with it, they would not have rejected the Lord who brought it; — as it is written, 'Eye *did not* see, and ear *did not* hear, and it did not enter into the heart of man to *preconceive* the revelations that God designed for all who love him.' But these revelations God has now made to our spiritual nature, — for it is only through that portion of his Spirit which he has communicated to ours, that we are enabled to enter into these deeps of God." The argument of St. Paul in this passage is simply this: — that Christianity, as not addressed to the speculative faculties, but as an immediate revelation to the diviner element in man, cannot be the subject of argumentative divisions, for that it is accepted only by that portion of the Spirit of God which is in a man, recognizing the same spirit dwelling without measure in Christ. Our translation in the tenth verse says, that God has revealed Christianity unto us by *his* Spirit. But this, though true, may not give the true import, — which is, that God has made the revelation *to the spirit;* not to the discursive or argumentative faculties, but to that higher principle in man which receives Jesus as from God, and rests in the sublime faith of *a moral certainty*, because the immediate oracles of God within the soul are found in harmony with, and bear witness to, the oracles of God in Christianity. This is the true source of Christian faith, — when the heavenly spirit that is in a man is thrilled and exalted by the greater fulness of the same spirit which is in Christ. No man who has not felt this is in any deep sense a Christian. His Faith stands not in the spirit and the power of God. And no man who has felt it can be in any doubt as to what constitutes Christianity.

No man, proceeds St. Paul, can know God, except so far as he has some portion of God's spirit in him; for as no man knoweth the things *of a man*, except the spirit of the man, that is in him, — so no man knoweth the things of God, except so far as he has something of the spirit of God: "Now we Christians, in so far as we are morally united with Christ, do not look with the dubious sight of worldly wisdom, — but have received of the spirit of God, that we might know, not speculatively, but by spiritual discernment, *his free gifts* in Christ; and we speak of these things not in words borrowed from speculative philosophy, but in words borrowed from the spiritual nature, — explaining spiritual things in a spiritual way"; or, possibly, "interpreting spiritual things to the spiritual." Our English version renders the last clause of the 13th verse, "comparing spiritual things with spiritual," which is not only of very doubtful meaning, but suggests no meaning at all that seems suited to the context. St. Paul meant to express, that neither in the discernment of spiritual things, which is the immediate act of a spiritual nature, — "the pure in heart see God," — nor in the method of communicating them, which is simply by presenting them for the spontaneous attraction of the spiritual faculty, could faction or schism find a place. The doctrine that pervades this whole argument of St. Paul, and of which every religious man must have had experience, is, that there is a divine element in the human soul, an intuitive spirit, which, when kept pure and exercised, and not clogged or dimmed by sinful passions, recognizes kindred goodness by a divine affinity, and is the immediate revealer of God. You will observe how, in the 14th and 15th verses, he speaks of the "animal man" and of the "spiritual man"; — by the one, meaning the worldly understanding, — the earthly mind, taste, sensibilities, and passions, — and by the other, the estimates and discernments of the diviner mind, — of the spirit that reveals God. Among the writers and philosophers of St. Paul's age there was a well-known division of the whole nature of man into the flesh, the soul, and the spirit. The Flesh was the bodily nature with all the desires and tendencies that arise out of it; the Soul was the common understanding, the judgment, the æsthetical and the logical faculties, applied to the various subjects with which mere Sense and Intellect are conversant; the Spirit was transcendental, — that portion of man's nature properly divine; — it had an inward intuition of God. The spirit was the voice and prompting of God within us. It could have no connection with evil, and nothing evil could proceed from it; but by the predominance of the senses, and of the lower powers of the soul, its activity could be depressed, or altogether suspended. "The Fathers," says Neander, "instead of endeavoring to prove the existence of God by logical inference, appealed to that which is most immediate in the human spirit, and is antecedent to all proof. They appealed to the originally implanted consciousness of God which human nature cannot deny. They appealed to an original revelation of the One God, made to the human spirit, on which every other revelation of God is founded. Clement appealed to the fact, that every scientific proof presupposes something which is not proved, which can be conceived only through an immediate agency on the spirit of man. To the Supreme Being — the Being elevated above all matter — faith alone can raise itself. There can be any knowledge or perception of God, only in as far as he himself has *revealed* himself to man. God cannot be conceived by means of demonstrative knowledge, for this proceeds only from things previously acknowledged, and from the more known to other things that are less known; but nothing in this way can be a prior premise in which the Eternal is included; and it is only by Divine grace, and by the revelation of his eternal Word, that we can recognize the unknown God." * There is another passage from one of the Fathers, given by Neander, which illustrates what St. Paul here intended by immediate revelations to the spiritual element in man: — "Just as the tarnished mirror will not receive an image, so the unclean soul cannot receive the image

---

* "The Training and Planting of the Christian Church." — *Cabinet Library*.

of God. But God has created all things in order that he may be known by his works, just as the invisible soul is known by its operations. All life reveals him; his breath animates all things; without him all would again sink back into nothingness; man cannot speak without revealing him, and only in the darkening of his own soul lies the cause of his being unable to perceive this revelation. He says, therefore, to man, Give thyself to the physician who is able to heal the eyes of thy soul; give thyself to God."

Again, to show the connection of all this with that subject of which St. Paul never for a moment loses sight: how can Christian unity be violated in relation to things which are only *spiritually discerned?* With these things the discursive and speculative faculties, which present various views, and create divisions, are not concerned; only the holy heart that is kept pure for God, only the divine eye of the mind, perceives them; and since it is God's spirit in us that makes us capable of discerning God, a moral sentiment of the Godlike in Christ must be the same in all souls, and the Divine Image in our Lord can leave but one impression on the hearts that are capable of taking the imprint.

And so, when we reach to any personal communion with God and Christ, to the deep utterances of the spiritual nature, controversy disappears. Our differences all arise out of our logical and argumentative faculties; but the revelations of the Spirit, that which the diviner mind approves, are in fact not ours as individuals, — they are derived from the spirit of our Father who is in us, and in all men they are the same. Within that Holy of Holies, where the spirit alone speaks, where, beneath all the errors and mistakes of feeble reason, there flow from a divine source, in the deep wells of the soul, the living waters of Conscience, — in that religious shrine of our nature, whenever they penetrate to it, there is harmony among all men. From this centre of communion with God, and from this alone, can the mind rightly discern the system which Providence has spread around it, and the attitudes of things; and the spirit that lives in communion with God cannot be judged, cannot be known, by the worldly mind.* In itself is the Holy Spirit, which no one can know, except those who have it, — and they are one family in God. "Now we Christians," says St. Paul, "inasmuch as we are Christians, have this spirit, for it is the spirit that dwelt in Christ."

With regard to this divine element in Man, which is the principle to which all Religion is addressed, — which is the source of immediate revelations in every holy heart unstained by sin, — which recognizes God in his works, not by a logical, but by a moral or kindred perception, and which, by the divine attraction of the Image of God in Christ held before it, may be lifted to holier and diviner revelations than the *unassisted* spirit could have reached, — I entreat you to remember that I am not offering to you views of my own, — that if I have but rightly read him, St. Paul is their Preacher.

---

* ii. 15.

I entertain, indeed, a profound conviction of their truth, — and that this is the only view of Man that does justice to the glorious nature that God has given us, and that appeals with fitting power to the divine affinities, to the solemn responsibilities, of children of God. One thing is obvious, in consistency with St. Paul's use of them in the maintenance of the inviolable nature of Christian unity, — that only from the rejection of these views, from substituting a speculative orthodoxy for a spiritual discernment, are still derived all the seeds of religious strife.

SECTION III.

DISSENSIONS, ARISING FROM THE PRETENSIONS AND VULGAR PASSIONS OF INDIVIDUALS.

CHAP. III. 1–23.

1 AND I, brethren, could not speak to you as to spiritual
2 men, but as to carnal, — as to babes in Christ. I fed
you with milk, not with meat, for not yet were ye
3 able, nor even now are ye able, to bear it. For still
ye are carnal: for since there is among you envying,
and strife, and divisions, are ye not carnal, walking
4 after the fashion of men? For while one saith, "I
am of Paul," and another, "I am of Apollos," are ye
5 not carnal? Who then is Paul, and who is Apollos?
Ministers through whom ye believed, even as the
6 Lord gave to each. I have planted: Apollos watered:
7 but God gave the increase. So that neither he that
planteth is any thing, nor he that watereth, — but God
8 that giveth the increase. Now he that planteth and
he that watereth are one; and each shall receive his
9 own reward according to his own labor. For we are
God's fellow-laborers: ye are God's husbandry, God's
10 building. According to the grace of God given unto
me, as a wise master-builder I laid the foundation, and
another buildeth up: but let each take heed how he
11 buildeth up. For another foundation can no man lay

in addition to that which is laid, which is Jesus the
Christ.
12 Now if any one build upon this foundation, gold,
13 silver, precious stones, — wood, hay, stubble, — the work
of each will be made manifest, for the day [time] will
declare it, because it is revealed in fire, and the fire
14 shall try every man's work, of what sort it is. If
any one's work which he hath built up endure, he
15 shall receive a reward. If any man's work shall be
burnt, he shall suffer the loss; but he himself shall be
16 saved, yet so as through fire. Know ye not that ye
are the temple of God, and that the spirit of God
17 dwelleth in you? If any man defile the temple of God,
him shall God defile: for the temple of God is holy,
18 which be ye. Let no one deceive himself: If any one
among you seem to be wise in this world, let him
19 become a fool that he may be wise. For the wisdom
of this world is foolishness with God, for it is written;
20 "He taketh the wise in their own craftiness." * And
again, "The Lord knoweth the calculations of the
21 wise, that they are vain." † Wherefore let no man
22 glory in men, for All Things are yours. Whether Paul,
or Apollos, or Cephas, or the world, or life, or death, or
23 things present, or things to come, All are yours; but
ye are Christ's, and Christ is God's.

The worst sources of Party spirit in Religion are the passions, the pride, the self-importance, of Individuals. In the peculiar language employed by St. Paul, these are connected, not with the natural

---

* Job v. 13. † Ps. xciv. 11.

man, but with the *carnal* man; they have their origin not in the errors, insufficiencies, or arrogance of mere intellect, but in the vanities, the jealousies, the intruding pretensions, the lowness and vulgarity, of the sensual nature. Their source is not in the Thoughts, but in the passions: they are not errors, but vices. St. Paul, as we have observed, points at the existence of a threefold nature in man; one of which is peculiarly the religious faculty, — whilst the others, whenever they presume to impress themselves on Christianity, and to mould it after their own tendencies, become the sources of divisions, intolerance, bigotry, mere human partisanship, and all the rest of the practical religious evils. In a broad and general way we may comprehend this triple nature under the heads of the Sensual or carnal man, — the Intellectual or animal man, — and the Religious or spiritual man. Every man is a compound of these three, and the moral question is, Which predominates, and subordinates the rest? There is order in the individual mind, and peace in the Church, only when the spiritual faculty, the recognized oracle and vicegerent of God, is the essential leader, — and when the dictates of speculation or corporeal feeling, however innocent or serviceable, as accessories, to the Individual, are never suffered to become *leading* principles in the mind, or to lay *foundations* in the Church. In our English translation these three elements in man are distinguished, as the carnal man, the natural man, and the spiritual man. It may perhaps place many in a position to form an independent judgment as to what St. Paul understood by this so-called *natural* man, to mention that it is the same conception, and the same word, as the *Psyche* of the Greeks. From the utterly indefensible and misleading use which polemics make of the expression, "natural man," in our translation, no one could suppose that it related to those parts of Man — the passions, loves, thoughts, and sensibilities of the earthly mind — which correspond with this impersonation of Mythology. By confounding the "natural man" with the "carnal man," and by representing that the "spiritual man" is not an original element in our nature, but a distinct endowment, like a new sense, of supernatural Grace acting arbitrarily, our orthodox theologians have removed St. Paul's conceptions of Man and Christianity, and substituted their own System. Our last chapter was occupied with the divisions which arise from the *speculative* tendencies, presuming to lay foundations and prescribe essentials in Christianity; — the present chapter is chiefly occupied with the meaner strife of personal pretensions, — with the vulgar ambition of Leadership in the Church, which has its main roots in the animal man, in the carnal envies and passions.

In Religion we may distinguish the End, which is the filial relation of the soul to God, from the Means, which are the agencies, of every kind, — moral, intellectual, liturgical, ceremonial, rhetorical, or imaginative and artistical, — by which the Church, for religious purposes, has sought to address and influence the nature of Man. Now here, as in all the other concerns of man, a livelier interest may improperly attach to the means than to the end; so that the Church, the outward instrumentality and appliances, may really attract to itself all the sympathies and feelings which ought to be devoted, and indeed are supposed to be devoted, to the religious relations of the soul. There is hardly any thing connected with himself, which a man, so disposed, cannot make a source of personal importance. It is in this way that the carnal element defiles Religion. The rank and standing of a congregation, the numbers and even the wealth of its members, the fulness and solemnity, or the poverty and bareness, of its outward worship, the comparative gifts of its minister, nay, the rival claims of the very Building, are all matters on which keen feelings can be excited, and partisanship exist, whilst Religion is made the mere occasion of these low interests. Of this nature are the pretensions of a sacred order, the claims of superiority on the part of Establishments, the emasculated character of the spiritual leaders of what calls itself the religious world by privilege of official rank, — and, what perhaps is more offensive still, the official importance of the ruling members in some dissenting communities, who sit in conclave on the rights of church-membership and issue permission to their fellow-Christians to attend the Lord's Supper. It is instructive to observe, and a warning that will be despised by none who know the human heart, over what an extent of foreign objects such men can swell their individuality, appropriating to themselves the genius of a preacher, the splendors of an edifice, the prosperity of a Church, — converting all these into sources of self-importance, whilst Religion is the mask under which these low passions find their gratification, and can exist without detection. The Roman Catholics and the Methodists recognized these carnalities, and acutely turned them to account. They made a place for the gratification of individual importance, — they used it to build up a Church, — as the Prophet complains, "calling in the Syrians to serve the Lord."

The only way to destroy the roots of Party spirit in religion is to regard the great end — the relation of the soul to God — as alone essential, and the instruments as utterly indifferent, provided only they are effectual; for then would the interests and the efforts of each mind fasten upon that which is universal in Christianity, and all the diversities of administration be but the special means best fitted to the individual, conducting the free mind to the same God. "There are diversities of gifts, but the same spirit. And there are differences of administration, but the same Lord. And there are diversities of operation, but it is the same God which worketh all in all." At the same time we ought to be aware that freedom from Party spirit in Religion is not an easy virtue, and that nothing but the purest and most earnest interest in the spiritual reality can save us from attaching a lower class of interests to the instruments and the accessories. "I was not able," says St. Paul to the Corinthians, "to speak unto you as unto spiritual, but as unto carnal, even as unto *mi-*

nors in Christ." The spiritual interest, the relation to God revealed in Christ, was not supreme and exclusive of every other; — the passions were not stilled in the intense life of the soul; the communion with Heaven did not preclude all earthly altercations; even within the sphere of Religion, the carnal nature could not contest with the spiritual the occupation of the heart, and find food for its gratification and occasions for its exercise. Those whose humble and supreme desire it was to feel the presence of God in the Temple of the spirit, and to find in Christ a divine light and guidance for the soul, could not merge these spiritual affections in the vulgar strife of Leadership, in the rival pretensions of distinguished Teachers. It is only among minds not engaged with the highest and purest sources of life and peace, — not lifted above the lower faculties, that Dissensions can arise, or Party spirit find a place. Those who truly seek to be one with God and with his Christ, do not breathe in the element of partisanship. "Whereas there is among you envying, and strife, and divisions, are ye not carnal, and walk as men? do ye not walk with a view to man's glory and pretensions, instead of centring all in God? For while one saith, 'I am of Paul,' and another, 'I am of Apollos,' are ye not carnal?" Is not this to have worldly contentions on holy ground; — to call the commonest passions a zeal for Religion, — and to forget, through the hot interest arising out of enlisted passions, that the whole Church has but one spiritual aim, and seeks, through the guidance of Christ, to be of God alone?

There were at Corinth — and until Christianity effectually realizes in the world the reign of God, there must always be — men belonging to a Church, and even passionately pledged to some of its interests, who yet do not find their chief attraction to it to be connected with the quiet nourishment of the inward life, — with the improvement and exercise of the spiritual nature. In such cases, when the true bond does not exist, — when the soul does not seek, in the simplicity of its affections, subjection and discipleship to Christ, the branch must either drop off from the vine, or some outward ligament supply the place of the living and organic connection; and the flame of zeal, if it burns at all, must derive its heat from some other source than the "baptism by fire." Such men are the worldly leaven of the Church, — its tempters and corrupters. They are worse than all external enemies, for they introduce the poison and agitation of low passions within its own bosom. They live upon coarse excitements, — they fasten with a carnal eagerness on some merely outward and instrumental interest, — they stir in other hearts the party spirit always too ready to be excited, that yet might have slept if the more elevated soul had not been rudely called away from deeper thoughts. Their element is external and superficial; they require stimulants addressed to the carnal and the natural man, — and they foster whatever in the administration of Religion may be connected with the importance of individuals, or with the vanity and ambition of Churches. The unspiritual Corinthians fed their zeal by disputing the rival qualifications of the principal Teachers of Christianity. The ambition of Leadership does not always originate with the Leaders: they are often tempted into it by the stimulants, and low-mindedness, of those who have no more spiritual source of interest in Religion. Mankind are willing to be led, are willing to have an Idol, and they are not displeased to believe that the lower interest of party, or personal excitement, is a true spiritual zeal. As Churches are constituted, and as the human heart is constituted, when the elements of ambition which every nature supplies are assailed by the very circumstances of temptation, — when the weakest part of man is purposely heated, — when, under the guise of spiritual power exerted in the highest services that man can render man, undue self-love is studiously inflamed, — who can wonder that minds, originally sincere and pure, have fallen under stimulants so coarsely administered? — and why should the ambition and miserable weakness of Church Leaders be more remembered, than the carnality and vulgar-mindedness of the Churches that corrupted them? It is not Apollos, nor Peter, nor himself, that St. Paul blames, but the unspiritual Corinthians, who, having no purer interest, must have the carnal excitement of party Leaders, even within the bosom of the same Church. In these times of religious fever, it requires some nobleness of nature in any gifted mind not to prostitute its high powers to the purposes of self-distinction, — of a superficial and pernicious popularity; — and Christian congregations of this day, no more than the Corinthians of St. Paul, are free from vulgarity and carnal-mindedness, if they minister to the self-importance of individuals, court Leaderships, and tempt the lower passions of men.

In the passage from the 5th to the 9th verse, St. Paul exposes the carnal character of Party spirit, by the consideration, that the Faith of the Soul, the confidence and repose of the moral being in relation to God, was the aim and rest of the Christian; and that to allow the soul to fall from this high desire to such unchristian work as a schismatical adherence to rival Teachers of the same truth, was in fact to derive their chief interest in Religion from low and passionate affections. "Who is Paul, and who is Apollos, but ministers by whom ye were led to the supreme rest of the spirit, to faith and trust in God, with such success as God gave to each of them? Shall your spirits forget the supreme End, that your passions may centre on the human means? The agents by which God works are, as to their officers, all alike in honor, — and the only distinction between them is in the *fidelity* with which they work; — in that relation alone does God make a difference between his servants, — rewarding each, not according *to his office*, but according to his faithfulness and labor. But God, through his instruments, is the supreme Teacher and Light of the soul. Ye are carnal if ye stop short of him; and if ye all rest in him, how can ye be divided? Ye are *God's* husbandry, — ye are *God's* building; — why range yourselves under the servants he employs?"

With respect to the peculiarities of opinion which

the rival sects of Corinth elevated into Heresies,—that is, sources of schism and contention, — St. Paul next lays down the doctrine, that there is but one thing fundamental in Christianity, namely, that Jesus is the Christ, the Leader up to God, the moral Lord and Master of the soul. If any man declares, that, in addition to this, something else is fundamental and essential,—then that man takes upon himself to preach a new Gospel;—but God's Gospel is, that men will be saved if they take his Christ as their guide. This is the literal meaning of the 11th verse: "Other Foundation can no man lay, in addition to that which is laid, namely, *Jesus as the Christ*," the moral Leader of the soul. The sectaries at Corinth did not reject Jesus as the Christ, but along with this, the only fundamental, they wished to connect some peculiarity of their own as equally fundamental. Such peculiarities, St. Paul declares, provided they are not taught so as to interfere with the only foundation, or to add to it, had better be left to the action of Time;—the *Day* shall test them, for it will place them in the burning focus of the universal mind, enlightened continually by God's truth. If these secondary views are in harmony with the Foundation,—if they are of the gold and precious metal of the soul,—they will stand the fiery test, and they will remain, eternal possessions to the Christian mind;—but if they are mere fancies, dross and stubble, they shall be burned up by the searching fire of Truth. Yet the man himself shall be saved, provided he has not lost sight of the fundamental truth that Jesus is his moral Lord,

— though, since his favorite theories and systems will burn like wood and hay, his salvation, if he has consumed time, and thought, and zeal in over devotion to such non-essentials, may be as a rescue from the flames, and not without scathe.

I mention it as a curious fact in the morbid Anatomy of religion, and as showing the appetite for horrors engendered by systems, that there is a class of interpreters, who, finding the last clause, as now expounded, too merciful for their theology, which would require that the man himself should be burned up along with the false views which he had added to the true Foundation, propose to translate in this way: "If any man's work shall not bear the force of the fire, he shall suffer its loss, — but he himself shall be *reserved*, as one kept for fire, to be burned for ever."

From the 16th verse to the close of the chapter, there is introduced a sublime view of the relation of the Soul to the vast system of Providence which is spread around us, and to the Infinite Father, who employs these influences not as ends in which his children are to rest, but as means to conduct them to himself. The spiritual Church is his temple: his spirit reigns in every member of it, — and not to be of that unity is to detach one's self from the spiritual building. "Know ye not that ye are the temple of God, and that the spirit of God dwelleth in you? If any man, by carnal strife, spoil this temple, God will cast him out of it, — so that he shall no more be one of its living stones. The Temple of God is holy, — but there is no holiness where there is no peace. God is not the author of divisions." And *all things* serve the soul: the Universe, all Life and Providence, are but its ministers and helpers to God. Why, then, glory in any of his agents, when, through all things that exist, God is inviting us to have our glory and our joy in him? "Let no man glory in men; *for all things* are yours, — whether Paul, or Apollos, or Cephas, or the world, or life, or death, or things present, or things to come, — *all are yours;* but ye are Christ's, and Christ is God's." This is the doctrine of Peace. There is unity in all hearts when they rise to and rest in God; their dissensions are all below, when they stop short among his means and instruments.

So unused are we to that elevation of thought which regards the spiritual life of his children as the central object of all God's works and agencies here, — all their influences to be transmitted to our souls, — all their beauty to open a thirst in our hearts for divine perfection, — all their teachings to build us up in heavenly knowledge, — so timid are we of assuming this providential attitude towards the vast system of Life and Nature spread around us, that the practical force of the Apostle's sentiment is feebly realized. *That all things are ours*, sounds strangely and unnaturally in our ears. It might be an unchristian sentiment, so little is it breathed forth by prevailing systems. Yet Christ lived, *and made all things his;* — and he left us the example that all should do likewise, — and that our Lord should be but the first-born among many brethren, — the first Son of God among men, but the guide to all the rest. And when we behold him with his universal spirit, in the midst of God's universal actings, directing every stream of experience inwards upon himself, to deposit in his soul its own freight of good; — when we see that to his understanding spirit and moulding love nothing was unavailable to spiritual uses; —when we read how full to his eye the world was of spiritual light, — how the frail flowers had connections with the Lord of Providence, — that in childhood's unshadowed heart his spirit beheld his Father's love of purity, — in the moral adjustments of an infant's mind discerning the earthly type of the children of the heavenly kingdom; — when we read those parables, the suggestions of an every-day experience, and perceive how each passing incident prompted the lesson of instruction, and opened a channel for the outward flow of holy wisdom, so that to his employment of God's commonest gifts and opportunities might be applied his own memorable words after the feast which miracle had spread, "Gather up the fragments that nothing be lost"; — when through his eventful history we find him neglecting no opportunity, however humble, of drawing strength and motive from the aids and instruments around him, — placing his nature beneath the influences which make Duty both holy and dear, — now gathering on his tasked heart the sustaining pressure of human love, — and now alone with God, watching out the stars in prayer, — calming nature's reluctance to pass through every darker scene by the summoned thought that God was proposing to glorify his Name, and that *for this end* came he to this hour; — then do we begin to understand, for we perceive how he understood it, that there is nothing which may not be instrumental to build up a meek and lofty spirit, — that for moral uses and the growth of the Christian mind, "all things *are* ours, — whether the world, or life, or death, or things present, or things to come, — all are ours, — and we are Christ's, and Christ is God's"; — for our Lord and Leader guides us to our common Father.

Now, it is easy to rail against other men's superstitions, but there is only one way of being true spiritual worshippers of God ourselves, and that is, by making *all things ours*. Nor would it be difficult to perceive, were we spiritually inclined, how this doctrine might be practically verified, *that all things are ours*. The World, — is it not fitted to educate and mature us until our dying day, — to teach wisdom, strong purpose, self-control, and patience, and love unwearied? Its trials, its uncertainties, its calls to exertion, its daily proffered means and instruments of usefulness, — are they not *ours*, and is there a day in which they are not available for our lasting good? *Life*, says the Apostle, — deep, sacred, mysterious life, with its first activities, its dreams of happiness, its struggles to realize them, — its visions and its hopes, all finding at last their noblest good in Christian duty, — in the patient and faithful doing of what our hand findeth to do, — and *Death*, breathing its hushing strain of tender and solemn wisdom over the turbulent agitations of too eager life, and all its fond and confident pursuits, — Death with its twofold beckoning, one to the available time that is passing away, and one to the eternity, the home of God, that knows no change; — "*Things present*," where all we have of holiness or hope has been learned, and where all of good that really belongs to us has been wrought out in trial; — and "*Things to come*," our Faith in which heals the wounds of life, and stores our hearts with undecaying affections; — all these *are ours*, if we are *Christ's*, for *he* made them ours by teaching us to use them, — and when we appropriate their power, we but take him for Master and Lord. And Christ is God's: his mission was to show us the Father, — to make us one with Him, even as *he* was; — he wrought in His power, he spoke in His name, he sought His glory; — and so we rise from the influences of earth to our Father's throne in heaven, and we rest in the faith, that as the shadow of his protection has been over us here, so shall it be, for ever and for ever.

And this is the Christian doctrine of Unity: — That we all are to be one in God, and that it is the mission of all things under God to lead us to our Father, and so promote his glory alone.

SECTION IV.

AN APOSTLE'S WAY OF APPLYING APOSTOLIC AUTHORITY TO THE STRIFES OF A CHURCH.

CHAP. IV. 1-21.

1 Let a man account us, as ministers of Christ, and
2 stewards of the mysteries of God. What remains is, that
3 it is required of stewards that each be faithful. But
with me it is a very small thing that I should be judged by
you, or by human measurement: nay, I judge not my-
4 self. For I am conscious of nothing against myself; yet
not by this am I justified, for he that judgeth me is the
5 Lord. Wherefore, judge nothing before the time, until
the Lord come, who will both bring to light the hidden
things of darkness, and will make manifest the counsels
of hearts; and then praise shall be to each from God.
6 And these things, brethren, I have transferred to myself and Apollos, for your sakes, that ye may learn by
us not to be wise above what is written, that no one be
7 inflated on behalf of one against another. For who
maketh thee to differ? and what hast thou that thou didst
not receive? But if thou didst receive it, why dost thou
8 glory as if thou hadst not received it? Now ye are full:
now ye are rich: ye have reigned without us: And I
would ye did reign, that we also might reign along with
9 you. For I think that God has set forth us, the Apostles,

last, as appointed to death, that we might be made a spec-
10 tacle to the world, both to angels and to men. We are
fools for Christ's sake, but we are wise in Christ: we are
weak, but ye are strong; ye are honorable, but we are de-
11 spised. Up to this present hour we both hunger and thirst,
and are naked, and are beaten, and have no certain dwell-
12 ing-place; and labor, working with our own hands: being
13 reviled, we bless: being persecuted, we endure: being
defamed, we entreat: we are made as the expiation of the
world, the offscouring of all things to this day.
14 I write not these things to shame you, but as my be-
15 loved sons I warn you. For though ye have ten thousand teachers in Christ, ye have not many fathers, for
I have begotten you in Christ Jesus through the Gos-
16 pel. Wherefore, I beseech you, be imitators of me.
17 To this end I have sent unto you Timothy, who is my
beloved and faithful son in the Lord, who will remind you
of my ways in Christ, as I teach everywhere in every
18 Church. Now some are puffed up, as if I were not com-
19 ing to you. But I will come to you shortly, if the Lord
will: and I will know not the word but the power of
20 those who are puffed up. For the kingdom of God is
21 not in word, but in power. Which choose ye? Shall I
come to you with a rod, or in love and the spirit of mildness?

It is only in the most advanced state of religious knowledge, that the individual mind takes confidence to abandon mere Symbols, as grounds of spiritual safety, and to trust itself with God alone. Long as it is since Christ taught the sublime doctrine, that the true worshippers worship in spirit and in truth, by the *reality* of an inward communion and not by outward signs, there is yet no universal disposition amongst men to rest themselves, or to permit others to rest, in this direct and immediate worship, and, satisfied with knowing that God is in his temple within, to be spiritually independent of the mere mechanism of Religion. Few are the minds so purely Christian, that they dare to trust themselves to God without a mediator, or to look within for the kingdom of heaven. In these days spiritual safety is made to consist, not in Christ's feeling of union with his Father, but rather in interposing as much as possible what are called Means of Grace, — in fact, in protecting ourselves against God, that, in the multitude of spiritual contrivances, we may get possession of the true watchword, or connect ourselves with some outward vehicle of favor, — sacerdotal, sacramental, or doctrinal, — to which if we but cling fast we may find a passage into heaven. Where are the Christians who can put aside all this intervening machinery, and say with the filial heart of Christ, "I am not alone, for my Father is with me"? Alas! to meet the Deity alone, without some intermediate protection, is just the most terrific idea that Theology has planted in the common mind. "Prepare to meet your God!" are words employed to awaken the terrors of the soul, — and the intervention of an Intercessor who will prevail for us, as the means to assuage them. To many minds, a Christianity in spirit and in truth, the filial relation of Christ to God, appears to afford no protection, — in fact, to be no *Religion*, — a word that seems to be used in the old heathen sense, of something so prescribed that a man can observe it with an outward exactitude and certainty, — and which when observed binds God to show favor. To profess that your whole Christianity consists in making your own spirit a living temple for God, employing as your greatest aid the study and imitation and spiritual attraction of his Christ, is held to be no definite answer to the question, What do you believe? what are your grounds of Hope? what is your Christianity?

How often are Unitarians met with that question, *What is* Unitarianism, — *what is* your Religion? And the question always means this: "What are your special reliances, that you have secured for yourselves a protection against God?" If you say, "Christianity has taught you to have faith in the divine Love, and to seek immediate communion with the Father of the soul, — and that the Son of God has shown us how to prepare the heart for some inward union with God's spirit," — you are thought to say a thing utterly vague, indefinite, shadowy, — in fact, to have no certain grounds of safety, no definite terms on the observance of which you can hold God bound to save you. For this is what is chiefly sought for in religion, — this is the refined selfishness of spiritual anxiety; — "How can I get assured of my safety, — how can I hold God pledged to me? — Let me know what I am to believe in as the terms of salvation, — what are the outward observances that God has appointed as the conditions of final Mercy?" — and so vanish, in this legal and covenanting temper, all the filial trusts of a religious mind, — the worship of the Father in the spirit of a child's faith and reality. There never was a time, since the Reformers, with a dim consciousness of spiritual freedom, made their ineffectual protest, when Christianity was so prominently an ecclesiastical, and so little a spiritual interest. On all sides the machinery is thrust upon you, as if it was the inward and essential life. Not the soul's communion with God, but the agency of a Church, — not practical discipleship to the Lord Jesus, the baptism of the affections into the spirit of his life and death, but the efficacy of the sacraments, — not faith in God, but belief in doctrines, — not reliance on divine Beings, but confidence in dead rites and propositions: — these are the essentials of which we hear so much, — the symbols every thing, the Realities forgotten. Even the dying wretch, on whose crimes man will have no mercy, is taught to lay hold on the symbol, and, naming the name of Christ, to exult in his safety. The man who has spent his life without God in the world, will yet close it with some feeling of protection if he has partaken of the Sacrament on his dying bed; — the most worldly deem there is some security in avowing an attachment to the Bible, — and the Ministers of the Gospel of repentance and newness of life not only assume, but, so little are they aware of the degradation, vindicate, their exclusive claims to the character of spiritual Magicians.

The Priest is the symbol that, in all ages, the common mind has substituted for a spiritual communication with God within the soul of the worshipper. The worldly man, occupied with low and perishable interests, and conscious of no sanctity or elevation of desire, has always shrunk from a direct intercourse with God, and interposed some mediator, set apart from common life, whose office it is to perform religious services for the people, — to pray not *with* them, but *for* them, — and through a sanctified medium to convey supplications which God would not listen to from profaner lips. There is no superstition that lingers so long upon the earth, for there is none that so accommodates the mechanical devotion of the material mind, as the peculiar consecration of places and of persons. There is something definite and tangible, conveying assurance of protection, — and this is what the worldly mind avowedly requires in a Religion, — in being able to go to some authorized intercessor who has access to the ear of the Almighty, — or to some holy *place* which imparts a consecration, makes prayer acceptable to Heaven, and communicates to the pilgrim, in virtue of his bodily presence, a spiritual charm. Religion in its common forms has ever been, and continues to be, an attempt to possess one's self of the low satisfaction of security, by means of prescribed services, so definite and tangible that the purchaser of heaven can be in no doubt that he has fulfilled *his* part of the covenant, — having transferred the terms from the spiritual qualifications of the soul, which might raise many a doubt, to a Creed, or a Sacrament, which may be reduced to a matter of absolute certainty. I mean not to say any thing so harsh, and I belive so false, as that those who adopt this mechanical religion expressly desire to divest themselves of any part of their moral obligations; or that they seek to have a claim upon the kingdom of God in a local heaven, without having the kingdom of God within. It is their want of *Trust*, not their avoidance of moralities, that materializes their religious character, and embarrasses the spirit of life within them by unnatural adjuncts, — fastening the dead to the living; — it is the absence of all Faith in a spiritual God, who manifests himself to the devoutly pure, and bestows immediate salvation on the filial heart, that narrows the religious sympathies, and makes bigotry the honest expression of a selfish alarm; — it is the spirit of *Fear*, seeking, not to evade a Duty, but to allay the torments of distrust, that by the bonds of express conditions desires to lay an outward hold on God, — and to have, as it were, at his hands, a title-deed to heaven. Does any one suppose that the bigotry, the exclusive and denunciatory spirit that may prevail, is primarily either the outbreak of positively malign passions, or the expression of a disinterested spiritual anxiety for the heretic's "salvation"? It is originally neither of these, — though, no doubt, it often partakes of both. It is neither pure hate nor pure love, but much more nearly *pure fear;* — it is the expression of irritation that you, with your doubts and your rationalism, have broken into its spiritual repose; you have disturbed its sense of security, — you have dared to question, and expose to rude investigation, the virtue of the spiritual charm, — and the bigot's anger is not so much zeal on your account, as discomposure on his own. You have shaken, what such minds chiefly seek, his *comfortable* assurance in Religion.

The development of the religious nature of Man, even under Christianity, though in many quarters it has disguised and refined, has not yet removed this substitution of the Priest for the Religion of the spirit and the truth, for the worship and consecration of the individual soul. The Religions of antiquity, including the Jewish, *recognized* the priesthood of peculiar individuals; they established and consecrated this elementary tendency to approach God by proxies and mediators, — for that which there was nothing in their own spirit to destroy, they necessarily sanctioned. Both Paganism and Judaism, at least in its later forms, appointed *priests*, — men set apart for the performance of holy offices, — who had an access to God denied to the people, — who offered sacrifices on especial altars, which would not be accepted from profaner places or less holy hands, — who had a power of calling down a blessing from above and of adjusting the relations of Heaven and Earth, which it would be the last impiety, only to be expiated by death, for any unanointed man to assume. And it is a remarkable evidence of how the unenlightened mind clings to the idea of a *material* consecration, and of mechanical conveyances, that the priest who presented the offering of the people, and drew down the answering blessing from on high, was so appropriated to dead things that never change, that he was not the person employed even to teach morality, — was not looked to as the national Instructor, — was not in any way concerned with the higher agencies of intellectual civilization, — was not expected to be, indeed was not permitted to be, one of the *Lights* of the age. Under Paganism this office belonged to the Philosophers, Poets, Orators, and Statesmen; — under Judaism it formed the peculiar function of the Prophets. The Priest uttered no burning word, — spoke no vivifying truth, — darted no light direct from God into the selfish heart of the world, — rebuked no oppression, — broke by moral force no oppressor's chain; — but there he stood at his altar, a dead symbol, — an official personage, — not acting on man but interceding with God, — a mechanical provision that certain religious formulas, in which the nation might be deeply concerned, should not be neglected. The Priest received no inspiration in his own heart; he was holy in no higher sense than one of the vessels of the temple was holy; he was professionally sacred, — officially pious, — set apart, not to receive by communion with God a divine life into his own soul, and thence breathe it out to others, but what is wholly a different matter, and not a spiritual but a cabalistic function, to communicate an outward consecration. I do not recollect, either in Heathen or in Jewish history, one single instance in which a Priest was one of the higher agents of God for the civilization of man. Moses, not Aaron, was the Lawgiver and Statesman; and Moses, not Aaron, understood and breathed forth the mind of God. The one received an inspiration: the other only imparted a consecration. Where is it on record that *a priest* ever purified the national worship, softened the national superstitions, — nay, even rebuked the national sins, — or, by his honest reading of the writing on the wall, made tyrants tremble? I profess not to know: for when the ministers of Christ have done these things, as their Master did, they were, like Luther, in arms against the sacerdotal principle; and let it be recollected that Christianity knows no hierarchy, and that the Prophet, not the priest, is the successor of the Apostles. Looking even to the priesthood of Judaism, it is evident that God made no account of these official persons, nor expected true service from them. They were the conservative symbols of the existing present, — not the reforming influences of the diviner Future; and, like all men used for official purposes, in which the free heart has no place and the intellect no exercise, they were timid, slavish, timeserving. It was a Priest who yielded and made the golden calf at the bidding of the people, — and no priest, but a Prophet, who dashed down the Tables of Stone in his burst of righteous sorrow, and summoned both priest and people to a severe account. In that noble legacy to all generations, the Bible, whose effectual inspiration the universal heart acknowledges, the Priest has left us not one word of immortal power. He whose devotion still flows through the world, like a refreshing stream, was no priest, but a man, who, though not faultless nor unstained by great sins, was yet, in the natural movements of his free spirit, in his *self-kindled* penitence, piety, and love, after God's own heart.

Isaiah, who evangelized Judaism, was no priest. Daniel, no unworthy image of Christ in the judgment-hall, was no official formalist, but one who communed with God, and spoke out the divine monitions of the living oracle. In the light of these facts, that Judaism tolerated an official priesthood at all, can only be explained on the principle, that Revelation itself has an historical development,— that it was not intended to teach absolute Truth, but to apply such aids to the mind, as, without destroying its own freedom, might introduce more spiritual ideas, and stimulate the unfolding of its own powers. It is the great peculiarity of Christianity, as a Religion, that it has abolished the priest,—that it teaches the priesthood of the soul,—and that to recognize an official mediator is to go back to Paganism or Levitical Judaism, and annul the distinctions of the Gospel. "The true worshippers worship the Father in spirit and in truth: and the Father seeketh such to worship him." "Know ye not that *ye* are the temple of God, and that the spirit of God dwelleth in you?" "If any man love me, he will keep my words; and my Father will love him, and we will come unto him, and make our abode with him." It is remarkable that the word which describes *the priests* of the Pagan and Jewish religions is never once applied in any part of the New Testament to the Apostles or ministers of Christ. He who knew what was in man recognized in every mind a divine element capable of entering into immediate communication with the spirit of God. He removed the barriers of materialism, of fear, and superstition, and outward devotions, and into the pure and seeking heart introduced a living sense of the intimate presence of God. Christianity is the only Religion the world has ever known, that has appointed no Altar, no Priest, no Sacrifice. Its altar is the humble and filial heart; its sacrifices are the passions; its oblations, the desires of a pure, merciful spirit; and its priest, the soul that devoutly communes with God. This is a remarkable fact, — and running counter, as it does, to the strongest tendencies of unspiritual man, — to the still unsubdued disposition to repose upon symbols, and approach God through ecclesiastical proxies, it augments the love and veneration with which we place ourselves at the feet of our divine Messiah.

The lower tendencies of human nature, however, have withstood the Gospel, and taken their own course, — and still a Priesthood makes pretensions to be indispensable mediators to the Church of God. Nor would it be just to say, that these superstitions originate in the designing policy of a few hierarchs: they have their roots in human nature; they are accommodated to the indolence, the weakness, the selfish fears, and unspiritual distrusts of man. It is altogether unphilosophical to call this state of things the craft of priests. It is priestcraft; but it is the priestcraft of the laity, to the full as much as the priestcraft of the clergy; — it is the low and mechanical religion of the one, that calls into existence the low and mechanical functions of the other. Priestcraft is not a business that Priests can carry on by themselves; the people must be abetting and consenting parties; — and when we look into the present condition of the religious world, and witness the ostentatious profession of attachment to *Symbols*, on the part of men not remarkable for purity of sentiment or nobleness of life, — to the Bible, the Church, the Creed, the Priest, — we must confess that the laity are often the tempting parties. The clergy are but made in the same mould; they have not the Christian elevation to refuse such functions as degrading, and to disown such allies as scandalous, — and they partake, themselves, of the material tendency to rest on Symbols, and to employ mechanical means of allaying the fears of superstition. Everywhere do we discern some traces of this the lowest tendency of the religious nature, — the desire for an official Person, on the part of those who are dimly conscious that their own souls are not in spiritual communication with God. I have witnessed it on many a death-bed, and, in moments when it is impossible to be unyielding, have felt conscious of the only degradation, in my own eyes, that the Christian ministry has ever exposed me to. I have known dying men ask assurances of security, and attach a painful importance to the prayer in which a fellow-man asked for them the blessing of God; — I have seen the Lord's Supper eagerly craved by those who never thought of it before; — I have been constrained to administer it in the last moments of trembling life, — not, I trust, without fidelity to the spiritual Lord of the soul; — and I have witnessed the bitterest lamentations of survivors because death had taken place, ere the rite had been partaken. Now if such things have fallen under my experience, what, I ask, must be the temptations which, in other churches, the laity throw in the path of the clergy? And is there not some trace of the disposition for an official Person in the very general feeling, from which perhaps no church is free, that what is entirely innocent and allowable in another man may be scandalous, or at least indecorous and unsafe, in a minister of religion? — and has not this impression its roots in the sacerdotal tendency, — in the belief which is natural to the lower religious states, that there is a professional sacredness, separable from personal sanctity, in which the community may have an interest? Now we readily admit that the ministers of religion deserve a deeper condemnation, if they scandalously fall away from the one standard of Christian duty, — because there are peculiar motives and influences acting upon them, and because they have voluntarily assumed a peculiar office. To the strictness of judgment, therefore, we do not object, — but we do object to the sacerdotal principle, that there are *different standards* for different men, or for different classes of men, — that guilt or innocence, however affected by knowledge and opportunity, has any relation to office or profession, — that there is a sacred — say rather a desecrated — caste, set apart as a compensation for the laxities of others, and who are denied any portion of the liberty that can safely, or righteously, belong to any Christian man.

It was the claim of *Priesthood* — the attempt by official and sacerdotal means to shut out the individual soul from God — that awoke the indignation of our own Wickliffe, who left the work of separation to be completed two centuries after, in more favorable times, by the more fiery strength, but perhaps inferior spirit, of Luther. It was the same claim, on the part of the Reformers themselves, — a claim if not to sacerdotal efficacy, to doctrinal infallibility, — that introduced Sectarianism, that unhappy offspring of Protestantism, into the bosom of Christianity. And now, in this freer day, it is the perception, openly avowed, that the doctrinal teaching of the Anglican Church cannot be sustained on the old Protestant grounds of the sufficiency of the Bible and the rights of Private Judgment, that has driven a large proportion of her clergy back upon the bosom of Authority, and forced them, if they would retain their Faith, to seek for it elsewhere. Such, in every age, has been the discord produced by official substitutes, and by an unspiritual disregard of the free priesthood of the Soul.

And in these days of Ecclesiastical pretensions, and of the wonderful assumption of Apostolical Succession, it is worth while to ask how an Apostle did deal with such difficulties when they came before himself, — what claim he set up when a Church, planted by himself, was split into factions, — what authority he claimed over rival teachers, when, in the very height and glory of his Apostleship, they broke the Christian unity which he had labored to establish, and sought to bring himself into contempt. He seeks to restore peace, simply by abolishing the pretensions of individuals, his own included, — and by awakening in each man the priesthood of his own spirit, — the sense of his accountability to God alone. Such is the great spiritual lesson of this fourth chapter as to the claims of Individuals in the Church; — and as it contained no material difficulties that required lengthened interpretation, and is much required at the present time, I have used it for this purpose alone.

I shall now simply present this Apostolic view of Apostolic Authority, intended by St. Paul as a lesson in the wisdom of peace and humility to the other Teachers of the Church: —

"Account us as nothing in ourselves, — being but servants of Christ, and stewards of the revelations of God. And as stewards we can deserve no praise but that of fidelity, — for a steward is but a dispenser of his master's bounty. And whether we Apostles are faithful or not in our stewardship of the Gospel, God alone must judge. With me it is a small thing to have the judgment of man, — nay, I dare not judge myself; for though I am conscious of no unfaithfulness [this clause is made completely unintelligible in our version by the translation, '*for I know nothing by myself*'] in myself, yet am I not therefore clear; for he that judgeth me is the spirit-searching God. Therefore, ye leaders of parties, judge nothing before the time, — until the Lord come, who will bring to light the hidden motives of men, and make manifest the counsels of the heart; — and then shall each have his due praise from God.

"And these things, brethren, I have applied to

myself and Apollos, through tenderness for you,— that ye might learn in our humility not to think of Leaders above that which is here prescribed, — and that no one party of you be puffed up for one Teacher against another. Who maketh thee to differ from another? What hast thou, that thou didst not receive? And if you are but a steward of it, why do you erect yourself into a party leader, as if it was your own? Witness us Apostles, and contrast the claims of your proud leaders with our low estate. Ye are full, ye are rich, ye have lorded it as kings without us, — and I would to God that ye did reign in the true supremacy of the Gospel, that we also might share in the peace of that kingdom. For I think that God hath set forth us the Apostles, — as those who are brought forth last on the Amphitheatre, to be devoted to death. We are made the suffering fools for Christ's sake, but ye are the wise in Christ; we are weak, but ye are strong; ye are honorable, but we are despised. Even unto this present hour, we both hunger and thirst, and are naked, and are beaten, and have no certain dwelling-place, and labor, working with our own hands; being reviled, we bless, — being persecuted, we submit, — being defamed, we entreat; — we are made the expiation of the earth, the offscouring of all things until this day.

"I write not these things to shame you by the contrast, — but, being my beloved sons in the Gospel, I admonish you. For though ye have ten thousand instructors in Christ, yet have ye not many *fathers;* for in Christ Jesus I have begotten you as my spiritual children, by preaching to you the Gospel. Wherefore I beseech you, be imitators of me. And to this end I have sent unto you Timothy, who is my beloved and faithful son in the Lord, that he may remind you of my ways in Christ, as I teach everywhere in every Church. Now some are puffed up, as though I would not venture to come to you. But I will come to you shortly, if the Lord will, — and I will know not the speech of those who are puffed up, but their inward power. For the kingdom of God does not manifest itself in Speech, — but in spiritual Power. Which choose ye? Shall I come to you with a rod, or in love and the spirit of mildness?"

PART II.

(CHAPS. V.–XI.)

THE IMMORALITIES AND PERPLEXITIES OF THE CORINTHIAN CHURCH.

PART II.

(CHAPTERS V.–XI.)

SECTION I.

SPECULATIVE PRETENSIONS AND MORAL ROTTENNESS.—INCEST.—LITIGATIONS.—DOMESTIC RELATIONS BETWEEN BELIEVERS AND UNBELIEVERS.

CHAPS. V.–VII.

V. 1. It is commonly reported that there is fornication
among you, and such fornication as is not even among
the Gentiles,—that a man should have his father's
2 wife. And *you* are puffed up! and have not rather
mourned that he that hath done this thing might be
3 taken away from among you. For I, verily, as present
in spirit, though absent in body, have judged already
as if I was present, him that hath so done this thing,
4 —In the name of our Lord Jesus Christ, when you
and my spirit are gathered together, with the power
5 of our Lord Jesus Christ, to commit such an one to
Satan for the extinction of the flesh, that the spirit
6 may be delivered in the day of the Lord Jesus. Your
boasting is not good. Know ye not, that a little leaven

7 leaveneth the whole lump? Purge out the old leaven
that ye may be a new lump, inasmuch as ye are unleavened, — since our Passover, Christ, is slain for us.
8 Wherefore let us keep Passover, — not with the old
leaven, nor with the leaven of evil and wickedness, but
with the unleavened bread of purity and truth.
9 I wrote to you in an epistle not to company with for-
10 nicators, not indeed absolutely, as including the fornicators
of this world, or the covetous, the rapacious, and the idola-
11 trous, for then must ye have gone out of the world; but
now I have written to you, if any one called a *brother* is
a fornicator, or covetous, or idolatrous, or a railer, or a
drunkard, or rapacious, with such an one not to keep com-
12 pany, not even to eat. For what have I to do with judg-
13 ing those without? Do not ye judge those within? But
those without, God will judge. Put away from among
yourselves that wicked person.

VI. 1. Dare any of you, having a suit against another, go
to law before the unrighteous, and not before the saints?
2 Do ye not know that the saints shall judge the world, and
if the world is judged by you, are ye unworthy to judge
3 the smallest cases? Know ye not that we shall judge
angels? how much more things that pertain to this life?
4 If then ye have judgments of things pertaining to this life,
do ye appoint those to judge who have no place in the
5 Church? I speak this to your shame. Is it that there is
not even one wise man among you who is able to judge
6 between brother and brother, — but brother goeth to law
7 with brother, and that at the bar of unbelievers? Now
therefore there is utterly a fault among you, that ye go to
law with one another. Why do ye not rather suffer wrong?
8 why are ye not rather defrauded? Whereas ye wrong,
and defraud, and that your brethren.

9 Know ye not that the unrighteous shall not inherit the
kingdom of God? Be not deceived; nor fornicators, nor
idolaters, nor adulterers, nor effeminate, nor abusers of
10 themselves with mankind, nor thieves, nor covetous, nor
drunkards, nor revilers, nor plunderers, shall inherit the
11 kingdom of God. And such were some of you: but ye
have been washed, ye have been sanctified, ye have been
justified in the name of the Lord Jesus, and in the spirit
of our God.

12 All things are lawful to me; but all things are not expedient: all things are lawful to me; but I will not be
13 brought under the power of any. Meats for the belly, and
the belly for meats; but God will destroy both it and them.
And the body is not for fornication, but for the Lord, and
14 the Lord for the body. And God has both raised up the
15 Lord, and will raise us up by his own power. Know ye
not that your bodies are members of Christ? Shall I
then take members of Christ, and make them members
16 of a harlot? Be it not so. Know ye not that he who is
joined to a harlot is one body? for it is said, they two
17 shall be as one flesh. But he that is joined to the Lord is
18 one spirit. Flee fornication: every sin that a man doeth
is without the body; but he that committeth fornication
19 sinneth against his own body. Know ye not that your
body is the temple of the holy spirit which is in you, which
20 ye have from God, and that ye are not your own? For ye
have been bought with a price: glorify therefore God in
in your body.

VII. 1. Now concerning the things whereof you wrote
to me: It is good for a man not to touch a woman;—
2 Nevertheless, because of fornication, let every man have
3 his own wife, and every woman her own husband. Let
the husband render what is due to the wife, and the wife to

4 the husband. The wife hath not power of her own body,
but the husband: and likewise also the husband hath not
5 power of his own body, but the wife. Deprive not each
other, unless with consent for a time, that ye may have
opportunity for prayer, and be together again, that Satan
6 may not tempt you through your incontinence. But this
7 I say on concession, and not by command. For I would
that all men were even as I myself: but each hath his
own gift from God, one after this manner, another after
that.

8 Now I say to the unmarried and widows, it is good for
9 them if they abide even as I. But if they cannot contain,
let them marry: for it is better to marry than to burn.
10 And to the married I command, not I, but the Lord: Let
11 not the wife be separated from her husband; but if she
be separated, let her remain unmarried, or be reconciled
to her husband; — and let not the husband put away his
wife.

12 But to the rest, I speak, not the Lord: If any brother
hath an unbelieving wife, and she herself be pleased to
13 dwell with him, let him not put her away. And if any
woman hath an unbelieving husband, and he be pleased
14 to dwell with her, let her not put him away. For the unbelieving wife is sanctified in the husband, and the unbelieving husband is sanctified in the wife: else were
15 your children unclean, but now are they holy. But if the
unbelieving depart, let him depart: a brother or a sister
is not in bondage to such; but God hath called us to peace.
16 For how knowest thou, O wife, if thou shalt save thine
husband? Or how knowest thou, O husband, if thou shalt
save thy wife?

17 But as the Lord hath distributed to each, as God hath
called each, so let him walk. And so I ordain in all the
18 Churches. Hath any one been called, being circumcised?

Let him not become uncircumcised. Hath any been
called in uncircumcision? Let him not become circum-
19 cised. Circumcision is nothing; and uncircumcision is
nothing; but the keeping of the commandments of God.
20 Let each remain in that calling [class], wherein he was
21 called. Wert thou called, being a slave? Let it be no
care to you; but if thou canst become free, use it rather.
22 For he that is called in the Lord, being a slave, is the
Lord's freeman; and likewise he that is called, being free,
23 is Christ's bondsman. Ye have been bought with a price:
24 become not the slaves of men. Brethren, let each remain with God in that state in which he was called.

25 Now concerning the unmarried I have no commandment
of the Lord, but I give my judgment, as one that hath ob-
26 tained mercy from the Lord to be faithful. I think, then,
that this is good, because of the present distress; that it is
27 good for a man so to be. Art thou bound to a wife? seek
not deliverance. Art thou free from a wife? seek not a
28 wife. But yet if thou marry, thou hast not sinned. And
if a virgin marry, she hath not sinned; yet such shall have
29 trouble in the flesh; but I spare you. But this I say,
brethren,—the time is short. It remaineth that both they
30 that have wives be as though they had none; and they
that weep, as though they wept not; and they that rejoice,
as though they rejoiced not; and they that buy, as though
31 they possessed not; and they that use this world, as though
they abused it not; for the fashion of this world passeth
32 away. But I would have you to be without anxiety: the
unmarried careth about the things of the Lord, how he
33 may please the Lord: but the married careth about the
34 things of the world, how he may please his wife. There
is difference between a wife and a virgin. The unmarried
careth for the things of the Lord, that she may be holy
both in body and in spirit; but the married careth for the

things of the world, how she may please her husband.
35 This I speak for your own benefit, not that I may cast a
snare upon you, — but for that which is becoming, and
for your assiduousness to the Lord without distraction.
36 But if any one think that he behaveth himself unbe-
comingly towards his virgin, if she pass her prime, and
accordingly it ought to be, — let him do what he willeth,
37 he sinneth not; let them marry. But he that standeth
steadfast in his heart, not having necessity, and hath liberty according to his own will, and so hath determined in
38 his heart that he will keep his virgin, doeth well. So then
he that marrieth doeth well; but he that marrieth not
39 doeth better. A wife is bound so long as her husband
liveth; but if her husband be dead, she is free to marry
40 whom she will; only in the Lord. But she is happier if
she so remain, — after my judgment; and I think that I
have also the spirit of God.

We enter now on a new division of the Epistle. The Apostle passes from the subject of the doctrinal Dissensions to the *Immoralities* of the Corinthian Church, with a sharpness and rapidity which serve to mark his own sense of the intimate connection between dogmatical presumption, spiritual pride, and practical remissness. Indeed, this very connection affords him the link of transition which conducts him from the one subject to the other, — and this appeal to their Sins may be regarded as the conclusive argument against their speculative Christianity. It is impossible, even in an argumentative view, to administer to that spirit which places the essence of Christianity in some superiority of speculative Doctrine, a more humiliating and crushing overthrow, than the moral test of the presence or absence of the purifying spirit of Christ, honestly applied to all such Orthodoxies, — than to be able to say to any man or Church, "Whilst you are presuming to build up an intellectual infallibility, there is moral corruption *within* you, — your *heart* and *life* are stained and guilty; — and is it for you, who in the inward springs of your practical being have no fellowship with Christ, to determine for others the essence of Salvation, — or to claim it as your own"? This is the condemning proof used by St. Paul in the first two verses of the fifth chapter: "It is well known that there is *impurity* in the midst of you, — and yet *you are the men* who boast of your advanced views of Christian Truth, — instead of giving yourselves to prayers and tears, that the evil thing might be removed from among you: your boasting is not good." In the clause "and *you* are puffed up," the Greek of the original throws a concentrated and scornful emphasis on the word "you," which, without tones or paraphrase, our language has not the power of expressing.

There is, in all minds not chastened by the spiritual symmetry of the Gospel, a tendency to substitute some favorite idea, strongly and vividly conceived, for the completed circle of important Truth. Not in relation to other men's opinions alone, but even within the sphere of our own, we are partisans, — singling out our favorites, casting into them our whole strength, determining them to be the sole essentials, making them captains over the life and the mind. In this way you will often find a man, or a society, living for a time under the dominion of a Thought, or a View, wholly given up to it, and only after a total exhaustion of whatever reality or power may be in it, as a child exhausts his childhood, lapsing from its control to pass under the same absolute subjection to the next dominant conception. "The one thing needful" with such men has indeed no long or perennial reign, but they are always under the fascination, and passing through the stages, of some new mental birth, which for the time is "the one thing needful." Such minds do not belong to the highest class, either of moral or of intellectual natures, — nor have the Societies on which they impress their own characteristics any thing of a catholic spirit; but they are often vivid, impulsive, and graphic; and they exert great influence on the less strongly marked of their fellow-men, — on the temporary mental states of a Community, through the very force and singleness with which they seize and depict some partial idea. They never give you *complete* views; but for this very reason there is no confusion in the mental image they present; — and since the singleness of one aspect of Truth is not interfered with by another and a qualifying one, they cut as with a diamond on the brain. The greater minds are deprived, by the very largeness of their views, of the use of this graphic power. The *number* of the elements which they combine and blend in a perfect Truth destroys that singleness of impression which is so often the effect of one-sidedness and of exaggeration. There is this compensation in all the gifts of God. The inferior talents are often of the readiest usury. The great minds can never be the immediately popular ones, except in some limited department of thought, to a smaller public; — their light is too broad for that, — it flows from them with the quietness of Nature's midday fulness, and does not impinge, like a fiery arrow, on the mental eye. Yet this partial and graphic form of mind, though an unsafe guide for others, is, in itself considered, a higher instrument of God than that sluggish intellectuality, which, because it sees the defects and incompleteness of every view, has earnest sympathy with none, loves nothing with a cordial heart, does nothing with the invincible might of a surrendered and unhesitating spirit, — is so doubtful, and so unsatisfied with every thing, that the hour of action, of free, unconstrained service, in entire trust of heart, to God and man, never comes to it; — and instead of passing from Saul the Jewish Zealot, to Paul the Christian Apostle, it remains for ever the undevout Gallio "who cares for none of these things."

The great Evil, however, takes place when this passionate and partial form of mind, which in the individual, if left free, is sure to exhaust itself, and pass on to nobler stages, becomes incorporated in a fixed System, and is made the outward bond of a Community, — when, arrested by the sudden paralysis of Creed or Church, denied the after developments which Nature would provide for the individual mind, and petrified at some elemental stage, it is entailed upon posterity as the full symmetry of Truth.

This fond clinging to the dominant idea of a Time, and eagerness to enthrone it for ever over the world of souls, falls in with the indolence of human nature, with an impatient demand for System that relieves from progress, and with the passionate tendencies with which men attach themselves to standards under which they have long been formed into Societies, and acted in corporate capacities. Under this weight of hereditary fidelity to a given Standard, there is no chance of sudden emancipation for the Society as a whole: — and if the associations formed under it have been coextensive with an entire People, individuals often struggle in vain, and minds, that, if left unfettered, would have gone rejoicing on their way through a succession of higher births of the soul, sink prostrate beneath its Rule.

The early Christians were not preserved from the common tendencies of Human Nature. Like other partial, and eager, minds, they seized *upon leading points*, and, in the exclusive interest attached to them, dropped out of view coördinate Truths. We find in the early Church two extremes, decidedly opposed to each other, but equally removed, in their opposite directions, from the spiritual Rule of the Gospel: — those who had their ideas of a Religion formed on the model of the Jewish Law, and never could emancipate themselves from the habit of allegiance to external authority and positive enactment, nor receive with any profound feeling of its reality the great doctrine, that the Kingdom of Heaven is within the soul; — and those whose heathen and philosophic tendencies led them to interpret this freedom from

Law in an immoral sense, — and to confound the Liberty of the Gospel with the Antinomian doctrine that the soul was independent of the impurities of the body, and was in fact elevated to higher perfection if it could dwell apart, in a cool region of its own, whilst it surrendered the physical nature to its native Evil, and placed it under no moral restraint. The first of these extremes, or the Jewish type of Christians, we find most distinctly characterized in the Epistles to the Romans and to the Galatians. The latter, *the Antinomian type* of Christians, are very distinctly alluded to in the chapter on Corinthian morals now before us, — and in the Epistles of St. John. For the true type of the Christian, the genuine subject of a Heavenly Kingdom, we must look to the Son of God, who felt the full force of the filial relation, and was the willing subject of paternal rule, — who destroyed the Law by fulfilling it, by spiritualizing and expanding it, imparting to it, from the unmeasured love within, a depth and fulness of meaning which no outward Law can be made to express; — and they alone are his subjects, modelled in his spiritual image, in the fellowship of his spirit, who have the springs of all holy living in the inward fountains of divine affections, — and, bound not by Law, but by Love, have their Blessedness in Obedience, and seek the Righteousness of God, even the Righteousness that is born of filial Faith.

St. Paul's Corinthian converts, led by the speculative tendencies of their philosophic schools, and nót preserved from that human weakness which, in its exclusive estimate of one class of interests, depreciates and neglects all others, adopted the dogmatical, instead of the spiritual type of Christianity, and, whilst boasting the superiority of their Views, turned away the earnest eye of Christian regard from the impurity of their Lives. If men place the essence of Christianity in correctness of Opinion, they will involuntarily, and in spite of themselves, regard as less essential inward communion with God, and holiness of heart and life. This arises from no turpitude of the will, but from the natural conditions of limitation, — the tendency to exclusiveness, under which all human faculties are constrained to work, — and of which it is the part of wisdom to cultivate a profound and solemn consciousness. Christianity has perhaps in no respect conferred a greater blessing on the world, than in the sense of importance it has attached to speculative Truth, — destroying all such indifference as was betrayed in Pilate's memorable question, and imparting an earnest and solemn tone to the deep convictions of the heart. But unquestionably this blessing has hitherto been purchased at a great expense to Christian charity, and to the sense of the supreme importance of the purely spiritual sources of Virtue and Piety, — and at present the profoundest want of the Christian world is some form of our Religion which will unite this supreme attachment to the spiritual faith of *the Heart* with a just sense of the undeniable importance of speculative Truth, — to make peace between the moral and the intellectual elements of our nature, and to educate us into harmony, not only with the affections, but with the mind of God. And who, that has any clear consciousness of this deep want, can doubt that God is preparing to supply it, and from the long ferment of its elements, and the exclusive development of some portions of its principles, that a full and perfect Christianity, to rise at length out of mixed agencies, to combine all partial truths, and to reconcile the warring world, is in the purpose of His providence? And with this view we mitigate our religious animosities; for, partial and incomplete as we all are, we learn to perceive that tendencies the most opposite to our own, may yet contribute something to the perfect form of Truth, the full and unmutilated Christianity which, uniting all real elements of Grace and Power, will appear at last, to explain the Past, and reconcile the Future.

The immoral tendencies and perplexities of the Corinthian Church, in contrast with their high speculative pretensions, which are described in the fifth, sixth, and seventh chapters, we shall now enumerate, noticing whatever difficulties may occur in the Apostle's treatment of these subjects.

I. He charges them with the scandal to Christianity, of retaining within its nominal communion a person notoriously guilty of leading an impure life. St. Paul, in this and in some other cases, advised excommunication, — but it was always the excommunication of immorality, and never of heresy. In this respect the Church has precisely reversed the practice of the Apostle, always excommunicating for heresy, and never for immorality. It is evident that infant and nascent Christianity, professing to exhibit a Kingdom of God upon the Earth, with its handful of disciples scattered in the midst of a Universal Heathenism, could prevail only through a true Christian power breathed forth from the lives of holy and devoted men, — that the salt of the earth must *be true salt*, and not unsound itself, — and that to let a Heathen man, with a heathen heart and a heathen life, be pointed at as an example of a Christian, was at once to destroy the Christian peculiarity, and to confuse the Kingdom of Satan with the Kingdom of God. St. Paul claims no jurisdiction over those that were without: he says that it was not for him to pass judgment on a heathen man, — let God judge him; but if any man professed himself a Christian brother; and joined himself to the small band of Christ's representatives on earth, and then brought disgrace on them by a scandalous life, — with that man he could have no association, — "no, not even to eat." If he acted in Satan's spirit, let him take his place on Satan's side; but why should one of the adversary's force, one of Satan's friends, be admitted, or openly retained, within the camp of the Lord? Let the contamination be removed; let him be taught his true place among Satan's followers, that, if there is any vestige of grace in his heart, he may be awakened to self-knowledge, and that by the present suffering of remorse his spirit may be saved in the day of the Lord Jesus. That by "Satan" no allusion was intended to any infernal Principle or Power, is very evident from the purpose which this committal to Satan was to serve, — "that the spirit might be saved." And we find exactly the same use of the expression — viz. assigning a man to the adversary's party, to the *worldly* side, if his *life* was worldly, — and for the same remedial purpose, — that he might be awakened to a knowledge of his gross inconsistency — in 1 Tim. i. 20; when St. Paul, speaking of nominal Christians who had made utter shipwreck of conscience, adds, "of whom is Hymenæus and Alexander; whom I have delivered unto Satan, that they may learn not to blaspheme." It is clear that the conception was that of two hostile Kingdoms, struggling for dominion on the earth, and that the Kingdom of Christ must not be weakened by communion with the allies of Satan, — and that these treacherous and fatal friends, if made to feel that their lives were *against* the Lord, that they were serving one cause whilst professing another, might be stirred unto repentance. This, indeed, is the essential idea that the Jews connected with Satan, — that of a tester and searcher of the spirits of men, with the probationary purpose of ascertaining, or confirming, their loyalty to conscience and to God. "Satan hath desired to have thee," says our Lord to Peter, "that he may sift thee as wheat." "Get thee behind me, Satan," is his reply to the same Apostle, when he suggested the *worldly* view of Messiah's kingdom. In the Book of Job, Satan is described as one of the angels of the Lord, whose function it was to prove by trial the hearts of men: — "Now there was a day when the Sons of God came to present themselves before the Lord, and Satan came among them. And the Lord said unto Satan, 'Whence comest thou?' Then Satan answered the Lord and said, 'From going to and fro on the earth, and from walking up and down in it.' And the Lord said unto Satan, 'Hast thou considered my servant Job, that there is none like him in the earth, a perfect and an upright man, one that feareth God, and escheweth evil?' Then Satan answered the Lord and said, 'Doth Job fear God for naught? Hast thou not made a hedge about him and about his house, and about all that he hath on every side? Thou hast blessed the work of his hands, and his substance is increased in the land. But put forth thine hand now, and touch all that he hath, and he will curse thee to thy face.' And the Lord said unto Satan, 'Behold, all that he hath is in thy power, — only upon himself put not forth thine hand.' So Satan went forth from the presence of the Lord."

When St. Paul urges the Corinthians to reject from the Christian Association the impure person, he employs the illustration, that "a little leaven leaveneth the whole lump"; — and following out the figure, he conceives of Christianity as the everlasting Festival of purity, when the old leaven was to be cast away for ever, and the unleavened bread of simplicity and truth, through an everlasting Passover, was to be the heavenly bread of life to the delivered of the Lord. The death of Christ dated the Era of Deliverance: the Passover is slain, — let nothing of the leaven of slavery and sin be found among the Lord's freemen. I know not under what strange misunderstanding this beautiful image can be applied to the common doctrine of the Atonement. The Passover marked a season of Deliverance,—and annually at the commemorating Feast the Jews cleansed their houses, and for eight days used only unleavened Bread. The Lamb slain on the occasion was not a sacrifice in any sense; it was a commemorative emblem of the Blood on the lintel, which the Destroying Angel observed, and left the house unscathed. And when Christ brought Deliverance from sin, and led the way to a heavenly Canaan, the Festival of Purity was to last *for ever*, the leaven of malice and wickedness was never to ferment in Christian homes or hearts again,—and those whose Passover from Heathen slavery commenced with the death of the Lamb of God (no more a sacrificial death than the Lamb of the Passover),—their relations to whom were now unbroken in the pure Heavens, spiritual and immortal,—were to keep for ever the Festival of Sacredness, and to have no more fellowship with the old Leaven, but to live as New Creatures, members of a Heavenly Kingdom.

II. In the sixth chapter, St. Paul exposes the utter violation of the Idea of a Christian Community implied in the injurious and litigious spirit, that, in the first place, could give cause for the interference of the Law,—and in the second, through the weakness of brotherly love, require the settlement of differences to be referred to the Heathen Tribunals. There was a double evil here;—the absence of the Christian bond in their own hearts, and the injury they inflicted on the cause of Christ, by failing to hold before the world the realized Image of a Christian Brotherhood. The Kingdom of God on Earth, the Reign of Love and Holiness, was as manifestly set at naught, and in the individual case proclaimed a failure, by the violation of its Peace, as by the violation of its Purity. It was too evident, that neither the litigious, nor the unholy, had established a Kingdom of Heaven.

In our Translation the fourth verse of the sixth chapter is unintelligible: "If, then, ye have judgments of things pertaining to this life, set them to judge who are least esteemed in the Church." Paul's meaning seems to have been: "If, then, ye have matters of judgment amongst yourselves, about affairs relating to common life,—do ye call in, to judge between you, those [unbelievers] who have no place in the Christian community? I speak this to your shame."

In the moral reasonings which St. Paul ascribes to the Corinthians, from the twelfth verse to the end of the eleventh chapter, there are the distinct suggestions of an Antinomian spirit. St. Paul, as his custom is, meets all such gross sophistry, such scandalous falsifications of the Liberty of the Gospel, by an appeal to first principles: "What did you profess, when you became Christians? To yield up your members to Christ, as instruments to work in his spirit, and do his will. What did you lay aside, when you professed Christ as your Master? The mastery over yourselves. You are not your own; your Master is in heaven,—and a holy spirit must rule you. Know ye not that your bodies are members of Christ, — and he that is united with the Lord must be of one spirit with him? Know ye not that your body is the Temple of the Holy Spirit which is in you, which ye have from God, — and that ye are not your own? — therefore, glorify God in your body."

Even in matters of indifference in themselves, St. Paul maintains that Christian Liberty is a great responsibility, which must be exercised under two conditions: that we infringe the Liberty of none, — and that at no moment, by indulgence in things indifferent, shall we be deprived of the mastery over our faculties, or be incapacitated for the severest Christian service. "Indifferent things are lawful for me: but they may be inexpedient. Indifferent things are lawful for me: *but I will not be enslaved by any thing*." How much are we all enslaved by enemies, that seem too trivial for the energy of Conscience to rise in its awfulness and slay! Petty weaknesses, and loose habits, creep over us and bind our giant strength. Small cares, some deficiencies in the mere arrangement and ordering of our lives, daily fret our hearts, and cross the clearness of our faculties; and these entanglements hang around us, and leave us no free soul able to give itself up, in power and gladness, to the true work of life. There is the profoundest moral truth in that doctrine of St. Paul's, that entire mastery over the physical nature is the only basis from which all the higher power of character must proceed. The severest training and self-denial, — a superiority to the servitude of indulgence, — are the indispensable conditions even of genial spirits, of unclouded energies, of tempers free from morbidness, — much more of the practised and vigorous mind, ready at every call, and thoroughly furnished unto all good works. In the lassitude and indulgence by which we deprive the soul of this physical fitness and freedom, many of us greatly sin; — nor is there a spiritual counsel that ought daily to penetrate the soul with more solemn tone than that high resolve of Christ's freeman, — I will not be brought under the power of any thing."

III. It could not but happen in the circumstances of the Early Church, that great anxiety and perplexity should arise in connection with the domestic relations. Ought a man, whom Persecution might at any moment leave no home upon the earth, to involve others in these trials of his faith? Must not the Cross be borne alone, rather than "a sword pierce through the soul" of family and kindred? Again, in the case of domestic relations already existing, if only one of the parties should be converted to the Gospel, how could that intimate communion of thought and spirit, without which the relation is a practical falsehood, subsist between a Christian and an Idolater? Did the spiritual change dissolve the temporal relation, in which there was no longer a soul of Truth? St. Paul gives his judgment on these points, which seem to have been brought before him in the form of questions by a Letter from the Corinthians, in the seventh chapter. His answers are avowedly given, in relation to the temporary circumstances of an infant Religion struggling for existence, and demanding the complete self-sacrifice of its first members,—and are framed, not upon unchanging principles, or laws of the Moral Nature, but upon considerations of present wisdom and expediency. He leans to the side of freedom from care and private relations; and in a case where fidelity to God and the domestic affections would cross, and make for each other severe temptations, he would be for giving no "hostages to Fortune." But he confesses that this was only what he deemed best for himself, and that he was no Law for others: "For every one hath *his own* gift from God; one after this manner, and another after that." The circumstances in which a man works out his mission of faithfulness to his highest convictions, may be of any nature whatever, if *in them* that faithfulness is preserved, and the spirit of Truth and Duty honestly wrought into outward expression. This was the noble Principle which Christ's Apostles announced, for the guidance of the Church in the most critical times. The spirit of Christianity is strong enough to sustain itself and sanctify Life, under any outward relations. Fret not against the outward Circumstance, but take up its burden with a Christian heart,—and the right soul will, in time, put all things right, and spiritually adjust the relations of life:—"Art thou called, being a Slave? Deem that your obedience is paid to God,—and care not for it; receive your external relations as from God,—for both the slave and the freeman are the servants of the Lord,—and he is the noblest who is faithful to his spiritual Master at the severest post." If Slavery was doomed to pass away before the Christian sentiment, every slave sustaining his hard relations in a Christian spirit, was exhibiting the inherent equality of all humanity, and emancipating the world. "Art thou called in circumcision, or in uncircumcision? Circumcision is nothing, and uncircumcision is nothing; — but the keeping of the commandments of God." "Art thou called, having an unbelieving husband? Desert not thine own faith for him, — but sanctify him with thy believing mind. Brethren, let every one remain *with God*, in that state in which he was called."

All external relations are alike to those who in them make no shipwreck of faith and conscience. Only, let no man's soul settle down upon present things, or fail to see that the essence of Joy, as of Duty, has no abode on earth, and, being divine and eternal, must soon change its transient form to inherit its imperishable substance. The essential character of joys and sorrows springing out of temporal relations is their transitoriness, — the essence of all spiritual bonds is their preservation by God, — their immortality with Him in the infinite world. "But this I say, brethren, Whatever be your outward relations, — *the time is short;* — it remaineth, that both they that have wives be as though they had none, — and they that weep, as though they wept not (as though God had already dried their tears), — and they that rejoice, as though they rejoiced not, sitting loose to life, — and they that buy, as though they possessed not, — and they that use this world as not abusing it: for the fashion of this world passeth away: and I would have you to be without vain anxiety." (vii. 29, 31.)

SECTION II.

PERPLEXITIES AND PERILS TO THE RECENT CONVERTS TO CHRISTIANITY, FROM THE CONNECTION OF GENTILE MANNERS WITH IDOLATROUS OBSERVANCES. — KNOWLEDGE WITHOUT LOVE NO PRINCIPLE OF CHRISTIAN ACTION. — PAUL'S APPEAL TO HIS OWN EXAMPLE OF FORBEARANCE FROM LAWFUL THINGS FOR THE SAKE OF OTHERS.

CHAPS. VIII., IX.

VIII. 1. Now concerning things offered unto idols, 'we
know'; for we all have knowledge. Knowledge puffeth
2 up; but charity buildeth up. And if any one think that
he knoweth any thing, he knoweth nothing yet as he
3 ought to know. But if any one loveth God, the same is
4 known of Him. As concerning therefore the eating of
things offered in sacrifice unto idols, 'we know that an
idol is nothing in the world, and that there is no other
5 God but one. For though there be that are called gods,
whether in heaven or in earth (as there are gods many,
6 and lords many), yet to us there is one God, the Father,
of whom are all things, and we in Him, and one Lord,
Jesus Christ, through whom are all things, and we through
7 him.' But there is not in all this knowledge: for some,
with a consciousness of the idol, to this hour eat as of
what was offered to an idol, and their conscience being

8 weak is defiled. 'But meat commendeth us not to God;
for neither, if we eat, are we the better; nor, if we eat
9 not, are we the worse.' But see to it, lest by any means
this liberty of yours become an occasion of sin to them
10 that are weak. For if any one see thee, who hast knowledge, at table in an idol's temple, shall not the conscience
of him who is weak be emboldened to eat the things of-
11 fered to idols? And through thy knowledge, the weak
12 brother for whom Christ died shall perish. But when ye
thus sin against the brethren, and wound their weak con-
13 science, ye sin against Christ. Wherefore, if meat make
my brother to sin, I will never more eat flesh, lest I make
my brother to sin.

IX. 1. Am I not free? Am I not an Apostle? Have I
not seen Jesus Christ our Lord? Are not ye my work in
2 the Lord? If to others I am not an Apostle, at least I
am to you, for ye are the seal of my Apostleship in the
3 Lord. My answer to those who question me is this:
4 Have not we privilege to eat and to drink? Have not
5 we privilege to take one of the sisters to wife, as well as
the other Apostles, and the brethren of the Lord, and Ce-
6 phas? Or have I and Barnabas, only, no privilege to
7 abstain from working? Who ever serveth in war at his
own charges? Who planteth a vineyard, and eateth not
of its fruit? or who tendeth a flock, and eateth not of
8 the milk of the flock? Say I these things as a man?
9 or doth not the law also say the same? For it is written in the law of Moses, "Thou shalt not muzzle the
ox that treadeth out the corn."* Is God's care for
10 oxen? Or does he not say it altogether for us? For
us it was written, that he who plougheth should plough in

---

* Deut. xxv. 4.

hope, — and he that thresheth, in the hope of partaking.
11 If we have sown for you spiritual things, is it a great
12 thing if we reap your fleshly things? If others partake
of this privilege with you, shall not we rather? Yet we
have not used this privilege; but we endure all things,
that we may give no hinderance to the Gospel of Christ.
13 Know ye not that they who minister in holy things are
fed from the temple? and that they who wait at the altar
14 partake with the altar? So also hath the Lord ordained
for those who preach the Gospel, to live by the Gospel.
15 But I have not used any of these things: neither have I
written these things that so it should be done unto me:
for better to die than that any one should make my glo-
16 rying void. For that I preach the Gospel is not my glorying; for necessity is laid upon me; for woe is me if I
17 preach not the Gospel. For if I do this willingly I have
a reward; but if unwillingly, I have been put in trust
18 with a charge. What then is my reward? That, whilst
preaching the Gospel, I make the Gospel of Christ without cost, so that I abuse not my privilege in the Gospel.
19 For being free from all, I have made myself the slave of
20 all, that I might gain the more. And to the Jews I became as a Jew, that I might gain the Jews; to those under the law, as one under the law, not being myself under the law, that I might gain those who are under the
21 law; to those without law, as one without law (not being
without law to God, but under law to Christ), that I might
22 gain those that are without law. To the weak became I
as one weak, that I might gain the weak. I became all
23 things to all, that by all means I might save some. And
this I do for the Gospel's sake, that I may be a partaker
24 in it. Know ye not that they who run in the race-course
run all, but one receiveth the prize? So run, that ye
25 may obtain. And every one that contendeth in the games

is temperate in all things: and they, that they may obtain
a corruptible crown; but we, that we may obtain an in-
26 corruptible. I therefore so run, as not uncertainly; I so
27 fight, as not beating the air: but I keep my body under,
and bring it into subjection, lest, having been a herald to
others, I should myself become dishonored.

It is but seldom that new moral Light comes so suddenly on the souls of men, that it enters into direct collision with the existing arrangements of Society, and requires violent changes in their modes of life. Even the greatest social revolutions, when they come in the natural course of human affairs, spring from the inward life and progress of Man: they are not sudden bursts of Enthusiasm or new-born Truth, but the eventual expressions of sentiments that had been long working in the popular mind, and that, after silently remodelling standard modes of thinking, pass at length into outward representation, and are livingly reflected in the Institutions, and the Civilization, which their spirit has created. Such natural Revolutions, if ushered into day by the quiet hand of God, whose preparations for progress are in the silent renovations of the heart, and whose Providence revolts from all violence of transition, — if left to the unconstrained ebb and flow of the vast human spirit moved and directed by influence and energy from on high, — if not artificially checked and fretted by selfish interferences and class obstructions, — would no more disarrange any existing interest, or come into abrupt opposition to any existing mode of life, than the Light of day, which reaches its meridian fulness without any human eye being able to detect the momentary gradation of its brightness, enters into an abrupt struggle with the Darkness, which insensibly it conquers. It is only the spirit of individual self-will, seeking to realize its own ends by precipitancy or resistance, that disturbs for a time the quiet flow of God's advancing providence; and under the natural government of the world, there are no violent changes introduced into human affairs, or into the moral adjustments of life, except those that spring from the selfish opposition of Individuals to the directions of the general Good, — from some powerful Class arresting, for a brief and desperate moment, the strong movement of Humanity. Such is the Law of God's natural providence; — violence never appears in it; — sudden changes never take place in it, — except when forced into existence by the selfish opposition of Individuals to the general directions of Mankind.

It might be supposed, that, in the times of a *supernatural* Influence exerted from on high, this Law of gentle and peaceful transitions would disappear, — that Revelation, by its very nature implying the coming of *new* Light into the world, not born within the heart but descending from heaven upon it, would at once, by a sudden enlightening of the moral nature, throw it out of harmony with institutions and modes of life which had been suited to its unregenerated state, the products of its lower and darker views; and that the perception of new and purer moral relations would require corresponding outward adjustments, and lead to immediate social convulsions. We can imagine, for example, what violence and disorder Christianity would have introduced into the commonest relations of Life, if, with a cold and hard exclusiveness, it had insisted on an immediate and complete harmony in all outward things with the final results of its own principles; — if, instead of planting a new sentiment in the heart, the seed of future change, and leaving it to work outwards, as it acquired fulness and strength within, it had commenced by enforcing the external Reformation; — if it had openly denounced consecrated observances, instead of gradually purifying the inward feelings from which their life was derived; — if it had commanded the *Slave* to assert his Freedom, and by physical resistance make good the spiritual claim; — if it had entered into the delicate and intricate relations of domestic life, and, regardless of the sacredness of existing bonds and affections, however theoretically imperfect, insisted on an immediate and forcible adjustment of all private connections in harmony with the purest realizations of Christian sentiment. God had provided, indeed, against the confusion that would in this way have been created, — by bringing the various nations of the world nearly to a moral level, when the Fulness of Time was come, so that the divine light of the Gospel fell with a remarkable uniformity of impression on the varied heart of Man, — and by meeting the diversities and conflicts of moral sentiment that were produced by that suddenness of illumination, even within the Church itself, with the healing spirit, the large wisdom, that flowed out of the heart of Christ, and that so eminently guided the administration of the great Apostle who was the principal agent in the establishment of his Kingdom. In more modern times, the history of Christianity has not been without exemplifications of the disorder created by violent attempts to remodel the outward life, before the Christian sentiment had taken possession of the inward springs of action. By the operation of Christian Missionaries a state of circumstances has been produced, that has no parallel in the times of the primitive Church: the highest and the lowest grades of civilization have been brought suddenly into moral intercourse, — and, instead of the patient heart, and spiritual eye, of Christ and Paul, there have too often been the formalism, the outward exactingness, of a precisian and a zealot. No cause of failure appears more prominent in the still noble history of Missionary effort, than an unyielding demand for violent changes in the habits of social life, — a hard enforcement of the outward realizations of Christianity before they could be the natural fruits of Christian sentiment,* — an attempt to subdue the sacredness of Nature in the savage heart by the power of

---

* A horrid, yet ludicrous, instance presents itself in the Paper of the day on which I was revising the MS. of this page: —

"Polygamy prevails in New Zealand, and a Chief with ten wives was told that he could not be baptized, unless he confined himself to one. At the end of about two months he repaired to the nearest Missionary, and stated that he had got rid of nine. 'What have you done with them?' was the natural interrogatory. 'I have eaten them,' was the unhesitating reply." — LECTURE by Lord JOHN MANNERS, *Inquirer* Newspaper, Feb. 1, 1851.

an outward Law, — a cause of failure that could never have come into operation, if the spiritual and catholic mind of Christ, his supreme regard for the smallest seeds of Life in the soul, the grains of living Faith, had been more profoundly sympathized with, or if the example had been followed, of "the Planting and Training of the Christian Church" by the great Apostle.

We have in these chapters remarkable examples of the practical wisdom of St. Paul; — and that not the wisdom of tact, nor of skilful address in the management of difficulties, — but the wisdom of a large and noble Nature, careful only that the principles of the Christian life should take root in the heart of the world, and undisturbed by small and unspiritual uneasiness about the external diversities, in which the Individuality of our nature manifests its infinite Variety. There was, in fact, a *truthfulness* in Paul's mind, that made him very patient of the slow and imperfect developments of Christian principles. He would not have accepted outward realizations of the Christian spirit, unless they had been forced into life by the genuine demands of the heart; — and the broken surface of the Christian world when the Light of Christ's mind first penetrated the moralities of Heathen and Jewish sentiment, the differences of form and degree in which it rent men from their old usages, in proportion to their moral susceptibility, showed the genuine truth and energy of the new Influence, — and that the Christian spirit had kindled its own fire in each separate breast.

We are presented here with the nearest approach

that the early records of Christianity contain, to a history of the unavoidable collisions between the new modes of Life required by the Gospel, and the old usages which affection, and even conscience, had long hallowed and endeared. We find ourselves in the midst of a warfare of Ideas: — Light from God has suddenly fallen on the confirmed habits of a people, — and the forms of a higher civilization and of a spiritual worship are slowly, and with many inconsistencies, developing themselves, as the results of a contest between fresh sentiment and long established usage. We must reproduce this state of things, with some little energy of the imagination, in order to look upon this Epistle from the Apostle's point of view. All is disorder, inconsistency, incompleteness. The new influence is partially disengaging some elements, and combining imperfectly with others, but as yet has produced no crystallized forms. The Christian spirit, introduced like leaven into the mass of heathen and Jewish ideas, has thrown them into violent fermentation, and an incongruous union of the old and the new Life is for a time the genuine and the right result of these mixing agencies. Nothing could have proved so fatal to the safe establishment of Christianity, as that, in such a crisis, a man of a conventional and narrow spirit, a rigid exacter of external consistency and symmetry, had taken the lead in the administration of the Church, and made it his first object to impress the Ideals of his own mind, the final results of Christian principles, on the natural and healthy disorder of the times. Here was the spiritual equality of all mankind — the doctrine of individual responsibility, and of course of an unlimited right over our own limbs and souls, that we may obey our own conscience — proclaimed in the midst of a civilization of which Slavery was a fundamental institution; — a doctrine which could not instantly be realized without, not only a revolution in the inward sentiment, but a total derangement in the daily life of a whole people, — such a derangement as, if immediately enforced, must have reduced Society to its first elements, and led to a direct collision of conflicting interests. Here, the pure sentiment of Christian Love, and a sense of the union of all spirits in holy relation to one Heavenly Father, was penetrating the bosom of Heathen families, and separating some wedded heart from a partner who still revelled in the worship and the license of Idolatry. Here were the very household usages of a People determined by the daily sacrifices to the gods, and interwoven with all the observances of Polytheism; — and to stand aloof from all contact with Idolatry would have been to renounce the World. Now it greatly increases the feeling of reality with which we conceive of Christianity coming as a new Influence into the world, when we thus historically find it engaged in collision with the modes of common Life created by a spirit so different from its own, — and can trace the moral inconsistencies, the first incomplete workings, of the partial penetration of its energy into the bosom of the Heathen and Jewish civilizations. And when we consider that the Authenticity of these Epistles of St. Paul has never been disputed by any party, we cannot conceive that any thing more is wanting to the substantial validity of the external evidences of Christianity, — nor how, amid such vivid pictures of its actual workings, the reality of that new Influence, introduced from on high into the affairs of men, can in its essential character be open to question, or received by so many earnest minds with vague and doubting Faith. The delineation of Christ's mind can be collected only from the Gospels; but as evidences of the Reality of *some* higher influence, introduced by God through the person of Christ into the common heart of the World, the Epistles afford the ground on which the Argument can decisively be conducted.

I. And if the actual appearance of these difficulties, in the midst of the common relations of Heathen and Jewish life, is the best proof of the *reality* of the Christian Influence, the spirit in which they were met and overcome exalts the *character* of that Influence to the calmness and comprehensiveness of God, by that "meekness of wisdom" which is the least questionable sign of whatever is Divine. *Knowledge*, superior enlightenment, the Freedom of a strong mind from religious weaknesses, St. Paul maintains, have their distinctive and Christian value, not in enabling a man to pursue his own way, but in enabling him to tread, with a quiet and sympathizing heart, in the harmless ways which, for a time, the comparative feebleness of others may compel them to adopt. In relation to things indifferent, who ought to yield, — the strong or the weak, — the scrupulous or the enlightened? — those who deem them essential and indispensable, — or those who deem them of no vital importance whatever, the one way, or the other? The weak cannot yield, without an injury and violence to Conscience, the worst of all evils; and if the strong *will not* yield, because they stand on the individual rights of their own Enlightenment, then Christian Unity is broken by those who follow the guidance of Knowledge alone, and take no guidance from Love. The Christian use of a spiritual discernment of things essential, is to enable a large mind to act with forbearance in things indifferent, — to yield to the scrupulous who conscientiously cannot yield, — and in its tenderness and comprehensiveness to manifest the catholic and healing spirit of true Religion. What is the moral use of Strength, if it does not enable us to bear with the weaknesses of others? The strong, unless they can vindicate their right to walk the world alone, and come into contact with no mind but God's, are the last who can, with a clear conscience, pass by the infirmities of the feeble. It is for the weak to be intolerant of the weak, — for his own helplessness is enough for each, and their mutual infirmities may come into selfish collision; but it is for the strong, *who can do it,* to forbear, and stoop, and lift the burden, in thankfulness of heart to God, by whose grace it is that he himself is not one of those who crowd, and straiten, and embarrass the way of Life. What is the boasted privilege of Liberty, if we are as much Bigots in our opposition to scruples as others are in their slavery to them? It is the glory of the free mind, that in things indifferent it can move off its own ground of abstract Knowledge, and with a clear and loving heart go, and join itself, to the weak and the bound, who cannot come to it. This is the Law of guidance in all such collisions, which St. Paul, with exquisite beauty and force of expression, lays down for those Corinthian leaders, who, severing Knowledge from Love, deemed themselves strong and independent in their religious enlightenment. Knowledge, unless placed under the guidance of Sympathy, is not a Christian principle of action, in relation to other minds. *Knowledge* alone only elateth *the individual;* but when guided by Love, it buildeth up the Church. "Knowledge puffeth up, but Charity buildeth up." "If a man thinketh that he knoweth any thing, and that his Knowledge makes for him an independent path in his moral relations to others, then he knoweth nothing as he ought to know: but if any man love God, and sinks all individual pretensions in his common relation to the universal Father, and so rises above self-love into a disinterested affection, — the same is known of God, — God recognizes in him His own spirit." Here it is remarkable that the man who loves God is not said to know God, — but God is said to know him. In the same manner, the Son of Man is represented as saying to those who do not manifest the mercies of his temper, "*I know you not.*" Such expressions show how thoroughly the spiritual sentiment had penetrated to the finest sources of language; and in both cases they mean, that the spirit of God, full of Grace as of Truth, has no intimate connections with self-centred, unsympathizing natures, — dwells not in such breasts. (viii. 1, 3.)

II. The particular case which required the clear expression of this practical Rule, arose out of the impossibility, in a Heathen City, of avoiding contact with the daily sacrifices of Polytheism. The Temples were, in fact, in a great measure the Markets of the Heathen world. The sacrifices were not entirely consumed on the altars, and what remained were the perquisites of the Priests, or the property of the offerers. A feast in the Temple was the usual sequel to a sacrifice; and a strong-minded Christian, who believed that an Idol was nothing in the world, and that, notwithstanding the Pagan worship of gods many and lords many, there was but one God our Father, and one Lord Jesus Christ, might have no scruple in partaking of the feast, which could not be an act of worship to the Idol, in whose very existence he did not believe. This is the case which, in the eighth and ninth chapters, St. Paul discusses with those who took their abstract Knowledge and enlightenment alone, unguided by a Christian sympathy for the scruples of the weaker brethren, as their only Law of social action. Admitting that the thing was in itself indifferent, and that an Idol was nothing in the world, and so could have no worship paid to it, he yet condemns a participation of the Feast in the Idol's Temple, as a wanton disregard of the consciences of others, and a dangerous snare for their own. The *Knowledge*, alleged in excuse, "that there was no God but one," and that

"God taketh no account of meats, for neither if we eat are we the better, nor if we eat not are we the worse,"—was indeed a self-justification, if they had been alone in the world, with God only,—and their conduct had reflected no influences on the souls of others. But no man, except in the silent depths of the spirit, sustains these exclusive relations with the Father of the Soul,—no man liveth to himself even in things pertaining to God, and a wise and tender sympathy for the interests of others must qualify and guide his Knowledge,—else, "he knoweth nothing as he ought to know." Others of weaker Faith, of temperaments more sensitive to the consecrated impressions of the Past, less free from the lingering vestiges of the old Idolatry, might not have this absolute conviction of the non-existence of the Idol God, and eat in trembling doubt, or with a scrupulous alarm lest the very act of eating might imply worship and recognition,—and so the weak conscience be defiled. "Take heed lest by any means this your Liberty become an occasion of sin to those that are weak. For if any one see thee, who hast Knowledge, sitting at meat in an Idol's Temple, will not his conscience, if he be weak, be encouraged to eat things offered to Idols? and *thus*, through thy Knowledge, without love or self-denial, the weak brother, for whom Christ in self-denial died, will lapse into guilt. And when ye thus sin against the brethren, and wound their weak conscience, ye sin against Christ. Wherefore if meat make my brother to offend, I will never more eat meat, lest I make my brother to offend."

III. The connection of the ninth chapter with this Christian Duty, of consideration for the wounded Conscience of the weakest Disciple, is not distinctly stated. Yet there can be no doubt that St. Paul appealed to *his own* Example, in proof that he made no claim on their forbearance or tenderness that he himself was not willing to observe, — and that the superior Knowledge, and spiritual Liberty, which had never exonerated *him* from tender adaptation to the wants, weaknesses, and susceptibilities of Jew or Gentile, could not be pleaded *by them* in excuse for the sin of self-concentrated disregard for the moral Temptations that belonged to any peculiar experiences, or forms of mind. There is a slight obscurity, or strangeness, in occasional expressions, arising, it would appear, from St. Paul's alluding, in an indirect way, to the injurious representations of his depreciating opponents at Corinth, — whilst at the same time he is pursuing the main current of his Christian argument. It is only on this supposition, that some unjust suspicion had been cast on the generosity of his motives, or some doubt hinted of the authority of his Apostleship, on the ground that he had had no *personal* intercourse with Christ, — that we can account for the necessity he seems to feel, of first vindicating his Character, which in the Second Epistle we shall find him obliged to do at great length, — and of claiming the fulness of his Office, before he proceeds to make application to their case of the Example he had shown of the voluntary resignation of his own Liberty, for the sake of the spiritual welfare of the Church. For the sake of unobstructed access to the Jewish mind, he had resigned his Liberty in ceremonial observances, in meats, and drinks, and fasts, and remained under the Law, — though no man made less account of such matters. For the sake of entire devotion to his missionary service, he had resigned all personal affections, and *wedded* his spirit only to the Church of Christ. For the sake of the loftier influence that belongs to an unrewarded service, he had resigned his Right of maintenance, — the Right of living by his work that belongs to every laborer, even to the ox that treadeth out the corn, — and he had toiled with his own hands, that he might burden no one, and the Gospel be a free gift. The early life of Saul the Persecutor, the enemy of Christ, left one indelible impression on the heart of the Apostle, — not in bitterness or remorse, but in the inextinguishable desire to do free service for the Gospel, — to atone for the Past by spending, and being spent, in its cause, without being placed in any connection with it to which the thought of a recompense could attach. How noble is this desire to do something *voluntarily*, over and above what he was bound to do, on the part of one who, though no victim of morbid memories, could not altogether efface from his heart its past history. "Though I preach the Gospel, I have nothing to glory of: because necessity is laid upon me; yea, woe is unto me if I preach not the Gospel. But if I do this *willingly*, I have a reward. What then is my reward? Verily, that, while I preach the Gospel, I make the ministry of the Gospel to be without recompense, — that I serve in Love." "And though free from all men, I have made myself the slave of all, that, by meeting their wants, I might win them to the Gospel. With the Jews I had intercourse as a Jew, that I might gain the Jews: to those without the Law, I became as one under Law to God and Christ only, — that I might gain those that were without the Jewish Law; to the weak I became as weak, that I might gain the weak: I have become all things to all men, that I might by all means save some. And this have I done for the Gospel's sake, that I, too, may have a share in its diffusion."

The application to the Corinthians, and to all men, lies in this, — that the Christian service is one of disinterested regard for the benefit of others, and that we must abjure our self-will whenever it interferes with this end, — and, instead of standing on our individuality, forget ourselves in sympathy. This is the incorruptible crown for which the Christian strives, this is the glory of Christ himself, — to find our life and joy, not in working our own pleasure, or seeking our own ends, but in blessing others, when and how *they can* be blessed, and finding, without seeking, our own blessedness therein. And if we seek this glory of the Lord, we must first strive for mastery over ourselves, and keep our self-will under, and have our affections directed not on ourselves but out of ourselves, fixed on those whom by our true service we may bless, else we "run with no definite object, and we fight as one that beats the air." Those who would be Victors in this contest, Athletes in this fight, must carry no dead-weights of selfishness, — must find their element in the spirit of self-forgetfulness, — their genuine blessedness in disinterested affections, — in the exercise of a pure Love, whose singleness of eye has no view to recompense, no self-directed glance. This was the spirit, the joy, the power, the crown, of him who reigneth from the Cross.

God give us grace to be in fellowship with that first-born of many Brethren!

SECTION III.

A CAUTION AGAINST SELF-CONFIDENCE; LEST AN UNSCRUPULOUS FAMILIARITY WITH POLYTHEISTIC HABITS MIGHT LEAD TO A RELAPSE INTO HEATHENISM.—THE PARALLEL CASE OF THE JEWS OF OLD.—COMMUNION WITH CHRIST EXCLUDES ALL DALLIANCE WITH IDOLATRY.—LOVE SHOULD CONTROL LIBERTY IN THINGS INDIFFERENT.

CHAPS. X. 1-33-XI. 1.

X. 1. For, Brethren, I would not that ye should be ignorant, that all our fathers were under the cloud,
2 and all passed through the sea; and were all baptized
3 into Moses, in the cloud and in the sea; and did all
4 eat the same spiritual bread, and did all drink the
same spiritual drink, for they drank from that spiritual rock which followed them, and that rock was
5 Christ;—yet with most of them God was not pleased,
6 for they were slain in the desert. Now these things
have become examples for us, that we should not lust
7 after evil things, even as they lusted: nor become
idolaters as some of them did; as it is written, "The
people sat down to eat and drink, and rose up to
8 play." * Neither let us commit fornication, as some of
them committed, and fell in one day three-and-twenty
9 thousand. Neither let us try Christ, as some of them
10 also tried, and were destroyed by serpents. Neither
murmur, as some of them also murmured, and perished

* Exod. xxxii. 6.

11 by the destroyer. Now all these things happened to
them as examples, and are written for our admonition,
12 upon whom the ends of the ages are come. Wherefore let him, who thinketh he standeth, take heed lest
13 he fall. There hath no temptation taken you but
such as is common to man: and God is faithful, who
will not suffer you to be tempted above that ye are
able, but will with the temptation make also a way of
14 escape, that ye may be able to endure. Wherefore,
15 my beloved, flee from idolatry. I speak as to wise
16 men: judge ye what I say. The cup of blessing which
we bless, is it not the communion of the blood of
Christ? The bread which we break, is it not the com-
17 munion of the body of Christ? That as there is one
bread, we, being many, are one body, for we all par-
18 take of the one bread. Behold Israel according to
the flesh: are not they which eat of the sacrifices par-
19 takers of the altar? What then do I say? that an idol
is any thing? or that what is sacrificed to idols is
20 any thing? No, but that what the Gentiles sacrifice,
they sacrifice to demons and not to God; and I would
not that ye should become in communion with de-
21 mons. Ye cannot drink the cup of the Lord, and the
cup of demons: ye cannot partake of the table of the
22 Lord, and of the table of demons. Do we provoke the
Lord to jealousy? Are we stronger than he?

23 All things are lawful; but all are not exepdient.
24 All things are lawful; but all do not edify. Let no
25 one seek his own, but that of another. All that is
sold in the market eat, asking no questions for con-
26 science' sake. For the earth is the Lord's, and the
27 fulness thereof. And if any of the unbelievers invite
you, and ye be willing to go, whatever is set before
you eat, asking no questions for conscience' sake.

28 But if any one say to you, "This hath been sacrificed to idols," eat not, because of him that pointed
29 it out, and because of conscience. Conscience I say,
not thine own, but that of the other. Why is my
30 liberty judged of by another man's conscience? If I
partake by grace, why am I evil spoken of, on account
31 of that for which I give thanks? Whether, therefore,
ye eat or drink, or whatever ye do, do all to God's
32 glory. Become occasions of sin neither to Jews, nor to
33 Gentiles, nor to the Church of God: even as I please
all men in all things, not seeking mine own benefit
but the benefit of the many, that they may be saved.
XI. 1. Become imitators of me, even as I am of Christ.

THERE is something of pleasing and graceful sentiment in the prevalent conception, that the Early Ages of the Church were the pure times of Christianity. The mind does not readily adapt itself to the idea, that Antiquity was the Infancy of human wisdom and development, — and that modern men are the Sages of Time. There is an instinctive tendency to regard that venerable Past as the Fountain-head of Knowledge, and to place ourselves in humble attitude, as juniors and disciples, at the feet of those "gray fathers" of the Ancient World. This indeed is but a sentiment, which reflection speedily corrects; and, as happens to most sentiments, even to those that have a divine Right of Rule, it is not suffered to stand in the way of any practical interest that touches the business and bosoms of men. Reverence for Antiquity will impede no man's gains, and the Wisdom of our Ancestors is seldom used as an argument against change, except when it is a profitable plea. There are minds, no doubt, abstracted from the world, with whom this worship of the Past is a lofty and enthusiastic sentiment, nor do we envy the man whose thoughts are never tinged by its solemn power. But still, wherever in the press of real life, in the great questions that practically affect Society, that sentiment holds its place as a guide to conduct, it will be found on the side of Interest and Ease, — that under its influence large classes of men neither make sacrifices for the good of others, nor resist advantages for themselves. It has indeed too slight a basis of truth to be of any practical force, except when allied with some secret motive of self. That no voice comes to us from the first Ages of the world for thousands of years, because, even as children write no Histories, undeveloped man had nothing to record; — that the earliest exercise of human faculties was in the helpless surrender of the Imagination, a dim, passive, and shadowy Mirror, to the forms of the Outward World; — that the first Worship and the first Civilization were in rude attempts to symbolize the Powers of Nature in vast and shapeless emblems; — that the period of authentic History commenced only when Man ceased to lie, like a dreaming child, on the mighty bosom of the External Universe, and awoke dimly to the consciousness of an inward Life and a spiritual Nature, designed to interpret and rule the Outward, not to lie prostrate beneath it; — that *Experience* is accumulative and her lessons most abundant, not in the earlier but in the latter Ages; — that all physical science is of modern date, and only in the sixteenth century an Englishman revealed the methods by which Nature should be studied; — that Revelation itself has had an historical development, and Moses and the Prophets are no longer the Lights of spiritual man: — these are facts, in the face of which mere veneration for Antiquity cannot reasonably be expected to hold its place, against any real interest, or temptation, of the world.

But no sooner is one Figure of the Imagination removed than another takes its place; for it is wonderful to what extent Metaphors rule the world. If length of experience belongs to modern men, and we, in the opportunities of knowledge, are the seniors of Antiquity, — then we change the emblem, and, since we cannot regard the olden Time as the hoary Age, we now call it the *Infancy* of the Race; and no sooner have we given it that name, than images of purity, and simplicity, and innocence, rise before us, — the golden light of Childhood fills our eye; — and the next error we fall into is, that, if the Primitive Times were not wiser, they were at least purer, gentler, with the first freshness of heavenly affections yet unsullied and unworn. Alas! we forget that this Infancy of the Race is all a figure; that the *ignorance* of a child was united to the *passions* of a man, — the most dreadful combination of moral elements that Humanity can present. The animal nature in its fiercest vigor, the moral and intellectual nature helpless as infancy, — are these, materials to produce a Golden Age? — or do they now, in the untaught masses, who have developed passions and undeveloped souls, produce the fabled tenderness and simplicity of the world's youth? That the former Times were better than the Present, is what no one with the least acquaintance with Antiquity will be forward to maintain, — and in fact only the total absence of any enlightened public sentiment, the silence and unconcern that suffered familiar inhumanities to pass almost unoticed, without a recording word or a resisting struggle, have left out the dark coloring of truth. The very protests of this Age against the ills that afflict it, contribute to swell our impressions that we have fallen upon evil times. That of which we hear so much, we imagine to be growing in amount. The constant denunciations of public injustice, and of private vice, never permit us to lose the feeling that we dwell in a bad world. There were Times, and not distant ones, when the evils were greater, and the denunciations less, because there was no enlightened Opinion to appeal to, and no public Virtue to speak out. I am not the apologist of the present Times, yet, however we may fail to detect the exact law by which Providence regulates the progress of Man, a successive progress History broadly declares, and though we are justly dissatisfied with our present condition, yet God has not deserted us, for in vain shall we search the past for a nobler Age.

Of all the delusions which have grown up as to the wisdom and virtue of primitive Times, that which affirms the perfection and purity of primitive Christianity is the most blind, both to the facts and to the reason of the case. "The light shineth in darkness, and the darkness comprehendeth it not," is a truer picture, and from a higher authority. Is it reasonable to expect that the Period of its conflict with Heathenism should bear the choicest fruits of its unadulterated spirit, — or that those from whose hearts it was expelling the gross darkness of the Pagan worship, should reach its most spiritual truths, and walk in its divinest light? Does it belong to the moral nature of man to be the subject of such rapid and perfect transformations, — to empty the mind completely of one set of influences, and receive at once the entireness and purity of another, — and, without a long term of intermediate mixture and struggle, put off the Heathen or the Jew, and exhibit, like a new creation, the truest symmetry of Christian development? And what are the facts? Do the Gospels, or do the Epistles of St. Paul, exhibit a more spiritual Discipleship, as we approach the person of Christ; or present a Model in the Churches that had an Apostle for their guide? Christ's life was passed without the conversion of a single soul; and when he died, the Jewish peculiarity had yielded to the Christian Idea of the Kingdom of God in not one single mind. In fact, the work of conversion, even in the Apostles themselves, took place after the death of Christ; and only when no longer Jewish notions could be made to cohere with a Messiah in the skies, did they gradually, and by necessity, adapt their conceptions of his Mission to his now spiritual and heavenly state. The Resurrection and Ascension of Messiah are usually represented as having their sole objects in the evidence they afford of human Immortality; — but in the actual History of Christianity, the first purpose they served was to spiritualize the views of the Apostles; — for with one who dwelt no longer on the Earth, all his relations to his Church must be of an inward, heavenly, and immortal nature, — and all Jewish apprehensions were disengaged from his person as he ascended to God, above all temporal connections. Still, however, did Judaism endeavor to fasten itself on as a necessary adjunct, even to spiritual Christianity; and those who had come nearest to the fountainhead of Truth, the personal companions and disciples of our Lord, were not the first to emancipate themselves from exclusive and unchristian views. Stephen the Martyr, in mind and character the evident prototype of Paul, had the first glimpse of the catholic nature of the Church of Christ; and St. Paul, who alone in the Apostolic Age conceived aright of the Universality of the Gospel, not in peace and triumph, but against controversy and resistance, proclaimed the essence of Christianity — that which rises above outward differences, and unites souls by an inward tie — to be, not a Righteousness with which any thing external can interfere, but "the Righteousness of God, proceeding out of Faith."

Or, are we to look in the Churches founded and taught by St. Paul for the purity and perfection of the primitive Christianity, — for examples of evangelical Unity, and humble submission to Apostolical

Authority? The Epistle to the Romans exhibits the Jewish and the Gentile form of mind looking upon Christianity from different positions; and the two partial views in bitter animosity threatening destruction to each other. The Epistles to the Corinthians exhibit schisms in Doctrine, immoralities in Practice, Factions organized under Leaders, a perilous observance of Idolatrous usages, proving a very imperfect emancipation from the Polytheistic sentiment, — and the most open contempt of the Authority of the Apostle. The Apostolic Age exhibits no Church Models, — no uniformity of Faith and Sentiment, — no gentle reign of Truth and Love, with quiet submission to legitimate Instructors, — no perfect realization of Christian Communion to serve as an example and a standard for successive ages, and by the claim of its Beauty and Repose to awe and silence the disturbing outbreak of individual Thought. These are not the Pictures which Christian Antiquity presents in the Epistles of St. Paul; nor will peace ever be restored to the Church by the endeavor to go back to a primitive Uniformity, that never existed. But the real Picture which that Age presents is full of the lessons of a true Peace for our present times; — it represents an attempt by Paul to combine a unity of Spirit with the utmost diversity of Forms, Sonship to God and Brotherhood to Christ with the freest varieties of national and intellectual differences, — and it exhibits an Apostle claiming no authority to settle controversies, to reduce to one common formula modes of worship, or inequalities of speculative view, but leaving every man free to be what he pleased, provided only he preserved uninjured the sentiment of Christian Love, and found his Rule of conduct, not in an intensely concentrated regard for his own Rights, but in the sympathy of the Christian spirit. The practical direction of the Apostle to the conflicting elements of the primitive Church was, to yield every thing external for the sake of a common sentiment of fellowship with Christ. The rule of "the Successors of the Apostles" is, to make every thing yield to the external Uniformity, and to let the unity of the Spirit and of Love pass for nothing, without the outward symbols of agreement. These are the great lessons we collect from a study of these Epistles:— that there never was a perfect realization of a Christian Church,—that only a Uniformity of the Christian *Temper* can gradually produce that Realization;—and that, meanwhile, he is working against Christ who adopts any other aim, than a desire for this inward unity of spirit and moral purpose, as a Christian Rule of conduct.

We saw, in the last two chapters, how St. Paul would not permit those Corinthians, who argued a question of Practice on the abstract ground of their individual knowledge and enlightenment, to avail themselves of that plea; that not even on a subject so little doubtful to a Christian as that of Idolatry, was *Knowledge* alone a safe guide; nor should Christian love forget the traces of Polytheism that might linger involuntarily with the weakest brother; and in his recurrence to the subject of this tenth chapter, he evidently fears, that those who violated *Love* were in imminent danger of violating *Knowledge* too, — and that a slight and vaunting estimate of a temptation overcome, gave no security that they were never again to fall beneath its power. Here then we have in a primitive Church, with an Apostle at its head, — what indeed we might reasonably have expected, — the distinctly announced danger, that, over the Christians of a heathen city, Polytheism might yet regain its sway. It is difficult to realize how thoroughly Polytheism was incorporated with the life of the Ancients. Every familiar salutation invoked the gods; the commonest utensils for household use were wrought in symbolic shapes; all the forms and courtesies of social life were associated with acts of worship; and even the daily meal had first been offered in sacrifice.

St. Paul, in guarding the Corinthians against this atmosphere of insensible temptation, compares, in this respect, the primitive Christian with the primitive Jewish Church; and warns the former that the lapse into Idolatry made by the Jews, when under the most signal guidance of God, was an example of what might happen again to a people who, if under the same guidance, were also under the same temptations. The opportunities which the Heathen Worship supplied for the gratification of the sensual and licentious passions, were in both cases the moving temptations to Idolatry; and in a city proverbially so corrupt as Corinth, the Baal Peor of old might be too closely paralleled by the Aphrodite of the Greek. Their external protections were the same, — and the inward vices that had seduced the

Jew to false Worship were also those that most abounded in the Corinthian character. If, argues St. Paul, some of the Corinthians have been separated by God from the practices of the Heathen World, — so also had the whole body of the Jews: — if the Corinthians had been baptized into Christ, — the Jews had been baptized into Moses, and had passed, under his standard, through that separating sea which left behind them, as a memory, their former and idolatrous Life: — if the Corinthians had perpetual remembrancers of that spiritual connection with Christ, in their participation of those memorial emblems which signified that they were of one Body with the Lord, — so also the Jew ate of that Manna in the Wilderness which, provided without toil or care, was as Bread from Heaven, and drank from that Rock whose gushing streams tracked their steps through the arid Desert, — an emblem of that Fountain of Living Waters, of which he who drinketh shall never thirst again: — yet these, though thus encompassed about with a divine Hand, fell away from God through the very lusts, and sins, and murmurings, that were rife in the Corinthian Church, — and, as the Examples of all former Times are for the guidance and admonition of those upon whom the latter ages have come, "let him that thinketh he standeth, take heed lest he fall." There hath no Temptation taken any one but such as is common to Man. Temptation is universal; it has its sources in human relations, and for him who is willing to be taught, there is no condition so peculiar, but in the past History of Man there is the failure to warn, and the example to guide; — and if he will not *make* temptations for himself, if he will not impair his own spiritual strength by contact and dalliance with Evil, God, who is ever faithful to the earnest mind, will not suffer him to be tempted beyond what he is able, but will with the temptation, to those that enter into no voluntary alliance with it, make a way to escape, that they may be able to bear it. Wherefore, says St. Paul, shaping this general principle to the special case, give no facility to the temptation, nor indulge in the careless pride of strength, but "*flee from Idolatry.*"

We are prone to imagine that our Temptations are peculiar; — that other hearts are free from secret burdens that oppress our energies, and cast a cloud upon our joy; that Life has for others a freer movement, and a less embarrassed way. But in no one has God made the human heart to carol its thoughtless song of joy; and the shadow of our moral being rests darkly on us all. We cannot take the world as it comes, enjoying what it offers, and passing by its sufferings and its burdens with our lightest touch; — we get involved in the deep questions of Conscience and Duty, and the sense of Responsibility stills the carol of the spirit, and suffers no man to repose without a trouble on the bosom of life. Infinite are the ways in which the devices and aims of the Moral Nature break the instinctive happiness that lives for the day, and forgets the morrow; but effectually this awakening of deeper and sadder life takes place in all; and struggle, fear, disappointment, the partial feeling of an unfilled Destiny, the restless wavings of uncertain Hopes, are in the heart of every man who has risen but a step above the animal life. The more we know of what passes in the minds of others, the more our friends disclose to us their secret consciousness, the more do we earn that no man is peculiar in his moral experience, — that beneath the smoothest surface of outward life lie deep cares of the heart, — and that, if we fall under our burdens, we fall beneath the temptations that are common to Man, the existence of which others as little suspect in us, as we do in them. We have but the trials that are incident to humanity; — there is nothing peculiar in our case, — and we must take up our burdens in faith of heart that, if we are earnest, and trifle not with temptation, God will support us, as, in the past fidelity of his Providence, he has supported others as heavily laden as ourselves.

St. Paul always places a practical question, however slight and passing, in the light of the largest and most permanent Principles, — and discusses the smallest outward matter in connection with the most spiritual views of Life. The propriety of a Christian, supposed to be an enlightened Monotheist, partaking of a feast in an Idol's Temple, which was to him no more than any other feast, introduces three leading principles of the Christian Life: — 1st. That mere *knowledge*, without a consideration for the influences we may exert on others, is not a Christian Rule of conduct; — 2dly. The Moral Law in relation to Temptation, that no man, whatever he may think of his own security, is safe, or in

God's keeping, who gives the Tempter opportunity; — and 3dly. The Principle that is contained in the passage from the 16th to the 22d verse, — that acts, the most indifferent in themselves, may yet be so eccentric *to us*, so unsuitable to our position, as to violate the harmony of our outward life, and even to peril the inward consistency of the character. "Is it consistent, is it sacred," such is the argument of this passage, "that *you*, who, by solemnly partaking of the emblems of the broken body and shed blood of Christ, bring before your religious affections your moral union with the Lord, — that his Church is as his Body, and draws spirit and life from him who is its Head, — that *you should*, in the wanton exercise of Liberty, be participant in a Feast, that others regard as implying the same spiritual communion with Idol Deities? You cannot be inwardly united to both; — why use the outward form, and tempt God by reservations?"

But the Sacrifice furnished the private meal as well as the Temple feast, — and a scrupulous Conscience might be oppressed with daily fears lest unconsciously it was touching things unclean, or, by eating things that had been sacrificed to Idols, dishonoring God. No man had ever less sympathy with a straitened, or false, Conscience; and he places no restriction on the utmost Liberty, except that which springs from another Principle altogether, and has no connection with straitened notions. "Let no man seek *his own*, but every man *another's* weal." "Whatever is sold in the Market, that eat, having no scruples of conscience," — "for the Earth is the

Lord's, and the fulness thereof"; — every thing is His, to be used and consecrated by a grateful heart. "If any unbeliever invite you to his house, eat what is set before you, asking no questions from scruples of conscience; but if a weak brother say unto you, 'This hath been offered unto Idols,' then eat not of it, — not on your own account, but lest you should tempt the weak to sin against his Conscience." The next words, forming the last clause of the 29th verse, if they are ascribed to St. Paul as the expression of his own feelings, are, as they stand in our version, in violation of the Apostle's sentiments: — "For why is my liberty judged, of another man's conscience; and if I by grace be a partaker, why am I evil spoken of, for that for which I give thanks?" This may be an objection which St. Paul supposes to be made by the Corinthian, to which the following verses would then form a pertinent answer: — "You must use your liberty, not for your own gratification, but for the good of others," — Liberty is not a principle of action, Love is; — "Whether ye eat, or drink, or whatsoever ye do, let the desire to do all to the glory of God protect you from injuring or obstructing another's Faith. Make no temptation for Jew, nor Gentile, nor for the Church of God: even as I serve all men in all things; not seeking my own profit, but the profit of the many, that they may be saved. In this be ye imitators of me, even as I also am of Christ." The passage, if the sentiment of it is attributed to St. Paul, must be understood thus: — "For why should I act so as that my freedom should fall under the condemnation of another man's Conscience, — should appear sinful or ill-used freedom through the offence that I give? — and when I partake of meat with thanksgiving to God, why do I act so as to injure a weak brother by means of that for which I give thanks?" *That is*, — "Is not this a contradiction? On the one hand, I thank God for my Liberty, and for the good things which He has bestowed, — and on the other I offend against Him, and make a mockery of my thanks, by my unchristian disregard for the infirmity of my Brother."

Either of these methods is admissible, preserving to St. Paul that guiding sentiment of Love as opposed to the individual pretensions of Knowledge, through which he sought to realize the sublimest Idea of Christianity, the universal Reign of Christ's spirit upon earth; in every heart kindling the same solemn ideas, and opening the same living springs; subduing the differences of class and country by the affinities of Worship, by kindred images of Hope, of Duty, and of God.

Such was the Christian vision of the Church Universal, — of the union of all good men in the Love of one God, under the Leadership of his Image in Humanity, — growing up into him, in all things, which is the Head, even Christ.

It is profitless to ask, — What has obstructed the Realization? — St. Paul at least is free. Let his spirit speak to us in one of his own Benedictions: — "Grace be with all them that love the Lord Jesus in sincerity!" *

* Ephes. vi. 24.

SECTION IV.

IRREGULARITIES FROM SOME ABUSE BY WOMAN OF HER SPIRITUAL EQUALITY, AND FROM A PROFANE AND HEATHENISH ABUSE OF THE LORD'S SUPPER.

CHAP. XI. 2-34.

2 Now I praise you, brethren, that ye remember me
in all things, and keep the instructions as I delivered
3 them to you. But I wish you to know that the Head
of every man is Christ; and the Head of woman, man;
4 and the Head of Christ, God. Every man that pray-
eth or prophesieth, having a covering on his head,
5 dishonoreth his Head. And every woman praying
or prophesying with uncovered head, dishonoreth her
Head: for it is one and the same thing as if she were
6 shaven. For if a woman is uncovered, let her also
be shorn, but if it is a disgrace to a woman to be
7 shorn or shaven, let her be covered. For man indeed
ought not to cover the head, being the image and
8 glory of God: but woman is the glory of man. For
9 man is not of woman, but the woman of man. Neither
was man created for woman, but woman for man.
10 Therefore ought the woman to wear *his* authority on
11 her head, because of the angels. Yet neither is
woman separate from man, nor man separate from
12 woman, in the Lord. For as woman is of man, so
13 also is man by woman; and all of God. Judge of

yourselves, is it becoming for a woman to pray to
14 God, uncovered? Does not nature herself teach us,
that it is a dishonor to a man if he have long hair?
15 But that if woman have long hair, it is a glory to
16 her? For hair is given to her for a covering. But if
any one thinks fit to be contentious, we have no such
custom; neither have the churches of God.

17 But I praise you not, in declaring this,—that not
for the better, but for the worse, ye meet together.
18 For first, when ye meet together in the church, I hear
that there are schisms among you, and in part I be-
19 lieve it. For there must indeed be separations among
you, in order that those of you who are sterling may
20 be manifest. When ye meet together in one place,
21 it is not to eat the Lord's Supper. For each taketh
before the other his own supper, in eating; and one
22 is hungry, and another is drunken. Have ye not
houses for eating and drinking? Or do ye despise
the church of God, and shame those that have not?
23 What shall I say to you? Shall I praise you? In this
I praise you not. For I received from the Lord, that
which I also delivered unto you, That the Lord Jesus,
on the night in which he was betrayed, took bread.
24 And when he had given thanks, he brake it, and said,
This is my body, which is broken for you: this do
25 in remembrance of me. After the same manner also
he took the cup, when he had supped, saying, This
cup is the new covenant in my blood: do this, as oft
26 as ye drink it, in remembrance of me. For as often as
ye eat this bread, and drink this cup, ye do show the
27 Lord's death till he come. Wherefore, whosoever shall
eat the bread, or drink the cup, of the Lord, unworthily, shall be chargeable with the body and the blood
28 of the Lord. Let a man try himself, and so let him

29 eat of this bread, and drink of this cup. For he that
eateth and drinketh unworthily, eateth and drinketh
judgment to himself, not discerning the Lord's body.
30 On this account many among you are weak and sickly,
31 and some sleep. For if we would examine ourselves,
32 we should not be condemned; but when we are condemned by the Lord, we are chastened, that we may
33 not be condemned with the world. Wherefore, my
brethren, when ye come together to eat, receive ye
34 one another. And if any one is hungry, let him eat at
home, that ye may not come together unto condemnation.
But the rest, I will set in order, when I come.

WHERE the spirit of the Lord is, there is Liberty: for Liberty comes into existence whenever Life is regarded from a spiritual centre, and each individual as the possessor of a soul for which he is responsible to God. Individual Responsibility cannot exist without individual Liberty: for no man must control that Conscience for which I alone am accountable to the External Judge. Where mine is the Peril, mine must be the Power over that soul which is to be judged; — and it would be a monstrous thought that the Power should be with one man, and the Responsibility with another, — that the Direction of my spirit should be in the hands of those who, in the last day, cannot take my place, nor bear my sentence. If, then, Christianity has brought upon the world the solemn feeling of Responsibility, which often lies heavy and oppressive on the heart, and restrains with grave thoughts the instincts of happiness, yet let us feel that, hand in hand with this Christian sentiment, comes the only true Freedom into the world, — that the glorious Liberty of the children of God is the gift of the same spirit, — and that where this sense of Responsibility does not exist, mankind are in a condition to be treated as children, or as slaves.

Nor is it necessary by *argument* so grave to *deduce* Individual Liberty as a necessary consequence from "the spirit of the Lord," — for the two *sentiments* that belong to Christ's view of Life, and to Moral Freedom, are incapable of separation. If I regard myself, and am regarded by others, as a being in filial relations with God, seeking new brightness for that Faith in all the dimness and struggle of the world, — and though that discipline, by which God tries how far we trust him, striving ever with a loyal heart to keep within the Presence of divine Light and Comfort, — that spiritual aim cannot cross the Liberty of any other child of God desiring to do likewise, — nor can it be exposed to wanton restrictions from any who reverence the inward Law of Conscience, and who acknowledge themselves to be independent members of a spiritual family, who draw their inward life from a common Source, and owe a common allegiance to its Lord. Limitations on Moral Liberty can arise only from some outward and material view of Life; — from the licentious abuse of our Free Will on the one hand, or the selfish tyranny of Power on the other; and in either case, the Christian view of Life is abandoned, and the spirit of the Lord is not there. Whether an abused Liberty requires restraint, or an arbitrary Principle exerts authority wantonly; whether the restriction is brought into existence by the encroachment of a usurping Power, or by such an arrogance of Liberty as in effect to cross and abridge the liberty of others; whether Licentiousness or Arbitrariness be the forger of the fetter, — the spiritual, the Christian estimate of Man and of his Destiny must grossly be violated, before it can be introduced. It is impossible, at one and the same moment, to contemplate others in the light of Children of God, seeking a spiritual connection with Him and doing the Work of Life beneath His eye, and to entertain the thought that any third Power may interfere. The sentiment of a spiritual Life, and the sense of subjection to other Direction than God's, cannot by any means be made to coalesce; and when Christ taught the Doctrine of Personal Responsibility, of the spiritual connections of the Individual Soul with God, he emancipated Humanity for ever. Oil and water may as soon flow together and form one crystal drop; as a Soul in living connections with God be in any moral subjection to man.

And not alone in this lofty moral sense does "the Spirit of the Lord" give Liberty, — but also in matters where Conscience is not so vitally concerned, — in conventional matters, — in matters where Usage, and Fashion, and the World's Law, have erected their standards, and drawn their fences. Through, and against, these, the Life that draws its impulse from a spiritual sentiment can, upon occasion, make its way, — without violence, indeed, without contempt, or any offensive self-assertion, but with a very calm and independent force, and with no oppressive solicitude as to what the children of this generation, sitting in the market-place, may choose to say. The spirit that is conscious of an earnest desire for communion with God, and for working sympathy with the meek and merciful Christ, *cannot* feel that Prescription has any right to guide its moral way through the Duties of the world, — to intrude into the inner sanctities of spiritual worship by any demand for Conformity to established usage; — nor in any other way to disturb the spontaneous impulses, and self-direction, of a Christian soul. It is this that often makes Religion so hollow, so insincere, so stale. We are not allowed to be religious in a genuine way: the inquisitorial eye directs its broad stare into the shrine of the Soul: and the freshness of individual sentiment is the most difficult of all possessions, in a world where every man affects the right of investigating your Religion, prescribing the proper character of its manifestations, and measuring it by some current standard of the times. Even those who aim to be most free, themselves, do not, in this matter, always respect the Freedom of others; and can profess to be scandalized by another's non-observance of Forms and Services, that are genuine and efficacious with themselves. This is an offence against Truth and Liberty, — an attempt to suffuse by the common breath of Public Opinion the pure mirror of the individual Soul,— and could proceed from no man, if he reflected for a moment, who reverenced supremely " *Truth in the inward parts*," the spiritual worship that the Father seeketh. Where the spirit of the Lord is, there is Liberty from all that may be characterized as the mere *Mode* of Religion; — and no offence against the God of Truth can be more gross than that Social Persecution, whether it springs from opposing Churches, or from the bosom of kindred, which exacts External Conformity, disregards the more spontaneous impulses and manifestations, and confuses the sincerity of Worship. Where the Heart is right with God, that is, *earnestly seeking to be right*, — and the Love that guided the spiritual Life of Christ is acknowledged as the animating sentiment, — let the World, as it reverences Holiness, and Truth, and all genuine manifestations of Christian Power, look after its own Salvation, and leave that spirit to worship God, and bless mankind, and image Christ, after the sincerity of its own nature. In this age of profession, the most devout of all sentiments is the worship of Sincerity, — the reverential recognition of individual Truth and Christian Freedom. And if this worship be true, it can sympathize with other forms of Freedom than those that are natural to ourselves.

Let it at the same time be acknowledged, that the Liberty which is derived from the Christian view of Life is not eager to assert itself, and rather avoids than seeks a declaration of its Rights. The Christian Mind does not permit of a dominant Impulse, which stands out in relief, and works in its single Will; it is a tempered Heart where no fiery passions exert an individual power, but where all true forces meet together, and produce that even movement which acknowledges the just sway of each, — where no forward faculty acts alone without the softening guidance of the rest, — where Knowledge seeks Light from Love, and in its eagle flight subdues itself to the temper of the dove, — where all thought of Self and Rights is blended with merciful sympathies, — and the meekness of wisdom when it appears in person, and comes forth to act and speak, is in the form of the Son of God, full of grace as of truth. Who can detect a prominent faculty, a projecting and self-asserting tendency, in that divine character? Who would dare to speak of *striking* characteristics in that full perfection? Even in that intensity of Love which gave itself to Death upon the Cross, there was the passionless serenity which ever shows the balance of our Powers. Such is ever the Liberty of spiritual Christianity; too comprehensive to be vehement, — too much centred in great interests to be a separatist for small ones, — too much influenced by sympathy to act with offence.

When, for the first time, a perception of spiritual Liberty entered among the unchastened elements of Heathen character, it were too much to expect that there should not be something of extravagance and excess in its immediate operations. The rude mind regards Liberty as a Law of License, a Charter for self-will; — but to the chastened heart, Liberty is Responsibility. The sentiment of the one is, — "I have a Right to do what I will"; the sentiment of the other is, — "My Free Will may lead me and others into evil, and throw me out of harmony with

God, — I must guard the sources of action, and place my Liberty under a divine Guidance." The Liberty which has regard to the *Rights of self* is always the form in which the sentiment *first* displays itself, — and not until the Christian and spiritual view of Life rules the heart, do we come to feel that Liberty is a Responsibility on Conscience, not a Charter of Independence and wayward Desire, — and that the more of Freedom we have, the more anxiously should we place our Free Will under the highest guidance of Love and of Law.

It was the first form of Liberty — that partial liberation from the control of others, ere we put ourselves voluntarily under the control of Christian sentiment — that had taken possession of the Corinthian Church in the times of St. Paul. Liberty, in the first flush of it, was enjoyed as the Power to gratify Self-will, and vindicate personal Rights. Superstition, just emancipated from its fears, treated with something of a natural rudeness and scorn the chains it had broken. It requires something of the spirit of Christ to deal respectfully with the moral fetters that you have cast off your own soul for ever; and the first moments of liberation from the daily and incessant anxieties of superstitious worship, were more likely to lead to wanton displays of self-gratulation, than to tender sympathy with the necessities of minds still beneath the yoke. We have already had some instances of this partial and wanton Liberty, enjoyed as a License, rather than reverenced as a Trust. The Corinthian, just liberated from the abject and never-ending bondage of an Idolatrous Ritual, went in idle or mocking unconcern to the Temple Feast, and physically enjoyed, where before he had spiritually served and trembled. It was an irreverent and indecent bravado, — the worst reaction of Slavery on a coarse heart, when its bond is broken, and the mean passions dare come forth. We are now to contemplate another instance of this partial Liberty manifesting itself violently, mistaking Rights for Duties, and by an eager forwardness violating the fulness of Christian sentiment. Christianity established the equality of the sexes; and, by restoring Woman to her place, removed the worst description of barbarism and inhumanity that ever poisoned the sources of Civilization. Slavery over a race of men, deemed inferior by caste or color, or serfs by conquest, would be a light injury to the heart, in comparison with a Home where the noblest affections trembled in vile dependence, and every tie of Love was under gross conditions of constraint. In the highest civilization of Greece there lurked that savage element, and Woman, except when a stain upon her name gave pungency to prurient taste, appears not in Grecian History. But in Christ Jesus there is neither male nor female, neither bond nor free. The soul that can hold an immediate connection with God, has a Right of independence of every other soul. We cannot be accountable to God, and bound to man; and where equal is the responsibility to the Father of the spirit, equal must be the Liberty. Can man be answerable for woman with his own soul at the final bar of God? — and if not, how can he have a Right over that Conscience which must answer for itself? But this Truth should work gently, and without violence, in the deep heart, not produce rent and confusion in the established arrangements of our outward Life. In the Corinthian Church this spiritual oneness, in relation to God, was by some conceived to carry with it the abolition of all social distinctions, as if moral equality implied sameness of place and mission in the world,—as if the Duties, and aptitudes, and grace of Sex, could in any way be relaxed, because its appropriate functions were now to be discharged in the meekness of freedom, and no longer under the bondage of constraint. Spiritual equality can in no respect affect, or alter, the principles which Nature establishes, and the common sentiment makes sacred. Yet who can be surprised, when the Slave breaks her chain and feels herself at large, that she should not discern the moral bounds of her Liberty, with as fine a tact as one who, never conscious of restraint, has long found her blessedness and her power within the wide circle of her natural gifts and aptitudes? This tendency to excess was but a broken wave from the first rush of long imprisoned waters; and when unfretted by constraint, it returned again to its still fountain and quiet flow, and we hear of it in the Church no more. There never has been shown, on any large scale, a tendency of Woman to overstep her sphere,—and the tides of ocean might sooner break from the gentle and heavenly forces that measure their benignant movements, than these aptitudes of Nature suffer any general violence. In fact, the single instance, in early Christian History, which the Corinthian Church supplies, of Woman assuming, not an equality of Rights, for that was conceded, but a sameness of Function and of outward manners, is mainly worthy of notice for the great lesson it teaches, that excess and reaction in an opposite direction are the natural consequences of abridged Rights. If you dread encroachments, stay the restless temper by full measures of Justice. If you fear Licentiousness, give ample Liberty. The chain you refuse to loosen will be a fearful weapon when it is torn from your hand by rude revenge. The passage I am about to quote from Hase's account of "The Public and Private Life of the Ancient Greeks" will remove all surprise at a momentary excess, which disappeared almost immediately from Christian History.

"The female citizens of Athens were bound in such rigid restraints of traditional usage, that their resigned submission to these antiquated forms is matter of no surprise. They grew up, guarded by bolts and bars, in a seclusion almost equal to that of an Eastern harem. The house-door was the threshold of the forbidden world to an honorable matron; and, to the maidens, it was fastened by a lock or seal, which was loosened with the greatest solemnity on days of high festival, when they walked in procession with downcast eyes."

"Nor did these privations of their early years receive the smallest compensation in after life, from the pleasures of freedom and of social intercourse. The early marriage into which they were often forced, was generally dictated by considerations of family interest; frequently, as in the case of heiresses, by legal obligation. In a connection in which speaking in company was esteemed a sort of indecorum, — in which to be absolutely unobserved was, according to Thucydides, the highest of all merits, and unconditional submission to the will or the caprice of their husbands the first duty of Woman, — the decent virtues of a housewife must necessarily have been the only ones which could be regarded with respect. Where, under such circumstances, any one of those talents that cheer and embellish existence unfolded itself, it must have been the irrepressible offspring of Nature, not the foster-child of Education. And these remarks apply generally to the States of Ionic extraction, so long as the ancient domestic constitution of society existed."

There is considerable obscurity in the details of this passage from the 2d to the end of the 16th verse, in which St. Paul rebukes that mistaken Liberty which led the Corinthian woman to speak in public with uncovered head. In the first place, there is supposed to be an inconsistency with a passage in the fourteenth chapter, in which women are absolutely forbidden to speak in the Church under any circumstances, — whilst here the prohibition applies only to the uncovered head. But the question of the Veil, or of exposure, contrary to all Grecian sentiment of propriety, was the only matter before his mind; and he deals with one point at a time. It is evident that he had been asked the question by the Corinthian Church, — and he meets it on his own ground, without superseding it altogether by the introduction of another principle. He takes another occasion of recommending Silence: he takes the present occasion of meeting the direct question that had been asked him, whether the Veil should be worn. It must be remembered, in examining this passage, that we are treading on the shifting ground of arbitrary notions. Decent respect for the usages of Society is not arbitrary, but a permanent part of Christian Sentiment. But the usages themselves are entirely so; and consequently the *sentiment* of St. Paul in this passage may be perfectly clear, whilst the observances referred to may have so totally disappeared as to render the individual expressions incapable of accurate explanation. Locke declares that some of these he does not understand; and after this it might be wise to pass them over, satisfied with extracting from them the general sentiment, about which there can be no doubt. But, perhaps, Interpreters have looked too deep for a meaning, and rejected the obvious ones, only because they were not just and natural to their own times and modes of thinking. I understand St. Paul to discuss this question on the grounds of reasoning, and on the grounds of sentiment. Now the reasoning may be inconclusive to us, because it proceeds upon social ideas that no longer exist, — whilst the sentiment remains in force, because it is the permanent feeling of mankind.

The Veil was the emblem of voluntary subjection, — and was never thrown off, except by Grecian Priestesses, when in moments of inspiration they claimed communion with a God. The flowing hair was regarded as the Veil which Nature herself had provided; and the Grecian man avoided it as disgraceful and unbecoming. Hence St. Paul argues, that in the natural course, not of their spiritual inequality, but of the due ordering and subordination of the offices and functions that respectively belong to them, it was becoming that the man should appear in the Church with uncovered head, as the representative of Christ, and the woman covered, as the representative of the man; — the one embleming the spiritual Head, the other the subjection of the Disciple; — and that Woman might with equal reason cast off the Veil which Nature herself provides, and adopt the mode of the man, as violate this habit. And for this reason ought the woman to wear upon her head the indication of her voluntary subjection to lawful power, because of the Angels; — according to the beautiful sentiment of the Jewish and early Church, which assigned to each individual an Angel,* whom they would offend by license or irreverent boldness. These ideas may seem arbitrary when made the grounds of a formal argument, but the usage itself the universal sentiment, that most irresistible of all moral reasoning, has everywhere sanctioned. In questions most vitally affecting the purity and harmony of character, there is often a felt boundary between Right and Wrong, for which Reasoning can assign no absolute grounds, nor define by palpable argument, — but which, nevertheless, the refined and educated sentiments, the moral *antennæ*

* This seems doubtful: but I can find, or suggest, nothing more satisfactory. There are guesses about *spies* and *male* messengers, but with no historical support or authentication.

of the mind, determine with a perfect accuracy;— nor can a greater violence be done to our nature, than to resist, or be careless of, the warnings and directions of this involuntary guide, which is in fact the finest and most ethereal judgment of the mind, — the very essence of our whole spiritual being, coming into flower.

There were other practical disorders in the Corinthian Church,— and St. Paul is naturally led to discuss them in this connection. The Lord's Supper — the Symbol of unity, of the one Body in connection with its Head, of the one spirit flowing through the members of the Church, of the branches meeting in and nourished by the one living Vine — had come to be celebrated at Corinth more in the spirit of the Factions that divided them, than after the Pattern of that last night, when the Lord, having loved his own which were in the world, loved them unto the end, and having symbolized his connection with the Church Universal by his Body, and his spirit ruling and living through it by his Blood, closed the celebration by the Prayer, "Holy Father, keep through thine own name those whom Thou hast given me, that they may be *one* even as we are!" — "Neither pray I for these alone, but for them also that shall believe on me through their word; that they all may be one; as Thou, Father, art in me, and I in Thee, that they also may be one in us!" We have already seen that this spiritual unity did not exist in the Corinthian Church, — that rival speculative pretensions had sundered the inward tie, and so unchristian was the temper of parties, that St. Paul, in the

19th verse, declares separations, even, to be necessary, in order that the pure spirit of the Gospel may not be overwhelmed, but have some manifest existence. In the true spirit which it emblemed, that of moral unity with Jesus, the Lord's Supper in such a Church could not be kept; and as the mystical view of that memorial Service, which regards it as a Sacrament and a Charm, had not yet come into existence, nothing remained but that its celebration, if celebration there was, should sink into the gross abuse of a common feast. It is painful, even at this distance, and in the cold way of historic explanation, to have to speak of sacred things profaned. But let the Truth be told: — it may serve to show, in these days, how far the primitive Church was from entertaining the Sacramental view of the Lord's Supper, — and how far the Apostle was from suggesting it. The Corinthians followed what, we learn from Xenophon, was a common custom at the Suppers of the Greeks, where each individual, or connected group, provided for themselves; and consequently, instead of brotherhood and union, the distinction of ranks and circumstances in a Church was rendered peculiarly and painfully prominent. Excesses were committed by the rich on these occasions, for which some were weak, and some sickly, and some slept in death. This was not to eat the Lord's Supper; it was to profane the Church, and shame the poor, and to eat and drink judgment against themselves, desecrating the body of the Lord. We can conceive that a *memorial* Service by a people of such habits might be thus abused; — but it is impossible that such a state of things could have existed if it had been the belief of the primitive Church that the sacramental Rite was the mystic medium of Salvation. St. Paul relates the original Institution of the Service, in order to recall them to a sense of its spiritual purposes, and of the gross irreverence of confounding it with a festal occasion, — of representing by symbols the divine Life and self-sacrificing Love of Christ, and then profaning, by disunion and intemperance, the emblemed Body and Blood. It is not necessary to suppose that St. Paul had a separate Revelation of the particulars of this Memorial Service; nor indeed will the words of the original naturally bear this construction. St. Paul had received through the sources of Apostolic testimony the words and purport of the Lord, — and he relates them in almost verbal agreement with the statements in the Gospels.

One point this whole passage does determine, — namely, that this Memorial Service was not confined to those who witnessed it, and that it had a fitness and application out of Judea, and beyond the circle of the first Disciples. It is the only symbolic Service, in its character of a Church, which Christianity possesses; and one sometimes wonders that those who are ready to complain of the bareness of our worship, coldly hold themselves apart from the breathing spirit of this Memorial Act. And how full of significance, of deep life, are those spiritual symbols! To show forth the Lord's death until he come! Can we pass a day, righteously, mercifully, meekly, resignedly, without the spirit of the

Lord's Death! Are we sure that it might not be good to watch with him one hour, as in a spiritual Gethsemane, before, in the world, we incur the risk of deserting him at the Cross? Might it not be well to bear about with us the Dying of the Lord Jesus, that the Life also of the Lord Jesus might be made manifest in our mortal flesh?

Sad at least it is, that a Memorial Act designed by Christ to symbol spiritual Union should become an occasion in which disunion is displayed!

PART III.

(CHAPS. XII.–XIV.)

THE OFFICE OF LOVE IN DRAWING INDIVIDUALS INTO A COMMUNITY; ENRICHING THE WHOLE BODY WITH THE GIFTS OF EACH OF ITS MEMBERS.

PART III.

(CHAPTERS XII.–XIV.)

SECTION I.

UNITY AMID DIVERSITY. — THE CHURCH AND ITS MEMBERS, AS THE BODY WITH ITS ORGANS AND LIMBS: EACH ESSENTIAL IN ITS PLACE; AND THE GIFTS AND GRACES OF EACH, THE WEALTH AND ADORNMENT OF ALL.

CHAP. XII. 1–30.

1 Now concerning spiritual things, brethren, I would
2 not have you ignorant. Ye know that ye were Gentiles, carried away unto dumb idols, even as ye were
3 led. Wherefore I give you to understand that no one speaking in the spirit of God calleth Jesus accursed, and no one can say, "Jesus is the Lord," but in the
4 holy spirit. Now there are diversities of gifts, but
5 the same spirit. And there are diversities of offices,
6 but the same Lord. And there are diversities of inward workings, but it is the same God who worketh
7 them all in all. But the manifestation of the spirit
8 is given to each, according to what is expedient. To

one through the spirit is given the word of wisdom:
to another, the word of knowledge, according to the
9 same spirit: to another, faith, in the same spirit: to
10 another, gifts of healing, in the same spirit: to another, the working of mighty powers: to another, prophecy: to another, discerning of spirits: to another, kinds
of tongues: and to another, the interpretation of tongues.
11 But all these worketh the one and same Spirit, distributing
severally to each as he will.

12 For as the body is one, and hath many members,
and all the members of that one body, being many, are
13 one body, so also is Christ. For we were all baptized
in one spirit into one body, whether Jews or Greeks,
whether bond or free; and have all been made to
14 drink into one spirit. For the body is not one member,
15 but many. If the foot should say, Because I am not the
hand I am not of the body, is it therefore not of the
16 body? And if the ear should say, Because I am not
the eye I am not of the body, is it therefore not of the
17 body? If the whole body were an eye, where would be
the hearing? If the whole body were hearing, where
18 would the smelling be? But now God hath placed the
members, each one of them in the body, according as
19 it hath pleased Him. And if all were one member,
20 where would the body be? Now are there many mem-
21 bers, yet but one body. The eye cannot say to the
hand, I have no need of thee: nor again the head to
22 the feet, I have no need of you. But rather, those parts
of the body that seem to be the weaker are necessary;
23 and upon those parts of the body which we think less
honorable, we bestow more abundant honor, and our
uncomely parts have more abundant comeliness; but
24 our comely parts have no need. But God hath tempered
the body together, giving more abundant honor to the

25 part that needeth, — that there should be no schism in the
body, but that members should have the same care, one
26 for another. And if one member suffers, all the members suffer with it: and if one member is honored, all
27 the members rejoice with it. Now ye are Christ's body,
28 and its members severally. And God hath placed in the
Church, — first, apostles; secondly, prophets; thirdly,
teachers; — then, mighty energies; then, gifts of heal-
29 ing, helps, governments, kinds of tongues. Are all apostles? Are all prophets? Are all teachers? Are all
30 mighty energies? Have all the gifts of healing? Do all
speak in tongues? Do all interpret?

Human Society, and human History, when *religiously* regarded, assume organized forms, of which classes of men, individual men, and individual eras are but articulated members. The present moment cannot be separated from the past and the future Providence of God. It is but a point of transition, not in itself a perfect and consistent whole. It is unintelligible without reference to the Ages that are gone: it is mutilated and incomplete without reference to the Ages that are come. History is a vast *Whole* not yet finished, of which the Eras are connected Parts; — and Society is an organic Body, of which each individual man is but a subordinate Member. Happy for him, if he has found aright his own position in the vast system, and is contented with his functions! It must be admitted, indeed, that this view of the organic connections of Time, and Human Growth, rests upon Faith as much as upon Knowledge, — that it implies a Trust in the Providence of God, and that it can be clear only to His Omniscience. For we border on *the Infinite*, when we contemplate the operations by which the Spirit that rules through all things worketh out the destinies of Humanity. Faith may receive it, and even have some insight into it; but no Intellect can reduce it to system, or find in it a Unity of Design. Who is competent to discern, and to unfold, the gradual working out of God's great Plan, as it is taken up and carried on by the successive generations of men! Who, through all action of the human Drama, — its Scene, the wide Earth, — its Characters, all the pilgrims of Mortality who have lived their hour upon the Stage, — its Time, from Creation to the present hour, — who is able to trace out an onward development of the Plot of Providence! Who will undertake to pass in review before us the distinct Epochs of Humanity, and declare to us how the great features that characterize each are but the several portions of a connected Scheme, — and how, amidst diversities of operations, the same guiding Spirit is continuously conducting the Education of our Race! And yet, the discovery of such a Plan must be possible, and to God's mind manifest, else is there no Providence in Heaven. The History of the whole World, if we could see it in one view, should present the same sort of connected growth and of attainment, the same consistent flow of character, as would the history of one mind, if we supposed it to exist from Creation until now. It is the noblest use of History to afford materials for discovering this Plan of God in the Education of our Race, and in that magnified Image of man which the large mirror of Time presents, to trace the order of succession in which the human mind passes to an advanced stage, and becomes a new reflection of the mind of the Eternal. When this is seen in History, then shall History be a new Bible, exhibiting God continually working out, over the wide Earth and for Man Universal, those results of Character which He has indexed in Revelation, and prefigured in Christ. Then only shall we have a Philosophy of History, when God is seen in it. Then shall Providence display its distinct outline and its just proportions on that ample sheet, — and each individual Man, perceiving that the Moral World has a plan, that all things progress together, and that nothing hangs loose, will discern also that *himself* is an instrument in God's hands, — that faithfulness of Life in him, in every one, is necessary to the full accomplishment of God's purposes, and so will stir his spirit to fulfil his own mission, and to do his own work.

And, to be in harmony with this view of Providence, — that God produces his noblest results by that organized Union of Members which Christianity calls a Church, — each man must forego all personal pretensions, all claims to individual independence and completeness, and regard it as his highest distinction that, in the vast subdivision of human service, he has a functional place, where he may do needful work under the eye of the Supreme Lord, and with an humble and loving devotion to the common Good. Whoever is thus incorporated with the Social Body, lovingly articulated into its frame, — so that, within his sphere of operation, the loss, as of a limb or member, would be deplored, if his Mind thought, or his Hand wrought, or his Tongue spoke, no more, — is so far in true spiritual connections with both God and Man; and if he holds this place, not as a part of a Machine, but with the freedom, and love, and conscious insight, of a devout Soul, consecrating itself to a voluntary service, he has opened for himself the pure fountains of unambitious Duty, of unselfish and perennial Peace; he has made himself to be a living Branch in that Vine of which God is the Husbandman.

But there is a tendency in human Nature to undervalue this functional service, and to seek a distinction more personal, — more individual to ourselves, — so as to stand out independently to receive a homage of its own, and not be obscured and lost in the general community of beneficence, in the silent workings of System. The organic structure of Society is disregarded, and every limb and member claims to be complete and perfect in itself. Our gifts and graces are not satisfied to be estimated relatively to an aggregate Result, which they contribute to produce; but must have a glory of their own, as if they had in themselves an independent existence, and were ultimate ends of God. That only possible Mirror to us of the perfections of God, with the single exception of the man who was His perfect image, — a vast Community, in which every variety of power, every manifestation of the

Almighty's spirit in separate men, works in harmony of heart and for a common Good, — is now broken into individual atoms, — each presenting only its own poor and partial reflections of the Infinite, — and this sublime image of the Power and Beneficence of Deity is reduced to the scale of a single imperfect mind. No individual can adequately represent the Civilization of which he is but a part, — the organic Body of which he is but a limb. The wisest, and the greatest, of men has but the merest fraction of the Knowledge and the Power that are in the world, — and the moment he makes a personal pretension, or claims more than his functional place, he has started aside from his sphere of service, and is guilty of that Sin by which, it is said, the Angels fell.

The efforts of Ambition, for the mere love of distinction, to stand out from the body of the Community and not be confounded with its other members, — the discontented spirit, that might derive Honor and blessed peace from the faithful exercise of its own Powers if it had no envy of a brother's gifts and place, — the divided Church, that finds sources of sectarian bitterness and selfish alarm in the spiritual varieties that, if properly understood, would afford the requisite materials of its own Universality and fulness of strength,— the partial Interests, that everywhere neglect and disorganize the Community, while they seek a Monopoly for themselves; — all these are examples of the tendency which Human Nature, in its unspiritual states, exhibits, — the tendency to make individual pretensions more prominent than the Universal Good, to sacrifice the Body to the Members. Human Nature, in the extraordinary awakening, in the rush of new spiritual Life which characterized the first age of Christianity, was not altogether in a natural state, — nor in that condition of liability to selfish temptations, which may be considered as its normal form. Nevertheless, under all variety of external influence, the same spirit betrays itself with more or less violence. And it is, perhaps, not more reasonable to expect that all exclusiveness of aim should disappear, when God pours out His Spirit to regenerate the heart of Life, and endows his servants with the rare gifts of utterance and spiritual energy by which a new Faith and Worship are established in the World, than when under his natural Providence He distinguishes his Agents by peculiar gifts and energies, and seeks, with an impartiality equally unlimited as the Gospel's Grace, the same result of Universal Good from the same diversity of Individual Endowments. The Corinthian Christians acted with the same narrow, and ostentatious, individuality under extraordinary circumstances, as other men do under ordinary circumstances, — and certainly the whole Scripture History leads us to attach no signal efficacy for sanctifying and exalting human nature to outward Wonders, — but shows that even the good seed, though sown by the hand of God himself, must fall also upon *the good soil*, before it bears fruit a hundred-fold.

That it was less excusable in a primitive Christian than it is in a modern Christian, to regard his individual endowments as sources of personal glory rather than as instruments in God's hands to establish the Kingdom of Heaven upon Earth, and beyond that, nothing in themselves, — is an opinion that ascribes to extraordinary influences, to miraculous interferences, a moral power to subdue and purify the ordinary passions, which nothing in the Gospel History would lead us to attribute to such an influence. A gift direct from God may inflame individual pretension and self-love, and convert the mere instrument of his Providence into the inflated favorite of Heaven, with even more of strong delusion than the rarest powers, or the most eminent attainments, disciplined by education, and acquired by toil, that come to us in the natural way, and do not separate us from the common necessities of men. How, it is asked in astonishment, could men like Judas and Peter, associates of Christ, and witnesses of Miracles, be base and false? — or, like the primitive Church, gifted with inspired utterance and Apostolic powers, be vain, selfish, ostentatious, uncharitable? St. Paul, at least, saw nothing impossible in the coexistence of such qualities, — for it is a supposition that he makes himself, — "Though I speak with the tongues of men and angels and have not charity, I am but as sounding brass or a tinkling cymbal." And surely in our own day, and to our own hearts, we may put the parallel question, — How is it that men taught by Christ, habituated from their earliest years to the idea of a Community in which one spirit, and one law, represent the Reign of God among His children of Earth, should manifest such regard for individual interests, such avidity for individual distinctions, such strong subjection to selfish aims and passions? Or how is it that those who *now* believe themselves to be in more intimate communion with God, — to be on "a higher religious level" than other men, — should live perpetually in the angry heat of unimportant controversy, and manifest so little of the Catholic and Apostolic spirit which would reunite the Church, and gather into one Body, as Members of Christ, all those who, inasmuch as with sincerity they call "Jesus their Lord," would be acknowledged by St. Paul "to speak in the spirit of God." "No man can say that Jesus is the Lord but in the Holy Spirit"; — some divine sentiment must be in the heart that recognizes the divine in Christ, — and all in whom that recognition livingly exists are in saving communion with him, and, under the Gospel conception, are members of the new spiritual Family of God.

The Corinthians, with the self-love of our Nature when unsanctified by the inner spirit of the Gospel, took the *individual* view of Life, as if each man was complete and independent in himself; and regarded their personal properties and gifts, not as instruments that were to work together for a common good, each indispensable, yet each nothing without the rest, — but as rival Endowments, — matters for jealous comparisons, — sources of self-importance. St. Paul reminds them of the Time when they were all equal in their Heathenism, — when the dumb Idol awake no divine spirit in any of them, — when no voice of God spoke through them, — when there was the leaden sameness of spiritual insensibility and death. And as then they were all on a level, in the absence of the Spirit, — all in that common blindness, that with one voice they would have called Jesus accursed, — so now, when the energy of the Most High had penetrated them with its living Spirit, and was manifesting its infinite variety according to the individualities and natural aptitudes of different men,— making, according to their fitnesses, some Apostles, some Prophets, some Teachers, — giving to one the word of Wisdom, to another the word of Knowledge, to another the gift of Tongues, — were those workmen of the Lord, thus brought by Grace out of the uniformity of Death into the diversity of Life, instead of joining together their hearts and hands to build up the Church (that spiritual Temple framed of living stones), to stand apart in their rival individualities, discussing the comparative importance of their several gifts and powers? They were spiritually dead, and dumb as their Idols, in their Heathen state; and now, when the Spirit of God spake and wrought through them, was Self-glory to forget *His* purposes, and commence its own wretched strife? "There are diversities of Gifts, — but they cannot enter into individual competition, for one Spirit gave them all. There are differences of Offices, but all contributing to a common Result, and in subordination to the same Lord; there are diversities of Energies, but it is the same God who works in each, and binds all together. And the manifestation of the Spirit has this variety of forms, according to the predominant capability of the individual, for the benefit of the whole: the manifestation of the Spirit is given to Each, according to the Law of the Common Good."

We must not altogether sacrifice the less interesting duties of an Interpreter, for the sake of pursuing the view that is here opened to us, of the organized nature of every Christian Community. God has regard for the Individual, — mental Peculiarities are not annihilated by Him; He finds an office and a place for all, but one Soul of Love must guide and combine the whole, as one Will directs the planning Thought, and moves the executing Hand: and all individuals must regard themselves as "forming reciprocal complements to each other, as parts of one vast whole in the Kingdom of God." — It is not possible to define the functions of the several Individualities of Office and Operation, to which St. Paul assigns a place in the administration of the Early Church. Some of these relate to the vivid communication of Spiritual Energy, which a Soul deeply moved itself can impart to others; some, to the more practical qualifications for the wise government and direction of a Church, at every moment liable to fatal collisions; — and some, to interior details of mutual assistance and coöperation, the particulars of which have for ever escaped us.

"The word of Wisdom" we find distinguished from "the word of Knowledge." The first corresponds with our ideas of practical Instruction, and denoted the application of Christian Truth to the various relations of Life, and the exercise of Christian Prudence in the collisions of the new Spirit with existing Social Institutions; whilst the word of Knowledge implied a more abstract and systematic Power, and presented Religion under a Theoretic view. The precepts and parables of Jesus might be regarded as his "Word of Wisdom,"—and some portions of the Gospel of St. John as his deeper "Word of spiritual Knowledge." *

The gift of Tongues, and the interpretation of Tongues, are described as portions of the instrumental Power of the Early Church,—and along with these are always mentioned, as in contradistinction, the Teacher and the Prophet. If we take the Epistles as our basis, which are of earlier date than the Acts of the Apostles, we must abandon the common opinion that the Gift of Tongues implied a miraculous power of speaking in Foreign Languages, with the view of facilitating among all nations a more rapid diffusion of the Gospel. In the Epistles, this "Gift" seems always to refer to the utterance of an elevated, and even ecstatic, state of mind, in which the language of Emotion transcends the style of ordinary communication, and to a mind cold and unsympathizing would border on the obscure. In the Acts of the Apostles, also, "speaking in Tongues" is always attributed to minds in the first glow of conversion,—under the freshest influences of Faith,—when pouring forth, not without excitement, the new feelings of spiritual Life with which their hearts were filled; and in

* Billroth.

such circumstances it is always described as taking the form of rapt prayers, singing the praises, and showing forth the mighty work of God in the believer's heart. Thus in the fourteenth chapter of this Epistle (at the 2d and 28th verses), he that speaketh with Tongues is said, not to speak unto men, but unto God, because he speaketh Mysteries in the spirit; — whereas he that prophesieth speaketh unto men for edification, and exhortation, and consolation; and unless there is an Interpreter present who can reduce his inspired and ecstatic utterance to intelligible language, he is enjoined "to keep silence in the Church, and to speak only to himself and to God." This cannot be made to consist with the common interpretation of speaking in a foreign Language; and as tongues, or *glosses*, was a common expression for forms of speech strange and unintelligible, for peculiar dialects, it would seem to be used for "the new language of that holy fire which was kindled in the hearts of believers," — for "the utterance of the new emotions with which the raised mind would be filled, in the new and more elevated language of a heart fresh glowing with Christian Sentiment."* There is undoubtedly a difficulty in harmonizing the account of the day of Pentecost, in the second chapter of the Acts of the Apostles, with this interpretation: but in the first place, the gift of Tongues in the Epistles will not bear the meaning of speaking in Foreign Languages, — and in the second, the passage in the Acts is involved in

* The "Gift of Tongues" often seems to signify the natural, *inarticulate* language of rapt emotion.

inextricable difficulties by the common interpretation. For example, — "It cannot possibly be supposed that all the nations who heard the disciples speaking with the new tongues of the Spirit, used different languages; for it is certain that in the cities of Cappadocia, Pontus, Lesser Asia, Pamphylia, Phrygia, Cyrene, and in the parts of Lybia and Egypt inhabited by Jewish and Grecian Colonies, the Greek would at that time be better understood than the ancient language of the country; and as this must have been known to the writer of the Acts, he could not have intended to specify so many different languages." * Again, it is remarkable, and fatal to the common interpretation, that the inhabitants of Judea are included among those who heard the Disciples speaking in the new tongues of the Spirit. Moreover, in the history of the first propagation of Christianity, no traces are found of a supernatural Power of speaking in foreign Languages. Indeed, the close intercourse then subsisting between all the provinces of the Roman Empire, and the universal prevalence of the Greek Language, superseded the necessity for such a miracle. And "as to the Greek Language, it is certain that the mode in which the Apostles express themselves in it, and the traces of their Mother-Tongue which appear in their use of it, prove that they had obtained their knowledge of it, according to the natural laws of lingual acquirement." We can only suppose, then, as the account in the Epistles is the older of the two, that some-

* Neander, — "The Planting and Training of the Christian Church."

thing of a symbolic and mythical character has mingled with the narrative in Acts; or, what appears to me highly probable, that all the foreign Jews pouring forth in their own dialects, as the most natural to an excited mind, with a rapt enthusiasm, the new experiences by which they were moved to the very depths of their natures, were afterwards viewed as an Emblem "that the new and divine Sentiment would reveal itself in all the Languages of Mankind, as Christianity is destined to bring under its sway all national peculiarities," — and, in relation to God, to fill Mankind with one voice and one spirit.

As it may be well to support this view by some unsuspected authority, I shall quote a passage from Neander, in which he attempts to define the characteristic differences of the Prophet, the Teacher, and the Speaker in tongues: —

"It is evident what influence the power of inspired discourse, operating on the heart, must have had for the spread of the Gospel during this period. Persons who wished for once to inform themselves respecting what occurred in Christian assemblies, or to become acquainted with the Christian doctrine, of whose divine origin they were not yet convinced, sometimes came into the assemblies of the Church. On these occasions Christian men came forward who testified of the corruption of human nature, and of the universal need of redemption, with overpowering energy; and from their own religious and moral consciousness appealed to that of others, as if they could read it. The heathen felt his conscience struck, his heart laid open, and was forced to acknowledge, what hitherto he had not been willing to believe, that the Power of God was with this Doctrine, and dwelt among these men. If the connected addresses of the Teacher tended to lead those farther into a knowledge of the Gospel who had already attained unto Faith, and to develop in their minds a clearer understanding of what they had received, — the *Prophet* served rather to awaken those to Faith who were not yet believers, or to animate and strengthen those who *had* attained, and to quicken afresh the life of Faith. On the contrary, to one '*speaking in tongues*,' the elevated consciousness of God predominated, whilst the consciousness of the external world vanished. — What he uttered in this state, when carried away by his feelings and intuitions, was not a connected address like that of a Teacher, nor was it an exhortation suited to the circumstances of other persons, like that of the Prophets; but without being capable, in this condition, of taking notice of the mental states and necessities of others, he was occupied solely with the relations of his own heart to God. His soul was absorbed in devotion and adoration. Hence prayer, singing the praises, testifying the mighty workings of God, were suited to this state. Such a person prayed in the Spirit; the higher life of the mind and disposition predominated, but the intelligent development was wanting. — Had St. Paul held the 'speaking in tongues' to be something quite enthusiastic and morbid, he would never have allowed himself to designate by the name of a spiritual gift an imperfection in the Christian Life, ... but it was consonant with that wisdom which took account of the interests of all classes in the Church, that he . . . . left the manifestations of such moments to the private devotions of each individual, and banished them from meetings for general edification ; that he valued more highly those spiritual gifts which gave scope for the harmonious coöperation of all the powers of the soul, and contributed in the spirit of Love to the general edification ; and that he dreaded the danger of self-deception and enthusiasm, where the extraordinary manifestations of Christian life were overvalued, and where that which was only of worth when it arose unsought, from the interior development of life, became an object of anxious pursuit to many, who were thus brought into a state of morbid excitement. Hence he wished that [in such moments] every one would pour out his heart alone before God ; but that, in the assemblies of the Church, these manifestations of devotion, unintelligible to the majority, might be repressed, or only be exhibited when what was thus spoken could be translated into a language intelligible to all." *

Whatever obscurity may attach to these details of Christian Antiquity, the great spiritual and providential View into which they are introduced as subordinate illustrations, is still full of the clearest and freshest truth, — and of truth which the World, like the Corinthians, in the strength of selfish partialities,

* "The Planting and Training of the Christian Church." — *Biblical Cabinet.*

still neglects. The world requires nothing more than for some Christian Apostle again to lift his voice, — "Now, concerning spiritual gifts, Brethren, and all other gifts of God, I would not have you to be ignorant. There are diversities of gifts, but all from the same Spirit; and his own peculiar manifestation of the Spirit is given to each, for the profit of the whole. And as the human body is one, although it hath many members, and all the members make but one body, so also is it with the Church of Christ. Be satisfied, that you serve the Community, whether with the directing mind, or the inspired utterance, or the working hand. All have not the same gifts or functions, but all may be members set in the Body by God himself. Dread nothing except to have *no* place in the body, and to be cast out as a *withered* branch, or a dead limb. But if you live, and do work, God hath tempered the Body together, that all the members are mutually dependent, and must have the same care one for another, — so that if one member suffer, all the members suffer *with it;* or if one member be honored, all the members rejoice with it."

A combination of the gifts, and powers, and peculiarities, of all individuals, makes a perfect Community, — as the freely contributed gifts of all climes and soils would make the wide Earth a perfect and blessed Home for that family of God.

Would to God that the spirit of exclusion, in every corner of this World which calls itself Christian, would take the Apostolic Doctrine to its heart!

SECTION II.

LOVE THE SOUL OF ALL THAT IS GOOD AND GREAT: ITS CHARACTERISTICS. — THE HIGHEST SENTIMENT IN SPIRITUAL MAN, AS THE ONLY ONE COMMON TO US AND TO GOD HIMSELF, AND THEREFORE ABOVE HOPE AND ABOVE FAITH.

CHAPS. XII. 31 — XIII. 1-13.

XII. 31. Be zealous after the best gifts; and yet I show
XIII. 1. unto you a more excellent way. Though I
speak in the tongues of men, and of angels, and have not
Love, I am become sounding brass or a tinkling cymbal.
2 And though I have prophecy, and know all mysteries
and all knowledge, and though I have all faith, so as to
3 move mountains, and have not Love, I am nothing. And
though I give all my goods to feed the poor, and though
I give my body to be burned, and have not Love, I am
4 profited nothing. Love suffereth long, and is kind: Love
envieth not: Love vaunteth not itself; is not puffed up;
5 doth not behave itself unseemly; seeketh not its own; is
6 not easily provoked; thinketh no evil; rejoiceth not in
7 iniquity, but rejoiceth in the truth; covereth all things;
believeth all things; hopeth all things; endureth all
8 things. Love never faileth. But whether prophecies,
they shall come to an end; whether tongues, they
shall cease; whether knowledge, it shall come to an end.
9 For we know in part, and we prophesy in part. But

10 when that which is perfect is come, then that which
11 is in part shall come to an end. When I was a child,
I spoke as a child, I understood as a child, I thought
as a child: but when I became a man, I put away
12 childish things. For now we see as by a glass, in
hints; but then face to face. Now I know in part,
but then shall I know, even as I also am known.
13 And now abideth Faith, Hope, Love, these three: but
the greatest of them is Love.

The Unity of Spirit apparent in Creation is the highest evidence of the presence of a pervading God. One Will must be the Author and Ruler of a Universe, amid whose infinite variety of kingdoms and regions there are no conflicting Purposes, and no inconsistencies of Law. This is not merely the argument from Design, which, from observing the adaptation of means to ends, and organs to functions, and faculties to the media through which they act, infers that there is a great Mechanician in the Heavens; — for all that this Argument from design establishes is an intellectual God, with a Power and Goodness commensurate with what appears in His works. It is good thus far: — "*If* the World proceeded from an originating Mind, then it affords evidences that it is the work of an Intelligence possessed of kindred qualities to that which we call Design in Man. But in this Argument, the only theological part of it is taken for granted. *If a living God* created this World, then the Argument from Design comes in to prove the commensurate depths of his Wisdom and resources of his Power; but it is of no logical force to establish the fundamental assumption, that wherever there are to us the signs of Design, there must have been a prior Creator. For if this argument is valid, then how can we avoid applying it to God himself? If Design necessarily implies a prior Designer,—then what bears such evidences of Design as the Constitution of a Mind? The Universe itself is not so wonderful for the compass of its harmonies. The World is not so full of the evidences of Design, as is the Mind of God:—by what valid argument do we infer a previous Designer in the one case, and not in the other?

As a *demonstration even of the existence* of Deity, this whole Argument from Design cannot, we think, be regarded as successful; nor any other of the philosophical reasonings of Natural Theology:—they all proceed upon logical assumptions which cannot be proved. If it be said, that we have but the alternatives of an eternally existing Universe, or of an eternally existing God, and that the latter is the more reasonable,—then it is obvious to reply, that where both are *incomprehensible* there is no *logical* choice,—no *logical* probabilities;—whatever grounds there may be for a *moral* conviction, a *spiritual* belief. In fact, our path to God lies not through the reasoning powers. Intellect proceeds from definite premises, and ends in definite and measured results. It can argue only from what it comprehends, from fixed points,—and it is a well-known logical principle, that a conclusion cannot contain more than the premises from which it is drawn. From the comprehensible you cannot *logically* deduce the Incomprehensible, — nor from the finite the Infinite. It is impossible, then, that the finite premises of human comprehension and experience should logically involve the infinite and incomprehensible God. God is revealed to *the highest* faculties in man: but these are not the logical ones, which are conversant only with definite measurements. But the moral God, the Father of spirits, is *spiritually* discerned. The Soul conceiveth Him, — the Spirit taketh hold on Him: — through the sentiment of a divine Faith, and not the discovering force of an all-sufficient Argument, have we access to and communion with Him. By the spiritual path He admits us into His presence: — when we attempt the intellectual one, we fall back into our own littleness, — for knowledge is human and defined. There is perhaps no real resemblance between the Intellect of Man and the Mind of God, between *the creative source* of Truth and Power and the mere observing and receptive mind, that slowly traces out some indefinitely small portion of their manifestations, — that originates nothing, but only deciphers, and painfully spells out a little of what the mighty Author has written in Nature. But in all moral and spiritual qualities, there is a oneness of kind, even between perfection and imperfection, — even between God and Man. The *affections* are of the same character; — they are touched by the same spirit, — they suggest the same sentiments, — they dictate the same actions, — they are framed and toned alike, and the difference is not of Nature, but of Degree. Even as it was no chain of inferences from the empty tomb, and the shattered seal, and the guards become as dead men, that led to the discernment of the Lord's Resurrection; nor even the presentation and recognition of himself in bodily form, — for the Disciples at Emmaus, and elsewhere, knew him not, and even Mary took him for the gardener, — but rather the moral tones of Jesus, which falling on the heart forced the faith that that heavenly voice, which they had believed stilled for ever upon Calvary, was once more a living Power, — so, they are the voices of God's spirit, toned by infinite tenderness, that awaken the vibrations of our own, and that, recognized by that portion of His spirit which God has given to each of us, intimate a moral Presence and Power, within the manifestations of whose Holiness and Love we live, and move, and have our being.

It must not for a moment be supposed, however, that the existence of God is *less certain* to us because He is spiritually discerned, — not logically inferred; — for in fact, whatever be the instruments and avenues of our knowledge, *Faith* lies at the foundation of them all, — nor have we any security for the reality of their communications except a Moral Trust. Man must have faith in God that his sensations, and physical expectations, do not deceive him, to the full as much as he must have trust that the intimations of Conscience, the self-sacrificing sense of Right and Justice, the spiritual discernment of the Perfect, do not lead him wrong: — and if

God can betray by the voices and aspirations of the spiritual nature, we cannot conceive what ground of confidence any man can have that the impressions of the Senses, or the deductions of the Intellect, are infallibly secure. It may be, as philosophers have thought, that this beautiful universe is all an appearance, — that there is no such thing, — and that, like the murderer's air-drawn dagger, it is but a creation of *the mind.* We know no ground that any man has that his senses are not deceiving him, but moral trust in God. It may be, if God and his Goodness are not to be taken upon spiritual Trust, that this world of *apparent order* is itself but a designed fallacy of the Senses, a contrived chimera of the Intellect, and that at some time, at Death for example, we may awake from this mocking Dream of Design in an everlasting Chaos; and certainly it is a gross inconsistency for any man to be free from this fear, who puts no faith in the pure revelations of Conscience and the Soul. If God can deceive upon one set of subjects, or by one set of mental Instruments, where can be the security that our whole mental Being is not a dreadful deception? The most irreligious of men unwittingly ground some of their deepest convictions, such as the constancy of Nature to her Laws, upon a religious foundation, even upon the constancy of God to his moral Purposes, — upon Faith in the Truth and Holiness of the Author of their being.

And when this Faith and spiritual sensibility are lively and tender, and trust *in the truth* of our faculties, in the religious intimations of our Nature, is regarded as the highest sign of a devout mind, how numberless are the concurring evidences of the one spirit and power of God, and, amid all the diversity of His operations, of one loved Design which His Providence pursues! When the soul has opened to the filial faith that the God who created the *human spirit* after His own Image is *also* manifesting Himself to it in his outward symbols of Creation, — a harmony of moral design appears to bind together the influences of his Universe, — one divine breath thrills through all things, — as even the smallest leaf has infinite connections, and feels the influence of earth and sky, of light and warmth, of air and moisture, — and the Apostle's vast doctrine becomes one of our own spiritual discernments, — "that All things are ours, whether the world, or life, or death, or things present or things to come," — that All are ours, — spiritual ties which our God holds with us.

And it is the Will of God concerning us, that the same unity of spirit which is apparent in Creation should be apparent in all the influences which we exert, and which are exerted upon us through the minds and characters of our fellow-men. God acts *directly* through the spiritual influences of the external Creation; — in these He is sole Agent; He has chosen His own manner of manifestation, and is undisturbed by the interference of man. Nothing is wanting but the religious sensibility in us, — the discerning spirit, — to open up all the communications with God which, in infinite ways, His Works, as the immediate expressions of his Mind, directly convey. And the same variety of divine manifestation which the outward Universe exhibits is repeated again in the infinite diversity of the gifts and influences *of individual minds:*—and nothing is required but the same religious sympathy, the divine power of Charity, as an animating sentiment in every heart, to impart a unity of purpose and direction, a convergence to one common end, to all the wonderful variety of mental working, faculty, and form. How gloriously are all the manifestations of its Creator which external Nature sets forth, exhibited afresh in the phenomena of Mind! The Sublime of Nature does not equal the Sublime of Thought; a good man is a truer Image of spiritual things than the loveliest landscape; the eye of devout Trust is more calm and holy than the watching stars; the light and the compass of Genius is brighter and vaster than sun or ocean; the sighing of the evening breeze is not so soft as the human whisper, so full of love and mystic meanings; and the faithfulness of Conscience, the inviolable Law in the soul, is more worthy to picture the moral constancy of God, than the orderly revolutions of the Heavens. God acts with as infinite a variety through the souls of Men, as he does through the forms of Nature; and if the divine grace of Charity dwelt in *us*, the one spirit and purpose of His Providence would show itself in the convergence of all our individual gifts and powers to the common centre of the Universal Good. Charity, then, is that Sentiment which imparts to whatever distinguishes individuals, the same common aim and tendency that belong to the Providence of God itself. We have not perhaps an unspoiled word in our language, that faithfully represents it; — and we cannot but think with humiliation, that if the sentiment itself had been more common amongst us, as the prime principle and method in our spiritual nature, — if our popular Religion had been more deeply imbued with it, valued it more justly, and sought it more fervently, as the essential element of the Kingdom of Heaven within, — the *Charity* of Christ would have shone out in our religious language above Faith and above Hope, as indeed their source, the well-head of all the living waters that spring up into everlasting Life.

This " Charity " is a sentiment, or pervading tendency of the character, rather than a particular affection. It is the constant temper of the heart, — not the warmth of individual attachments. It acts universally, and before personal affections have time, or opportunity, to be formed. It does not depend on association, or local connections, or the relations of mutual interest, which create so many of the strongest and most faithful bonds of earthly fellowship. It exists independently within the heart, and is not excited into life, as the passions are, by the attractions and solicitations of its objects. It acts at all times, and amid the most novel or the most revolting circumstances, as truly as amid scenes most familiar, and with beings most endeared. It is *the sympathy* of the spirit with God, with Humanity, and with Nature. It is the quick and living sentiment to which *the Divine* in Life is never long obscured,—which keeps the spiritual ear open to the still, small voice, and the heart, undimmed by self-seeking or the soiling breath of sensual desire, as a pure mirror to receive the images of Grace and Truth, from the Spirit of Holiness and Love that dwells in all things. It is that spirit which, without effort, and by an unbidden impulse, finds itself in gentle communication with every condition of Humanity,—to which no joy of another's heart is unnoticed, no grief of another's heart indifferent;—which feels an involuntary thankfulness rising up to God for every scene of human happiness it is permitted to witness,—for every evidence that the world is not so wretched as we sometimes deem it to be,—for the cheerful voices of labor,—for the song that shows the still light and uncrushed heart of tasked poverty, and for the laughter of children in dismal and neglected streets. It is the spirit that feels the bond of a common nature with all sentient things,—and that, in fact, has acknowledged that bond in the most emphatic way, by giving to a sympathy with the animal creation the remarkable name of *humanity*. It is a spirit which, when not a natural gift from God, it is the last and most perfect result of the discipline of life, and of the religious care of the character, to frame within the heart; for it is not an affection that can be excited by its objects and nurtured by outward warmth, but the very temper and spirit of the soul itself,—the mild and reconciling eye of meekness and sympathy that looks with one love on all things. It is the uniting, reconciling, atoning Power of the moral and spiritual Universe.

Intellect may give keenness of discernment. Love alone gives largeness to the whole Nature, some share in the comprehensiveness of God.

We have attempted to describe a Sentiment, which it is impossible to define. Let us, to show its living presence, instance some of the moments in the life of Christ when this sentiment of "Charity," rather than an affection for any particular beings, gave its color and direction to his thoughts and deeds. — When he understood the Baptist who understood not him, and chose a moment when John had given expression to his distrustful impatience, to do full honor to one so unlike himself in views, methods, temper, and expectations, — "Wisdom is justified of all her children": — when he passed out of the Temple for the last time, knowing it to be the last, — the rejected and despised, — and his eye happened to fall upon the widow and her mite, and his whole soul passed into hers, — and the blessing of the Lord's rejected fell in fullest sympathy upon her: — when for one short hour he was the accepted Messiah, and with an absent mind stopped distractedly on Olivet, and amidst shouts of triumph, unheard by him, was weeping for woes not his own: — when with sinking frame, and as long as his wasted strength could support it, he bore his cross to Golgotha, — and some hearts wept for him as he passed along, — and the spirit on the freshness of whose love no weariness had fallen seemed to lose the sense of his own position in his intense sensibility to theirs, — "Women of Jerusalem, weep not for me; weep for yourselves and for your children":

— when, upon the cross, the Love that never faileth rose above the sense of suffering, and sustained itself by the suggestion of Mercy, in the truth of which, since he urged it, let us believe, — "Father, forgive them, *they know not what they do*": — and, as a last instance, when he returned again to Earth, and the possessor of Immortality, now God's acknowledged and exalted, breathed unchanged the tenderest "*charity*" of human brotherhood, and singled out one heart that had been faithless but now was anguished, and which the bitter shame of recent desertion and treachery would have forbidden to approach his Lord, — to drop into that heart, through special words of remembrance, the balm of his reconciliation and forgiveness, — Go tell my disciples, and *Peter*, that they meet me in Galilee." Such, in living manifestation, is the *Charity* "which thinketh no evil, and seeketh not its own, — which rejoiceth not in iniquity, but rejoiceth in the truth."

Respecting this, the inward Sentiment of all large natures, of every peace-making Life, the following statements are made in this celebrated Chapter. That it is the Soul of whatever is great and good, whether in intellectual, or in practical excellence, — without which they either perish, or by becoming spurious and self-idolatrous lose their power to bless; that there are certain Characteristics, by which its existence in any heart is infallibly made known; and that it is not only of a more divine and immortal nature than any of the intellectual endowments of our being, but is the highest*

* This, of course, is true only of that Love which loves all that God loves, and loves nothing that God does not love.

form of the moral element in Man, and ranks first among the things of the spirit, above Faith and above Hope.

I. Let us take the outward forms of intellectual and practical excellence in the order in which St. Paul states them, and examine for a moment their spiritual dependence upon Charity. Suppose an eloquence without disinterestedness, without simplicity, without earnest sympathy with the wants, sufferings, happiness, and improvement of Mankind. Suppose a Demosthenes without patriotism, with a venal heart. Suppose a Paul preaching the Gospel without divine Love, or Christian affections in himself. What would then be the sustaining spirit of such Eloquence? Ambition, the love of power, self-seeking, ostentatious vanity. Every noble thought would have a base origin, — and every generous sentiment be a mean falsehood. Is such the inspiration that gives to gifted speech dominion over the souls of men? Or is such the Eloquence that refreshes the very heart from which it came, by the burning glow of elevated principles and honest sympathies? The most effective utterance is ever the most direct, simple, earnest, truthful. Unrivalled is the energy of persuasion, that proceeds from the tones, and looks, and kindling eye of unselfish sincerity. What is Rhetoric, to the simplest word of Love and Truth! Only that which comes from the heart long continues to go to the heart; — and the world has not been without examples of the highest Eloquence of intellectual genius, because suspected to be unsound at heart, losing the faith of men, and becoming as sounding brass or a tinkling cymbal.

Next, suppose intellectual Eminence, vast knowledge, without the bond of Charity, — unconsecrated by beneficent connections with mankind, by coöperation with God. Could the pride of unused, or abused, Knowledge sustain, and dignify, and give a sense of satisfaction, to that lonely mind? Or, is any thought more dreary and awful than to pass a life in the study of the truths and laws of that Infinite Mind, with the spirit of whose Providence the heart had no sympathy, — to live in the cold pursuit of Infinite Wisdom and Eternal Order, and have no bonds of the affections with Him, — to know ourselves gifted with such capacities, and gain by them no approving Love, standing out of spiritual harmony with Earth and Heaven?

Once more, suppose the outward semblance, and actions, of practical excellence, without its inward truth, — almsgiving without charity, — prayers without devotion, — fastings without humiliation of heart, — the martyr's stake without the martyr's trust in Truth. Does this do good to any one, or deceive any one? It cannot imitate even the outward mien of goodness. The false spirit works out through it, and betrays it. The heart is false, and perishing before God. Of such semblance we can only say, in the words of St. Paul, — "It is *nothing*, and it *profiteth* nothing."

II. There are unfailing "signs," by which it is manifested whether this Sentiment of Charity is the spirit of the Character. The tree is known by its fruits. The religious and the moral character, though they bear infinite variety of fruit, have but one root; — this holy love, this divine sympathy with goodness and happiness, and the desire to reproduce them, — this harmony with the merciful tendencies of Providence carried into all things, — and all the virtues of the Christian Life, active and passive, are the flower, and bloom, of this one Spirit. Then, the Spirit of Love must work the works, and speak the tones of Love. It cannot exist and give no sign, or a false sign. It cannot be a spirit of Love, and mantle into irritable and selfish impatience. It cannot be a spirit of Love, and at the same time make Self the prominent object. It cannot rejoice to lend itself to the happiness of others, and at the same time be seeking its own. It cannot be generous, and envious. It cannot be sympathizing, and unseemly; self-forgetful, and vainglorious. It cannot delight in the rectitude and purity of other hearts, as the spiritual elements of their peace, and yet unnecessarily suspect them. Love taketh up no malign elements; — such are not its natural affinities, — its spirit prompteth it, to cover in mercy all things that ought not to be exposed, — to believe all of good that can be believed, — to hope all things that a good God makes possible, — and to endure all things, that the hope may be made good. It is not that Charity is slower to recognize actual evil than Malignity itself, — but that it is quicker to see good. The purest spirit must ever have the finest sensibility to the presence of evil, — but it suggests it not, and it loves not to linger with it, or to dwell upon it; —"Whatsoever things are true, holy, just, pure, lovely, — it thinks on these things."

III. The Intellectual distinctions and graces of our Being are relative and temporary.* It may be that the very Faculties by which our present knowledge is attained are only adapted to the present condition of man, and are of a perishable essence; — but in all ages, and in all worlds, the spirit of sympathy with the pure and good must be of *the substance* of our peace, our principle of harmony with the will and the works of God. Charity never faileth: Love, the very same Love that we experience now, can be superseded in no world where God and blessed Beings are. Knowledge may fade, like a star out of the meridian sky, as a light unsuited to that diviner Day. What vast stores of Knowledge prized on Earth shall find no scope in Heaven! The erudition of the Critic, the learning of the Biblical Student, — a few words of actual converse with the Church of the first-born, with Prophets and Apostles, will sweep it all away, — if *there indeed* its doubts and questions have any significance at all. The profound knowledge of Law which a lifetime has acquired, — the science of Disease to which only the finest discernment and the most unwearied patience can attain, — the theory and practice of the

* A distinguished philosopher, Dr. Thomas Brown, has suggested that a greater keenness of Sight might make visible the constituent elements of all bodies, and so render unnecessary the analysis of Chemistry.

common arts of Life; — these can have no application to a world spiritual in its framework, and not subject to want or death. The Powers that have been exercised and trained therein may, indeed, be nobler instruments for eternal progress, — but this *Knowledge* is for the Earth, and the Immortal Faculties may cast its burden off. Our partial knowledge of God, and of divine things, may have to be utterly transformed in that perfect state whose full Light is attended by no shadows, nor manifested under the conditions, which possibly a state of Discipline may here impose. As the guesses and fancies of a child are to the insight of a man, may be the relation of the Earthly to the Spiritual Mind. Here we see as through a glass, catching reflections and hints. This material universe is often a veil over God's Presence, — a hiding of His power. In this state, then, our knowledge of Divine things has no analogy to God's knowledge: but we love as *God* loves; the moral affection is the same in essence.

And even of the imperishable directions of the Spirit, Love is the only one that is common to us with God; — it is the only element in which we are partakers of the Divine Nature. *Faith* must be for Man eternal; — never can confidence in God be dispensed with, and Heaven shall fully establish the childlike Trust; — but God has no part in this sentiment, — the Faith of the everlasting Father cannot be tried. Hope can never die out of the deathless Soul; for ever must a noble and blessed being, a child of the Infinite, aspire to higher perfection, and reach forth to things before; — yet Hope is not for God, — He knows not the sentiment, — it belongs not to the Perfect One, the Blessed for Ever. But Love is God's as ours; and it is ours only because it is God's; and out of it spring our Hope and Faith. Love is the very essence of the Eternal's Blessedness, — the moral Spirit of the Divine Nature. Love is therefore the highest part in Man; — the source of whatever is divine in us; — our only fellowship with the Father, — our sole Salvation, and fitness for the inheritance of the Saints in Light. This is not for a moment to exalt Love above Holiness, — for we speak not of the Love of the Heart only, but also of the Love of the Soul, the Mind, the Strength, and so Love cannot remain inviolate, Self cannot be extinguished, except in a holy being.

Now abide for ever Faith, Hope Charity, — these three, — but the *greatest* of these is Charity.

SECTION III.

LOVE GIVES PRECEDENCE TO THE GIFTS THAT EDIFY; AND OBTRUDES NOT ON THE CHURCH WHAT IS PERSONAL TO THE INDIVIDUAL SPIRIT, PRIVATE TO ITSELF AND TO GOD. — PROPHECY. — TONGUES. — RULES OF ORDER.

CHAP. XIV. 1–40.

1 Follow after love, and be zealous of spiritual things,
2 and chiefly that ye may prophesy. For he that speaketh
in a tongue speaketh not to men, but to God, for no one
3 hearkeneth, and in spirit he speaketh mysteries. But he
that prophesieth speaketh to men, edification and exhorta-
4 tion and consolation. He that speaketh in a tongue edifi-
5 eth himself; but he that prophesieth edifies the Church. I
wish indeed you all to speak in tongues, but rather that ye
prophesied, for greater is he that prophesieth than he that
speaketh in tongues, unless that he interpret, so that the
6 Church may receive edification. Now, brethren, if I come
to you speaking in tongues, what shall I profit you, unless
I shall speak to you, either in revelation, or in knowledge,
7 or in prophecy, or in doctrine? So things without life,
giving sound, whether pipe or harp, unless they give a
distinction to the sounds, how shall it be known what is
8 piped or harped? And if the trumpet give an uncertain
9 sound, who shall prepare himself for the battle? So also,
unless ye utter by the tongue well-marked speech, how

shall it be known what is spoken? For ye shall be speak-
10 ing to the air. There are, it may be, so many kinds of
voices in the world, and none of them without expression.
11 If then I know not the meaning of the voice, I shall be
to him that is speaking a barbarian, and he that is speak-
12 ing shall be a barbarian to me. So also ye, when ye are
zealous of spirits, seek that ye may abound to the edify-
13 ing of the Church. Wherefore let him that speaketh in a
14 tongue pray that he may interpret. For if I pray in a
tongue, my spirit prays, but my understanding is without
15 fruit. What then? I will pray with the spirit, and I will
pray with the understanding also; I will sing with the
16 spirit, and I will sing with the understanding also. Because, when thou shalt bless with the spirit, how shall he
that occupieth the place of the ignorant say Amen to thy
thanksgiving; seeing that he knows not what thou sayest?
17 For thou indeed givest thanks well; but the other is not
18 edified. I thank my God speaking in Tongues more than
19 ye all: but in the Church I choose to speak five words
by my understanding, that I may teach others also,
20 rather than ten thousand words in a tongue. Brethren,
become not children in understanding: but in evil be
21 ye children, and in understanding be ye men. In the
Law it is written, "In other tongues, and with other
lips, shall I speak to this people, yet neither then will
22 they hearken to me, saith the Lord." So that tongues are
for a sign, not to those who believe, but to the unbelieving: but prophesying, not for the unbelievers, but for the
23 believing. If then the whole Church be come together
in one place, and all speak in tongues, and the ignorant
or unbelieving come in, will they not say that ye are mad?
24 But if all prophesy, and an unbeliever, or one ignorant,
come in, he is convinced by all; he is searched through
25 by all; the secrets of his heart are made manifest; and

so, falling on his face, he will worship God, declaring that
26 God of a truth is in you. How then is it, brethren?
When ye come together, each of you hath a psalm, hath
a doctrine, hath a tongue, hath a revelation, hath an inter-
27 pretation. Let all be done to edification. If any speak
in a tongue, let it be by two, or at most by three, and in
28 succession; and let one interpret. And if there be no interpreter, let him keep silence in the Church, and speak
29 to himself and to God. And let two or three prophets
30 speak, and let others discern. And if, to another who is
31 sitting, a revelation be given, let the first be silent. For
ye can all prophesy, one by one; that all may learn, and
32 that all may be comforted. And the spirits of prophets
33 are subject to prophets. For God is not the maker of
34 confusion, but of peace. So, in all churches of the saints,
let your women be silent in the churches, for it hath not
been permitted to them to speak, but to be subordinate,
35 as also the Law saith. And if they wish to learn any
thing, let them ask their husbands at home, for it is disgraceful for women to speak in the Church.

36 Did the word of God proceed from you? Or did it
37 come to you alone? If any one seem to be a prophet, or
spiritual, let him acknowledge the things that I write to
38 you, that they are the commandments of the Lord. But
39 if any one is ignorant, let him be ignorant. Wherefore,
brethren, be zealous of prophecy, and forbid not to speak
40 with tongues. But let all things be done decently, and in
order.

The twelfth, thirteenth, and fourteenth chapters of this Epistle form a connected Argument, and should be embraced in one view. The eminent beauty, and practical importance, of the celebrated description of Love, has given to the thirteenth chapter an independent interest which has loosened its place in the Apostle's reasoning. The temporary circumstances of Corinthian contentions are forgotten,— and the *special* application of the divine principle of Christian sympathy is obscured by the sense of its still abiding truth and power. So that, even in this respect, it has come to pass, that "the tongues have ceased," and "the prophecies have come to an end," and the questions about "knowledge have vanished away,"—and to the eye of the Christian reader, that part of the record which relates to the Corinthian pretensions is dimly marked, and only "the Charity that never faileth" shines forth from out the page.

It becomes necessary, therefore, having paid our separate tribute to the universal and everlasting interest of that divine Sentiment, that we should now exhibit, in a more exegetical spirit, its particular connections with that portion of the Epistle into which it is introduced.

We must, again and again, call upon ourselves for a certain effort of the Imagination, to bring before us the real condition of the primitive Churches, —and on this historic point, as much as with reference to any scientific pursuit, it is necessary to say, that the only preparation for the reception of Truth is the dismissal of all such crude and hastily adopted notions as may tend to preoccupy or mislead. As an eminent modern Philosopher* has

* Sir John Herschel.

beautifully said, upon all subjects such an effort "is the 'euphrasy and rue' with which we must 'purge our Sight' before we can receive and contemplate, as they are, the lineaments of Truth and Nature." And we are especially liable, from feelings akin to veneration, to misconceive the actual condition of the Early Churches. In the absence of distinct historical knowledge, which indeed does not exist, and must be collected from hints and incidental notices, a religious sentiment of what would be *natural* to such a season, of what would harmonize with our own ideal conceptions of the men and the manners that ought to have been produced by such a rending of the Heavens, and such an outpouring of divine influences from God, covers with a solemn haze that holy Time, and peoples it with the mystic forms of spiritual and unearthly men,—just as Palestine itself, to many a mind, appears not to have belonged to this common earth, but to be a Shadow Land where spirits walked, and the Angel's wing might be daily seen amid the haunts of men. Our religious feeling of the sacredness and elevation of heart that must *needs* characterize Apostolic men, and of the lofty element of piety and love, above the agitation and disturbance of the lower passions and meaner thwartings of Life, in which we suppose them to have habitually breathed,—is transferred also to the Apostolic Churches;—and notwithstanding very significant hints to the contrary, the historic picture of strife and spiritual pretension—alas! of common humanity—is too dim to rob us of the fairer vision of simplicity, self-surrender, heavenly-mindedness, and superiority to all minor things, which we naturally ascribe to the Primitive Christianity. I know nothing more painful than to have one's heart disenchanted of such a picture; and there is no task one less willingly undertakes, than to make such a benignant vision fade away, whilst the cold, hard features of the Reality are gradually exposed. A man who reveres his nature, and believes that all that was ever imaged of its Purity and Love might well be nothing short of true, will not exhibit an inhuman eagerness to dissolve any fair and blessed belief in a realized sacredness and peace, which, though it belongs *to the Past*, and claims no place *in the Present*, still shows, by the facility with which it is received, the Faith of the common heart in the divine affections of humanity. But perhaps even the tenderest sympathy with Man should disincline us to favor that tendency, which only shows our instinctive faith in Goodness, whilst it transfers its energy to some *distant* scene of Action; and whilst it finds, or creates, but little that is divine in the Present, satisfies and expends the ideal sentiment that is in us, by dwelling on a transfigured Past, and a celestial Future. Every man has a Belief in the capabilities of Humanity to realize a life of peace and sacredness; but, alas! Eden or Heaven, or some mythic and unhistoric period, is always the scene of the Picture; — whilst it is forgotten that such a Faith presses with the whole of its practical responsibility on the *present* hour of Life, — and that whoever *believes* in a blessed capability which he does not aim to manifest, is a spirit fallen and unprofitable in the eyes of God. Assuredly God gave us our Belief of a fairer and nobler state for Man, — a Belief universal to every form of the religious, or the irreligious Mind, — not that untasked Fancy should locate it in the Past, or dreaming Hope transfer it to the Skies, but that with our own hearts and hands, with the energy and patience of true Believers, we should transfigure the Present, build up the living Temple, and realize outwardly the spiritual Beings that we are. This, essentially religious, Faith has been delivered over to be a luxury to the Imagination, — whilst the Conscience has scarcely felt the burden of its Greatness. Trust in our diviner capacities, and in a more blessed state for Man, has sought its justification in uncertain traditions of the Past and dim visions of the Future, whilst for *the Present* it assumes humble dejection, and self-distrust, and the miserable confessions of infirmity, as the religious attitudes of this Christian Faith. Now this is in reality to burlesque Humility, — for it is not only to distrust one's self, but to distrust God, — it is not only to have no confidence in our own strength, but to have no confidence in Him who perfects His strength in the weakness of those who cast themselves in Faith upon Him. God loves not the Humility that is as distrustful of Him as of itself; and *he* is the meekest child of the Heavenly Father, who, knowing his own weakness, has yet a divine Faith, that, if he aspires to be true to his holier nature, the everlasting Grace will bear him through. To be humble and self-abased is nothing, — but to be humble and at the same time to lift the eyes and stretch forth the hands towards heights of Heavenly Goodness, and regard them as attainable through reliance upon Him who, within the sincere and pure heart, works effectually to will and to do of his own good pleasure, — this is the true meekness of a Christian Soul. Wherever there is Christian Faith there must also be something of the spirit of Christian Enterprise, and that from no mere confidence in man, but from filial trust that God never deserts those who follow, in love and self-forgetfulness, the highest guidings of His Spirit. Who ever did so much to create Faith in the divine powers of Human Nature, as Jesus Christ? Yet who ever so entirely cast himself upon God for strength? In him were united Humility, and the feeling that all things were possible to him. Never do we read of a moment of depression, but it is followed by the record, that a fresh sense of connection with God came upon him, — that he rejoiced in Spirit, — and that the eye which Prayer had brightened, or any symptom of success kindled into hope, "saw Satan like lightning fall from Heaven." — Now, perhaps, the feeling that the primitive Church caught and continued this spirit of our Master, has rather directed us to the Past for the realizations of Christianity as a thing once accomplished, than created the sentiment of Responsibility, that its realizations are still for us to accomplish, — and that the justification, which in fact no past condition of the Church has yet given, of the divine Faith in Humanity which Jesus taught, it is still for *us* to give. And if this be so, then have we less scruple in presenting that Apostolic Age in its own colors; if to do so may create the sentiment that Christian Enterprise, in order to justify by our own realizations the divine trust and spirit of the Lord, has still to show, what as yet the world has never seen, the due fruits of such a faith. It is in this spirit, — to do away with the enervated impressions that there ever was a realized Church of God from which the world has deteriorated, — and to show that on every new generation of advancing Man rests the responsibility of consummating the faith and divine expectations of the Lord, — that we would now speak the plain and unvarnished Truth of that Apostolical Period.

There never was a time when the Community of Believers, by their realizations of brotherly Love, and their communion with the Holy Spirit, approximated to the Saviour's idea of a Kingdom of God upon Earth. That the influence of a new and more quickening spirit in Religion, which brought the living heart into immediate connection with God, wrought powerfully upon individual minds, and produced results that can only be attributed to a divine movement of the mightiest elements in Man, is, in our view, an established Fact. But we can nowhere find, either in the small community that assembled around the Lord, or in the Apostolic period, or in the times of the early Fathers of the Church, any traces of a *Society* in which the mind of Christ subdued the infirmities of man and the passions of the world. And the more we look into the details of these times with a calm and quiet eye, when the prejudice of sacred expectation has yielded to an investigation into the Facts, — the more we are disappointed and startled to find how often the lowest elements in man dwelt in close proximity with Christian influences, and appropriated the privileges of Faith for the mean indulgences of a common, vain, worldly, and unregenerated heart. We would not imply that Insincerity was at the root of these evils, for there is no question so difficult to determine as the degree in which spiritual self-deception may connect itself with the lower passions of the mind; and when made the grounds of social elevation and distinction, Religion has always manifested a peculiar tendency to part with its diviner spirit, and to give intensity to the fanatical selfishness of man. We might suppose that, if anywhere in the primitive times, around the person of the Lord, a Christian Society, a Church of God, would be formed: but of the Twelve, we have it on record, that James and John desired spiritual dominion over their Brethren, and sought to turn the love that the Lord bore them to their own glory; — that Peter was carnal in view, and savored not of the things that be of God, and, as might be expected, without spiritual self-knowledge and thoughtfulness, was unstable and faithless in trial; — that Thomas could not recognize the divine mind in Christ, and put the material question, "Show us the Father," and was obtusely sceptical, as such a man naturally would be, of his Resurrection from the dead; — that Iscariot embittered the heart of Jesus, and introduced a sense of painful discord into his last and parting hours, — "I have chosen you twelve, and one of you is a Traitor," — "He that eateth bread with me hath lifted up his heel against me"; — and that of the rest, though so distinguished in privilege and place, nothing but their names is known to preserve their existence from oblivion. And neither in this respect was the disciple above his Master; — a Church of Christ did not gather around the Apostles more rapidly than around their Lord. We read, indeed, of one period when the multitude of those who believed were of one heart and of one mind, and great grace was upon them all; — but the next passage records the judicial death of two of their number who desired to combine the semblance of Christian Communion with reservation and falsehood of heart; — and when we look further, we find these first believers, with an exclusive nationality, ignorant of the Liberty of the Gospel, and looking coldly on the evangelizing spirit of St. Paul. St. Paul's enumeration of the qualities that should be found in a Bishop of the Church, might give us some insight into the nature of the materials on which Christianity spent its first influences, and the impossibility that a Kingdom of God on Earth should be the immediate fruit. "A Bishop must be blameless, vigilant, sober, of good behavior, — not given to wine, no striker, not greedy of filthy lucre, — not a brawler, — not covetous, — not a novice, lest being lifted up with pride he fall into the condemnation of the Devil." Such a passage, to those not voluntarily under the influence of religious enthusiasm, is full of information as to the slow and natural workings of the Spirit of the Gospel, — and pictures but too plainly the coarse and common natures, with which, even in its highest offices, the Church had to contend.

The Image conveyed to us by this First Epistle to the Corinthians, is that of a Community in which the first stirrings of a higher life combined with the unsubjugated passions of common men, — and the personal distinctions conferred for the Gospel's sake, instead of tending to the destruction of the ambition, spiritual pride, and vainglory of our lower nature, were rather seized upon as especial instruments for their gratification. The various gifts of God's Spirit are disposed in rival attitudes, and discussed in their relations to the glory of the individual. Paul cannot plant, and Apollos cannot water, whilst the Debate rages as to their spiritual Leadership, — and the factious Church perishes. The *Teacher*, whose mental gifts qualified him to present in clear and systematic view the connected Truths of Religion, is at strife for precedence with *the Prophet*, whose more inspired utterance kindled into intense life the spiritual elements in man, and carried away captive the Conscience and the Heart; whilst the *rapt Mystic* who *spoke in Tongues*, and addressed God in ecstatic words, or in the inarticulate cries and sighings of an excited spirit, which, though expressive of real states of inward feeling, were unintelligible and uninstructive to the Church, would naturally act most powerfully on the weak and morbid forms of religious temperament, and be ranked accordingly, by those who required a spiritual excitement of this mixed nature. Now in this picture we see a real

Power, the first influence of Christian Truth, acting naturally on the common elements of our nature; — and if we deem it strange and disappointing that such should have been the first condition of the Church, it is because we contemplate it under the false apprehension that not only was the Christian *influence* supernaturally given, but also that *its practical operation* was supernaturally conducted on the Community of the first Believers. For this apprehension there is not a shadow of support, — and we must regard its prevalence as a sign of that moral weakness in man which inclines him rather to direct his gaze to some distant scene for the consummations of Christian excellence, than to feel on Conscience a personal responsibility to manifest that Perfection in his own circumstances, — than to feel that to *himself*, to every true lover of our Saviour, it is confided, as a sacred trust, to justify by his own realizations a Kingdom of Heaven upon Earth, and the long predicted Ages of our Lord.

In the twelfth Chapter, St. Paul exhibits the variety of individual endowment as designed to contribute to the complete edification of the Church; — for which if we seek an illustration, we have the common parallel of the division of employment and office contributing to the perfection of mechanical Art. In the thirteenth Chapter, he shows that amid this mental diversity moral unity must be obtained by Love, which is itself the divinest grace of God, combining with all other endowments, and giving them their direction to the common good. And in the fourteenth Chapter, he states that, in harmony with this preëminence of Love, the highest value attached to those spiritual gifts by which the Church might be edified, exhorted, or consoled, — whilst all the more enthusiastic manifestations of spiritual feeling, and rapt utterances of piety, were not for the public Assembly, but for the private Devotions of the Closet and the Heart.

We had before occasion to observe that the common interpretation, which makes speaking in Tongues equivalent to the power of using Foreign Languages, cannot be reconciled with this Chapter. As a single proof, take the fifth verse: — "I would, indeed, that ye all spake in tongues, but rather that ye prophesied, — for he that prophesieth is greater than he that speaketh with tongues, unless he interpret, so that the Church may receive edification." Now the common interpretation would here require us to suppose, that, for mere ostentatious purposes, a man miraculously gifted addressed the Church in a foreign language which they did not understand; whilst at the same time he had the power of interpreting to them in their common forms of speech. This would not be the comparison of various Gifts, but the gross and wilful *abuse* of a Gift, — an abuse which, if it had existed, St. Paul would assuredly have dealt with in a very different manner. He does not seek to destroy that rapt state of spiritual emotion in which ejaculatory prayer, or mystic hymns, or inarticulate cries, might break forth from the moved soul, and be its truthful language; — it was not in the nature of St. Paul to deny the existence of such spiritual frames, or to refuse them their expression;

— he would only confine them to the private communion of the heart with God; for in the public assemblies of the Church, where instruction, and consolation, and exhortation were the requisites, the Trumpet must utter no uncertain sounds. The *Prophet* might speak to the still, small voice, and give it in every heart the force and clearness with which it spoke in his own earnest soul. Or the *Teacher* might place the truths and principles of Christian Knowledge in the light of a calm, strong mind. But the unstable in the faith, seeking to be edified, or the weak and tempted seeking to be strengthened and refreshed, were not to be disappointed, or distracted, or misled, by manifestations with which they could have no safe sympathy, by the unprofitable raptures and the incoherent utterances of the ecstatic states of religious Emotion. If the authority of St. Paul be claimed for the reality of such ecstatic frames, and of their peculiar language of expression, then, to say nothing of the difference of circumstances, let it be remembered that he would allow them no *public* manifestation, — and that until they unfolded themselves in the light of the Understanding, so as to become edifying and elevating to others, they must keep silence in the Church, and be known only to the secret heart and to God. In the Church he would rather utter five words so as to be understood, than ten thousand expressions of the peculiar relations of his own heart to God, which might be an unprofitable mystery to others. In the Church he would pray with the spirit, yet so as to unfold to the understanding of others his pious thoughts; and he would sing with the spirit, yet so as to unfold in the hearts of others the devout feelings of his hymn. Only children in the spirit,—those who were weak, and babes, in religious intelligence and knowledge, would prefer the ostentatious display of mystic utterance to the awakening appeals and the clear instructions of the Prophet and the Teacher. And it was not in *this* respect that the Church of God was to resemble children. "Brethren, be not children in insight and understanding: in your knowledge of evil, indeed, and in the innocency of your hearts, be children,—but in understanding be men."

This Section of the Epistle opens to us many interesting views of the influences and constitution of the first Churches. And, first, it leads us to doubt whether, exclusively of the Apostles, it was ever intended to be conveyed that there was any supernatural operation of the Spirit of God on the early believers. We find here that divine energy which produces the various forms of Mind, following the same Laws of manifestation which universally obtain,—in one man exhibiting the productiveness of a creative spirit,—and in another the penetrating and reflective powers of Judgment and Discretion. The same relation that Genius holds to the Critical Faculty did the Prophet hold to the Discerner of Spirits. I need not remind you that in the Scriptures the *usual* sense of the word Prophet is not a Predicter of future events, but the earnest utterer of awakening and elevated moral Discourse. The man who could penetrate the Heart, and speak to the

Conscience, was the Prophet of the Scriptures. In the Prophets mentioned in this Chapter, it is evident that St. Paul did not recognize "pure organs of the spirit of God, in whom the divine and human might not easily be confounded. On the contrary, the excesses of such a mixture, and the delusions which might prevail from regarding the suggestions of human feeling as the promptings of God, are distinctly guarded against."* The Prophet submitted himself to the judgment of the Church; and a distinct class of minds was recognized, whose function it was to determine what really proceeded from the mind of God, — and to apply a sound discretion to test the worth of the utterances of Impulse.

We see, also, the free and equal spirit that prevailed among the first Communities of Christians, with no mingling whatever of the Ecclesiastical element. The meetings of the Church were evidently those of a Popular Assembly; — and, no doubt, were liable to the evils and abuses of so free a constitution. Its members would naturally occupy themselves with those offices for which they possessed peculiar qualifications, — but every form of the religious mind and life was permitted the utmost freedom of expression. The passage from the twenty-sixth to the thirty-third verses is a vivid description of the confusion that might arise from so popular a constitution, unless each individual was under the habitual direction of the spirit of Love and of a sound Mind.

---

* Neander.

The only exception to the perfectly unlimited constitution of the Primitive Church, was in the case of its female Members. But in this respect, Christianity created no restriction; — it only gave a sacred voice to the almost universal feeling of Mankind, and sanctified the dictate of Nature.

And, lastly, we find everywhere instilled, as the essence of all well-being, and well-doing, — without which the wisest Constitution is but a lifeless formula, and the highest Powers of individual endowment profitless or pernicious, — the spirit of a divine Sympathy with the happiness and rights, with the peculiarities, gifts, graces, and endowments of other minds; which alone, whether in the Family or in the Church, can impart unity, and effectual working together for Good, to the communities of Men. It is this which produces the highest and the lowest virtues, and cements them in the unity of one spirit and one purpose, — which represses the impatience of selfish eagerness, — which secures what St. Paul calls "the decency and order" of the Christian mind, — which takes the sting of envy out of the heart, and blesses it with the cordial enjoyment of whatever in others is Good or Great, with that loving Coöperation which assimilates the temper of each man's heart to the spirit of Providence itself, — and through its action gives him at once the full sweetness of his life, and the full use of himself, uncankered by self-seeking.

PART IV.

(CHAPS. XV., XVI.)

CORINTHIAN AND PAULINE VIEWS OF THE RESURRECTION. — CORINTH AND JERUSALEM ONE CHURCH OF CHRIST, ONE FAMILY OF GOD. — CONCLUSION.

PART IV.

(CHAPTERS XV., XVI.)

SECTION I.

STATE OF OPINION ON THE DOCTRINE OF A RESURRECTION. — ST. PAUL'S ARGUMENTS. — CHRIST'S RESURRECTION A PATTERN AND A PLEDGE. — THE CASE OF THE APOSTLES, ON THE SUPPOSITION OF NO RESURRECTION. — THE ANALOGIES OF NATURE. — CELESTIAL BODIES. — BEFORE CORRUPTION CAN INHERIT INCORRUPTION, THE NECESSITY OF CHANGE; AND THE NEW BIRTHS OF DEATH.

CHAP. XV. 1-58.

1 And I declare unto you, Brethren, the Gospel which
I preached to you, which also ye received, in which also
2 ye stand; by which also ye are saved, if ye hold by the
word which I preached to you; otherwise ye have be-
3 lieved in vain. For, first, I delivered to you that which
I received, that Christ died on account of our sins accord-
4 ing to the Scriptures; and that he was buried; and that
he was raised up on the third day, according to the Scrip-
5 tures; and that he was seen by Cephas, afterwards by
6 the twelve. Afterwards he was seen by more than five

hundred brethren at once, of whom the most remain till
7 this time, but some of them have fallen asleep. Afterwards he was seen by James; then by all the Apostles.
8 And last of all he was seen by me also, as by one born
9 out of due time. For I am the least of the Apostles, as
one not worthy to be called an Apostle, because I perse-
10 cuted the Church of God. But by the grace of God I am
that I am: and his grace which was towards me was not
in vain, but I labored more abundantly than they all, yet
11 not I, but the grace of God which is with me. Whether,
12 then, I or they, so we preach, and so ye believed. But
if Christ be preached that he was raised from the dead,
how say some among you that there is no resurrection of
13 the dead? If there be no resurrection of the dead, then is
14 Christ not risen. And if Christ be not risen, then both
15 vain is our preaching, and vain is your believing. And
we are found also false witnesses for God, since we have
testified concerning God that he raised up Christ, whom he
raised not up, if so it be that the dead are not raised up.
16 For if the dead are not raised up, then has Christ not
17 been raised up. But if Christ has not been raised up,
18 your faith is vain; ye are yet in your sins. And then
they that have fallen asleep in Christ have perished.
19 If in this life only we have hope in Christ, we are of
20 all men most to be pitied. But now has Christ been
raised from the dead, the first fruits of those that slept.
21 For since through man was death, through man also was
22 a resurrection of the dead. For as in Adam all die, so
23 also in Christ shall all be made alive. But every man in
his own order: Christ the first fruits; then they that are
24 Christ's at his coming. Then is the end, when he shall
deliver up the kingdom to God, even the Father, when
he shall have put down all rule, and all authority, and
25 power; for he must reign till he hath put all enemies

26 under his feet. The last enemy that shall be destroyed
27 is death. For he hath put all things under his feet. But
when he saith that all things are put under him, it is manifest that it is with the exception of him who did put all
28 things under him. And when all things are put under
him, then shall the Son also himself be subject unto him
that did put all things under him, that God may be all
in all.

29 Else, what shall they do who are baptized for the dead,
if the dead are not raised at all? Why then are they
30 baptized for them? And why are we in danger every
31 hour? By your rejoicing which I have in Christ Jesus
32 our Lord, I die daily. If I have fought with beasts at
Ephesus, as a man, what advantageth it me? If the
dead are not raised, let us eat and drink, for to-morrow
33 we die. Be not deceived: evil communications corrupt
34 good manners. Awake to righteousness, and sin not; for
some have not a knowledge of God: I speak to your
shame.

35 But some one will say, How are the dead raised up?
36 and with what body do they come? Thou inconsiderate!
that which thou sowest is not quickened, unless it die.
37 And that which thou sowest, thou sowest not the body
which shall be, but bare grain, it may be of wheat, or of
38 some other grain. But God giveth to it a body as it hath
39 pleased him, and to each of the seeds its own body. All
flesh is not the same flesh: but there is one flesh of men,
another of beasts, another of fishes, and another of birds.
40 There are also celestial bodies, and bodies terrestrial:
but the glory of the celestial is one, and the glory of the
41 terrestrial another. There is one glory of the sun, and
another glory of the moon, and another glory of the stars,
42 for star differeth from star in glory. So also is the resurrection of the dead. It is sown in corruption: it is raised

43 in incorruption. It is sown in dishonor: it is raised in
glory. It is sown in weakness: it is raised in power.
44 It is sown an animal body: it is raised a spiritual body.
There is an animal body, and there is a spiritual body.
45 And so it is written, the first man Adam was made to be
a living soul: the last Adam to be a life-giving spirit.
46 But not first was the spiritual, but the animal; afterwards
47 the spiritual. The first man was of the earth, earthy:
48 the second man, the Lord from heaven.* As was the
earthy, such are they also that are earthy: and as was
49 the heavenly, such are they also that are heavenly. And
as we have borne the image of the earthy, we shall also
bear the image of the heavenly.

50 But this I say, brethren, that flesh and blood cannot
inherit the Kingdom of God: neither doth corruption
51 inherit incorruption. Behold I tell you a mystery: we
52 shall not all sleep: but we shall be changed, in a moment,
in the twinkling of an eye, at the last trump; for the
trumpet shall sound, and the dead shall be raised incor-
53 ruptible, and we shall be changed. For it is necessary
that this corruptible put on incorruption, and that this
54 mortal put on immortality. And when this corruptible
shall have put on incorruption, and this mortal shall have
put on immortality, then shall be brought to pass the saying that is written, "Death is swallowed up in victory."
55 O Death, where is thy sting? O Grave, where is thy
56 victory? The sting of Death is Sin: and the strength
57 of Sin is the Law: but thanks be to God, who giveth us
58 the Victory, through our Lord Jesus Christ! Wherefore,
my beloved brethren, be ye steadfast, unmovable, always abounding in the work of the Lord, knowing that
your labor is not in vain in the Lord.

---

* Or, "The second man, from heaven, heavenly."

The Unity of an Epistle is not analogous to the Unity of a Discourse, a Treatise, or a Fiction. The only Unity that ought to belong to a Letter is in its close relation to the individual circumstances and prominent interests of those to whom it is addressed; — and its very completeness in this respect, — the fulness with which it embraces the many detached questions and anxieties which may, at the same time, be pressing on the minds addressed, — will necessarily destroy that Unity of Thought, which in writings of another class is properly required. It is the perfection of a Letter, that it touches on every point of immediate interest between the communicating minds, — that it leaves no painful doubt unresolved, — omits no question, whose unrelieved solicitude is pressing for an answer. The Unity of such a composition must consist in the fulness with which it meets the wants, and satisfies the expectations, of the receiver. There is nothing in the preceding fourteen Chapters of this Epistle to the Corinthians, which, judging merely from the orderly development of Thought, would require or justify the introduction of the subject of the Resurrection in the fifteenth. It appears there as a distinct and independent Topic, and points to some peculiarity of Belief, among a portion at least of the Corinthian Church, on this central Doctrine, which would have rendered the Apostle's advices of instruction and admonition essentially fragmentary and incomplete, if he had not addressed himself to its enlightenment and relief. And here we encounter the grand difficulty in the interpretation of this Chapter, when we seek to discover what was the peculiar state of Belief among the Corinthians respecting the Resurrection from the dead, to which St. Paul points his arguments and exhortations. We have no historical account of their peculiar views, — and "no information is open to us, but what we can infer from the objections against the doctrine of the Resurrection which St. Paul seems to presuppose, — and from the reasonings employed by him in its favor, — adapted, as we may conclude, to the positions from which they assailed it."

That both the Fact, and the Doctrine, of the Resurrection should call forth formidable objections on the part of professed unbelievers, could create no surprise; but that scepticism on these points should appear in the very heart of a Christian Church, and should *coexist* with their faith in Christianity, is a matter that requires to be explained. If this Chapter had been found in his first address to some Heathen City by the Missionary Apostle, there could have been no more question about the fitness of its topic, than there is of its cogency and power; but that a labored argument in defence of the Resurrection should be addressed to those whose acceptance of the Gospel is not disputed, and who, in every verse, by the very terms of the Argument, are acknowledged to be Disciples, is a circumstance that opens an inquiry of no common difficulty into the state of opinion in the Early Church on the mystic subject of the Second Coming of the Lord, and its relation to Believers, according to the Messianic conception of the Reign of Christ.

The first point to determine is, *what was it* that the Corinthians doubted. Was it the *Fact* of the *Lord's* Resurrection, — or the *Doctrine* deduced from it of a *Universal* Resurrection? It was the Doctrine solely; and there is no trace that the Fact of the Resurrection of Christ was implicated in their peculiarity of view. On the contrary, St. Paul takes his stand on the *Lord's* Resurrection, as on admitted ground, and reasons from it to consequences subversive of their peculiarities. He recalls indeed to their minds the leading evidences of that Event, but only with the view of placing in full light a fundamental position, the legitimate consequences of which were inconsistent with the other tenets in connection with which they held it. The whole Chapter has logical coherence only on the principle that belief in the Lord's Resurrection was common ground.

There is no part of our Lord's language which was more misunderstood by his followers, than that which related to the coming of the Son of Man; — and the adoption by him, according to our Gospels, of a style of expression that accorded with, and must have encouraged, some of the Jewish ideas of the Messianic Kingdom, is a circumstance that must always be connected with the gravest and the freest speculations into the authoritative character, and literal perfection, of the New Testament Records. Either his words have come to us through a Jewish coloring; — or he himself, and at the latest period of his life, participated in the common expectations of the Jewish Messiah, a supposition which I can mention only to reject; — or the conceptions of the Apostles respecting our Lord's future coming were erroneous, with this addition, that the imagery in which he pictured it, and which they misunderstood, was especially liable to such misapprehension: "For the Son of Man is coming with the Glory of his Father, with his Angels; and then he will render to every one according to his deeds. I tell you, of a truth, there are some of those standing here who shall not taste of death, till they see the Son of Man coming in his Kingdom." Whether it arose from a misconception of such words, combining with the Millennial elements in the Jewish anticipations of Messiah, — or whether the tendency to these anticipations was so strong that it colored, or even projected, the words, — it is certain that it was a prevailing belief in the Apostolic Age, that the second coming of the Lord might be looked for within the lifetime of the first Disciples; and that with this event St. Paul connected the end of the present World, and the opening of the Life Eternal. This distinctly appears in the First Epistle to the Thessalonians: "If we believe that Jesus died and rose again, even so will God bring with him those also who sleep in Jesus. For this we say unto you, that we who are alive, and remain unto the coming of the Lord, shall not prevent [or anticipate] those who are asleep. For the Lord himself will descend from heaven with a shout, with the voice of an archangel, and with the trump of God; and *the dead* in Christ will rise first; afterwards we who are alive and remain shall be caught up, together with them, into the clouds, to meet the Lord in the air: and so shall we ever be with the Lord." In the Chapter before us we find the same anticipations, of the resurrection of those who had died in Christ at the second coming of the Lord,—of the possible occurrence of that event within the lifetime of the Apostle,—of the glorious and instantaneous transfiguration of those who, being still in the flesh, had not, through the refining processes of death, developed the spiritual from the natural body; and of the opening of the Eternal Reign of God over all the enemies of his Moral Government: "Behold I show you a mystery: we shall not all sleep; but we shall all be *changed*, in a moment, in the twinkling of an eye, at the last trump; for the trumpet shall sound, and the dead shall be raised incorruptible, and we shall be changed; for this corruptible must put on incorruption, and this mortal must put on immortality." "As in Adam all die, even so in Christ will all be made alive; but every man in his own order,—Christ the first fruits,—afterwards *they that are* Christ's at his coming. Then cometh the End; when he shall deliver up the Kingdom to God, even the Father,—when he shall have put down all Rule, and all Authority and Power; for he must reign till he hath put all enemies under his feet.—And when all things shall be subjected unto Him, then will the Son himself also be subjected unto Him that put all things under Him, that God may be all in all."

With this coming of the Lord the Apostles always connect the General Resurrection, and the Immortal Existence of mankind. With the Early Fathers a different conception prevailed. "They believed, and appealed to the Apocalypse as their authority, that Jerusalem was to be rebuilt, adorned, and enlarged; that there was to be a resurrection, in which the followers of Christ who were dead, together with the patriarchs and prophets, and other pious Jews, were to return to life; that these, with the body of Christians, were to inhabit that city with Christ, rejoicing for a thousand years, at the end of which would follow the general Resurrection and Judgment of all. This is the doctrine of the Millennium, — of the visible reign of Christ in person upon Earth; a doctrine which the earlier Christians would be disposed to receive the more eagerly, in consequence of the oppression, persecution, and deprivations they were suffering." *

The prevailing expectation of the immediate return of Christ, with which they connected the fulfilment of his Promises, and the perfection of the Messianic Reign, led to that peculiar state of Belief in the Corinthian Church to which this Chapter is addressed. Living in the daily hope of the Lord's return with the glory of his Father, and looking for the Sign of the Son of Man in Heaven, they naturally regarded Death as an intervening Enemy that might separate them from that Day of the Lord, and deprive them of the joy of being the living Witnesses of his Triumph, the immediate sharers in his Kingdom. The peculiar aim of the Messianic Christian would thus be not the life *before*, but the life *after* Christ's return, — and his natural anxiety

* Norton's "Statement of Reasons for not believing the Doctrine of the Trinitarians on the Person of Christ."

would be to outlive the intervening period, and be found alive when the Lord came. It appears also, both from the passage in the Epistle to the Thessalonians, and from this Chapter, that this anxiety to be found alive at the daily expected coming of the Son of Man was heightened by coarse and material doubts of the possibility of the Resurrection of the Body. We read in the Second Epistle to Timothy, of some who believed that the Resurrection *was past already*, understanding it in a purely spiritual and figurative sense, — that it was the regeneration of the Believer's soul, the awakening from the death of Sin to the life of Righteousness, — in accordance with language which we find used, figuratively no doubt, by St. Paul: — "If, then, ye *be risen* with Christ, set your affections upon things above."

Such, then, was the state of opinion in some portion of the Corinthian Church. They looked daily for the return of Messiah, — and they feared that none but those who survived till that day could be sharers in his Kingdom. St. Paul addresses himself to this state of mind: he sympathizes with their expectation of the immediate return of the Son of Man; — but he allays their fear of Death by his Doctrine of the Resurrection, — that all who have fallen asleep in Christ shall be raised up to enter into his Glory. We shall now drop these early peculiarities of Belief, and consider the Apostle's argument in its more universal relations.

I. There was no doubt entertained as to the Resurrection of Christ. "I delivered unto you, first of all, that which I also received, that Christ died,—that he was buried, and that on the third day he rose again according to the Scriptures." — "So I preach, and *so ye believed.* Now if Christ be preached, that he rose from the dead, how say some among you that there *is no Resurrection* of the dead? For if there be *no* Resurrection of the dead, then is Christ not risen;—and if Christ be not risen, then is our preaching vain, and your *faith* is vain also." Now this argument proceeds on the admitted fact, that the Resurrection of Christ, at least, was not questioned amongst them. And if *one* Resurrection was admitted, why not a Universal Resurrection? One established case destroys the theoretic impossibility. There is no difficulty in the Resurrection of all Mankind, that does not equally attach to the Resurrection of one Man. With what consistency, then, could they *deny the possibility* of a Resurrection for Man, and yet believe in the resurrection of *the man* Christ Jesus, — or believe, *as they did*, in the Resurrection of Jesus, if, as was said by some among them, there was *no* resurrection from the dead? Either a universal Resurrection was possible and credible,—or Christ was not risen at all. Either the inductive fact must be denied,— or the induction from it must be admitted. But to deny that the Lord was risen, would be to deny their own faith,—and so their own faith in the Resurrection of one Man contended with the fear that those that had fallen asleep in Christ had perished.

II. St. Paul employs the admitted fact of the

Resurrection of Christ as a more *direct* argument for the Resurrection of all Mankind, — as not only demonstrative of its *possibility*, but as the pledge and pattern of a Universal Destiny. Had the Resurrection of one Man been merely an isolated case, without proof that he was intended to be the Representative of our Father's purposes for all men, — still it would have done much to create and confirm in the heart the faith in Immortality. It would have demonstrated at least the *possibility* of Revival. "There would be an end," as has been said, "of the Antagonist proof set up by those who look scornfully down on the Valley of Death, and demand, '*Can* these dry bones live?' It would have been the decisive reply of Nature and Providence to the inquiry, — their decisive refutation of the implied assertion of impossibility. Such an event would be a declaration, if not that man shall, yet that he *can* and *may* live again. There would be an end of the System whose doctrine is Annihilation, and whose precept is Licentiousness." But when to this proof of the possibility of a Universal Resurrection by the actual Resurrection of one Man, you add, that by the hypothesis *that one man* was the Representative of the spiritual destinies of Humanity, that his Mission was to embody in all things the will of God concerning us, — to show forth the *completed existence* of a human soul, — that death was one of his links of Brotherhood with us, and that the severing grave only makes us one in and with Christ Jesus, — that all Mankind have a common nature and a common relation to God, — and that the Son of Man is the Example, set forth by Heaven, of their common inheritance, — then do we feel the full force of St Paul's argument, — "Now is Christ risen from the dead, the first fruits of them that slept. For since by *Man* came death, by Man came also the Resurrection of the dead." If Adam is the representative of the animal and mortal nature, Christ is the representative of the spiritual and immortal; — and not more universal shall be the Death of the Perishable, than the Resurrection of the Immortal. In this argument St. Paul proceeds upon the two great facts of Christianity, — that Jesus was one in Nature with all Mankind, — and that he was set forth by Providence as the Representative of the spiritual destinies of all the Sons of God. If either of these is denied, there is no coherence in his words.

III. St. Paul argues for the Resurrection of all Mankind, from the moral consequences that would follow from the denial of that Doctrine. And here we may trace distinctly the peculiar state of opinion to which we have referred, though it does not confine within its own limits the sentiment of the passage. "If in this life only we have hope in Christ, we are of all men most to be commiserated." If only those who remained to the coming of the Lord had hope of the glory of Christ, then the zeal of Apostleship, and the missionary spirit of the Gospel, and all the chances of persecution and violent death in that glorious warfare, were but elements of fear and misery to the Disciple, who, through very faithfulness to his great trust, might perish before that Day of the Lord, and have no participation in his Kingdom. Such a fear would counsel the Lord's Apostles to be silent about the Gospel before the face of its enemies, lest the Death that sealed their tongue should also seal the Tomb from which no Resurrection was expected; — and, with such views, if there was any certain prospect of Death before the coming of the Lord, what unanswerable refutation could be given of the wisdom of the maxim, — "Let us eat and drink, for to-morrow we die." St. Paul does not charge this licentious precept upon the Corinthians as the root of their unbelief; — on the other hand, he exhibits it as one of the natural consequences of their state of opinion, the mere presentation of which should make them recoil from such a Doctrine. Errors of belief, though they do not spring from corrupt sources, may yet have a natural connection with immoral consequences, and insensibly lead to them. The Doctrine of the Resurrection, or of Immortality, might be doubted by the purest mind, — but such a mind would have especial need to awake up to Righteousness, lest its belief should unconsciously unstring the Soul, and take away the spiritual supports of Virtue.

In the argument for the Resurrection of the dead from the admitted faith and practices of the Corinthians themselves, there is a passage of considerable obscurity: "If the dead rise not at all, what shall they do who are baptized for the dead? Why are they then baptized for the dead?" What was understood by Baptism for the dead, it is now very generally admitted that it is impossible to determine. It is said that in the Early Church there was a representative, or vicarious, baptism for one who died before the rite had been administered. There is no proof, however, of its existence in the Apostolic age, — nor is it likely that St. Paul would have noticed such a superstition, however indirectly, without some rebuke or exposure of its unspiritual character. The simplest explanation, though not flowing from the words without some obscurity of expression, is that which regards "baptism for the dead" as a baptism into the views of the Gospel of Christ in relation to the dead, — with an implied reference to their state, and faith in their Resurrection.*

IV. St. Paul meets the objections which a sceptical materialism would most obviously suggest to the doctrine of a Resurrection. These objections are of two kinds: How can a mouldering frame revive, — and what *quality* of body could be adapted to an immortal existence? "How are the dead raised up, — and with what body do they come?" St. Paul, borrowing the illustration from Christ, meets the difficulty by an analogy drawn from our experience of other organisms: Unless a grain of wheat fall into the ground *and die*, it abideth alone, — but if it die, it bringeth forth much fruit. The perishing of the *seed corn* is not only no difficulty, but is an es-

* Some commentators suppose the Apostle to have reference to an idea, that all who were baptized were baptized *for the benefit of the dead*, by contributing to a certain Complement of believers, or Fulness of the Body of Christ, which must precede his coming.

sential condition of the germination of the new body. Cut the seed or the bulb, and there to the eye of science the fair form of the perfect plant is distinctly traced; and so, to the eye of God, in the corruptible seed of the human frame may be enveloped the germ of the immortal and spiritual body. If we had no experience of those delicate and splendid forms springing, in the freshness of their glory, from the bosom of decay, Scepticism, no doubt, would be ready to interpose its rash fiat of impossibility: and because we have only experience of the planting of the mortal germ of Humanity, and have not seen the wondrous bursting into Life of the celestial body, shall we disregard the analogies by which God would aid our Faith, and fall under the Apostle's charge of having a mind without spiritual perception, and slow to learn? "O man without understanding, that which thou sowest is not quickened except it die." And, then, as to the second objection, of how can this human frame become accommodated to a spiritual and imperishable Life, the same analogy suggests an answer: "That which thou sowest, thou sowest not the body *that shall be*, but bare *grain;* — but God giveth it *a body* as it hath pleased Him, — and *to every seed its own body.*" A root, a seed, is dropped into the Earth, and from it the chemistry of God educes the loveliest forms, the most delicate tints and odors, the most ethereal and spiritual beauty. Follow the analogy: — and if such are the new Bodies that God gives to the seeds of unconscious Matter, and to the spring-times of Earth, — what may be the glory of the spiritual Body from a seed that is now an organism for the souls of His children, and whose spring-time is reserved for the Celestial World? Nor are we confined in our conceptions of that spiritual Body by our present experience of organized existences; for there are bodies terrestrial, and bodies celestial, — and as much as the glory of the one transcends the glory of the other, may our Resurrection Body transcend the imperfect seed of our Earthly frame. "The glory of the terrestrial is one, and the glory of the celestial is another. So also is the resurrection of the dead. It is sown in corruption; it is raised in incorruption: it is sown in dishonor; it is raised in glory: it is sown in weakness; it is raised in power: it is sown a natural body; it is raised a spiritual body." The natural Body is an organism fitted for the development and action of the animal man: the spiritual Body is an organism fitted for the development and action of the spiritual nature; and the spiritual Body holds to the natural Body a relation, which is emblemed by that which the most glorious of Nature's forms bears to the seed from which it springs.

V. Lastly, St. Paul explains the Mystery of the change passed upon us by Death. We die, — because Flesh and Blood cannot inherit the Kingdom of God, — and we must all *be changed*, in order that this corruptible may put on Incorruption, and that this mortal may put on Immortality. Not from our ashes, but from our spirit, should we take the lesson of Death, — and seek the interpretation of its mystery. Not into the grave of the body, but to the home of the soul, should the gaze of a *thinking* Being be directed; and if we have *any Christian Faith*, as often as the great change passes on a familiar form, in order that the Mortal may put on Immortality, — to us should Death be swallowed up in Victory. Death has no sting but Sin: — the pure, the righteous, the faithful, — whatever to themselves may be the passing fear and doubt of nature, — in the sight of others are blessed in their death; they fall asleep in Jesus, and are found with God. Sin is the Shadow in the Valley of Death; — take away the fear of a violated Law, and in its place fill the heart with the Love of God as it wrought, and suffered, and freely laid down its life, in Jesus, — and we, too, should be ready to lie down in death with Christ, that we might rise and live with him for ever.

Thanks be to God who giveth us the Victory through our Lord Jesus Christ, — the victory of the Spirit over the Senses, — of Faith over Sight, — of Love and the filial heart of Duty over the fears of a legal Obedience and a grudging Service! Sons of God, — this is the Victory of our filial Faith, — that " God hath not given us a spirit of fear, — but of power, and of love, and of a sound mind!

" Wherefore, my beloved brethren, be ye steadfast, unmovable, always abounding in the work of the Lord, forasmuch as ye know that your labor is not in vain in the Lord."

SECTION II.

SYMPATHY OF THE CORINTHIAN CHURCH FOR THE DISTRESSED BRETHREN OF JERUSALEM. — CONTRIBUTION TOWARDS THEIR RELIEF: AND ST. PAUL'S VIEWS OF DUTY IN MATTERS OF MONEY. — HIS NEXT VISIT TO CORINTH. — TIMOTHY. — APOLLOS. — EXHORTATION. — CONCLUSION.

CHAP. XVI. 1–24.

1 Now concerning the collection for the Saints, as I have
given direction to the Churches of Galatia, so do ye also.
2 On the first day of each week let each of you lay by
him, storing according as he hath prospered, that there
3 may be no collections when I come. And when I come,
whomsoever ye shall approve, I will send them with let-
4 ters to bear your gift to Jerusalem. And if it be right
that I also should go, they shall go with me.

5 Now I will come to you when I pass through Macedo-
6 nia, for I do pass through Macedonia. And it may be I
shall abide with you, and even winter with you, that ye
7 may send me forward, wherever I shall go. For I do
not wish to see you now by the way; for I hope to re-
8 main some time with you, if the Lord permit. But I will
9 remain in Ephesus, until Pentecost. For a great and
effectual door is opened to me; and there are many op-
posers.

10 Now if Timothy come, see that he be without fear
among you; for he worketh the work of the Lord even
11 as I. Let no one then despise him, but send him forward
in peace, that he may come to me; for I wait for him
with the brethren.
12 And concerning our brother Apollos, I much entreated
him to go to you with the brethren, and it was by no
means his wish to go now; but he will go when it is sea-
sonable.
13 Watch ye; stand fast in the faith; acquit ye like men;
14 be strong. Let all your things be done in Love. And I
15 beseech you, brethren, (ye know the household of Stephanas, that it is the first fruits of Achaia, and that they have
16 addicted themselves to the service of the saints,) that ye
submit yourselves to such, and to every fellow-worker
17 and laborer. I am glad of the coming of Stephanas, and
Fortunatus, and Achaicus: for what was deficient on your
18 part they have supplied. For they have refreshed my
spirit and yours: wherefore acknowledge them as such.
19 The Churches of Asia salute you. Aquila and Priscilla
greet you much in the Lord, with the Church that is in their
20 house. All the brethren greet you. Greet one another
21 with a holy kiss. The Salutation by mine own hand, of
22 Paul: If any love not the Lord Jesus, let him be separat-
23 ed; the Lord is at hand [Anathema, Maran-atha]. The
24 grace of our Lord Jesus Christ be with you. My love
be with you all, in Christ Jesus! Amen.

It is said that the manifestation of a brotherly interest by one *Community* towards another, a general direction of effectual sympathy toward distant sufferers, is peculiar to Christianity. It dates with the

Gospel, and appears there for the first time, as a new fact in History. There is no parade made of it in the Records, nor any claim of appropriation on this new development of the spirit of Humanity. It appears there as the natural fruit of that spiritual sentiment which connects the Brotherhood of Man with the Universal Father, — and it is left to the philosophical Critic, in some after age, to discover and proclaim, that it is an entirely new phenomenon in the Moral History of Mankind. Such is the unconsciousness in which the Spirit and the Truth of Goodness ever brings forth its fruit, in quietness of heart. Acting from an inward movement, from the growing life of an affection, its noblest deeds are but simple faithfulness to itself; and what appears extraordinary in the eyes of others not stirred by the same sentiment, is but spontaneous and natural to it. The Christian heart, like Christianity itself, ripens its own blessed fruits, but makes no note of how far it differs from the common world.

But now, after the fact has been pointed out by the historical philosopher, it is not difficult to perceive how this last and purest development of the spirit of Humanity — an approach on the part of His children to the tenderness and universality of the Providence of God — should be reserved to be the product of the Christian sentiment. Christianity first placed men in spiritual relations to one another. It recognized their identity of Nature, and their one Heavenly Father; and on each child of God necessity was laid to act in God's spirit, — in every man to recognize a Brother, and to unite that brother with the whole Family of the Heavenly Parent. Before Christianity, there was no example of a Community applying itself to the elevation and enlightenment of another and distant Community. Polytheism could never make of all Mankind one Church and one Family.

St. Paul, who acted in the spirit of this relationship, had the satisfaction of awakening it wherever he went, and of making it fruitful in charities like his own. Corinth becomes united to Jerusalem by mercy and beneficence; — so true is it that the spiritual sentiment, the relation of each individual to the same God, is the fountain of the practical virtues, of the tenderest and strongest sympathies, and of all the finest humanities of Life. The parent Church had sent the blessing of the Gospel to the distant Grecian City, — and Corinth sends what she has, and can spare, to lighten the afflictions of the persecuted Christians in Jerusalem. It was no slight progress of the Spirit of Jesus, that within half a century Greece and Judea had been brought into such connections; — and it is no slight call to individual faithfulness and courage, that one man was the main agent of that change.

The Christians of Palestine were depressed and persecuted. They were poor in circumstance and station, — and sunk below even their natural poverty by the exclusive and persecuting spirit of the privileged order, and of the established Priesthood. They were losing their life in this world, that they might keep it unto Life eternal. In their behalf Paul enlisted the brotherly affections of the Gentiles. The treasures of Faith and Knowledge, the spiritual riches of Christ Jesus, flowed from Palestine, and it was no mean proof that they had accomplished that whereunto they were sent, that there flowed back again from the Gentiles a stream of Mercy. "Now concerning the collection for the saints, as I gave order to the Churches of Galatia, so do ye likewise. Upon the first day of each week, let each of you lay by him in store, as he hath prospered, that there may be no collection when I come." The *Duty* is not insisted on, — the Spirit of Liberality is not urged, — the Principle and Affection are taken for granted, and only the best method of Administration pointed out, — that time and trouble may be economized, and the fullest effect given both to their capacity, and their will to help.

It is commonly supposed that the mention of the first day of the week fixes that early date for the ecclesiastical observance of Sunday, as the Lord's Day. But this is by no means implied in the passage; — it contains no allusion to a public collection, — on the other hand, it distinctly states, more distinctly than in our English Version, "Let each man lay by him, *at home*, according as he hath prospered"; — and it is certain that, in St. Paul's view, *the observance of "Days"* did not belong to the Christian estimate of the fulness of the spiritual Life. St. Paul mentions the first day of the week as that in which they were to examine, and lay aside for purposes of Mercy whatever could be spared from the prosperity which God had given them, — because it was evidently expedient that some marked day should be allotted for that work, — and the last day of the week, as being the Jewish Sabbath, still regarded by the Jewish converts, was not available. It would appear that the first Christians assembled every day, as opportunity offered, for worship and communion of spirit, — and that the first day of the week was gradually set apart for these purposes, because the interferences of worldly business, and the outward relations of different men, rendered such undetermined Communion liable to interruption and uncertainty. It is obvious, too, that not until Christianity had spread so extensively as to be able to dictate its own Laws to a Community, could it appoint a Day for general Worship, without interfering with all the relations of Society, in a manner most foreign to its Spirit. "According to the doctrine of the Apostle Paul," says Neander, "the Mosaic Law in its whole extent had lost its value as such to Christians. Hence a transference of the Old Testament command of the sanctity of the Sabbath to the New Testament point of view was not admissible. Whoever considered himself subject to one such command, in St. Paul's judgment placed himself again under the yoke of the whole Law; his inward life was thereby brought into servitude to outward earthly things, and, sinking into Jewish nationalism, denied the Universality of the Gospel; for on the ground of the Gospel, the whole life became in an equal manner related to God, and served to glorify Him, — and thenceforth no opposition existed between what belonged to the world and what belonged to Him. Thus all the days of the Christian Life must be equally holy to the Lord; hence St. Paul says to the Galatian Christians who had allowed themselves to be so far led astray as to acknowledge the Mosaic Law as binding, — "After that ye have known God, or rather (by his pitying love) have been led to the knowledge of God, how turn ye again to these weak and beggarly elements, whereunto ye desire again to be in bondage. Ye observe days, and months, and times, and years. I fear for you, lest I have bestowed labor upon you in vain." He fears that his labors among them, to make them Christian, had been in vain, and for this very reason, because they reckoned the observance of certain days as holy to be an essential part of Religion. The Apostle does not here *oppose* the Christian feasts to the Jewish, but he considers the whole reference of Religion to certain days as something quite foreign to the exalted spirit of Christian freedom, and belonging rather to the genius of Judaism or Heathenism.

"An unquestionable and decided mention of the ecclesiastical observance of Sunday among the Gentile Christians, we cannot find in the times of the Apostle Paul. In 1 Cor. xvi. 2, if we examine his language closely, he says no more than this, — that every one should lay by, in his own house, on the first day of the week, whatever he was able to save. We may fairly understand the whole passage to mean, that every one on the first day of the week should lay aside what he could spare, so that, when Paul came, every one might be prepared, and, by putting the several contributions together, the collection of the whole Church would be at once made. The origin of the religious observance of Sunday must be deduced from the peculiar circumstances of the Gentile Christians. Where the condition of the Churches did not admit of *daily* meetings for devotion, — although in *the nature of Christianity* no necessity could exist for such a distinction, — although on Christian ground all days were to be considered as equally holy, in an equal manner devoted to God, — yet on account of peculiar outward relations, such a distinction of a particular day was adopted for religious Communion. They did not choose the Sabbath which the Jewish Christians celebrated, in order to avoid the risk of mingling Judaism and Christianity, — and because another day was more closely associated with Christian sentiments. The sufferings and resurrection of Christ appeared as the central point of Christian knowledge and practice: since his resurrection was viewed as the foundation of all Christian joy and hope, it was natural that the day which was connected with the remembrance of this event should be specially devoted to Christian Communion." *

There is another point, in connection with this benefaction to the persecuted Christians at Jerusalem, which claims notice, as disclosing something of the individual character of St. Paul. He constantly refuses to be placed alone in matters of trust, into which, from the absence of examination

* *Biblical Cabinet.*

and inspection, it was possible abuse might creep. "And when I come, whomsoever ye shall approve, those will I send with letters to carry your gift unto Jerusalem: and, if it be meet that I should go also, they shall go with me." In all such cases there was a strictness which, with St. Paul's unsuspected character, might appear scrupulous and fastidious: but the unsuspected character is that which never needlessly consents to be placed in circumstances of suspicion. And in matters of this nature, and in a world where virtue is weak, and calumny is strong, and temptation is perilous, and suspicion, as far as reputation is concerned, is almost as fatal as guilt, the example of the Apostle in the strict demand that responsible colleagues, "elected for that purpose by the contributors themselves," should be associated with him in the distribution of public bounty, is worthy of all imitation, — an admirable proof that an honorable prudence, a care for reputation in the smallest things, may unite with the loftiest enthusiasm of the religious mind; and if some of the greatest names in our history had possessed something of this practical wisdom and salutary fear, we should not have had the mournful and corrupting spectacle of genius and character, great in all things else, fallen under the meanness of petty degradation, — their glory associated in everlasting remembrance with the depths to which they stooped, — and all because they reverenced not the Christian principle to avoid even the appearance of evil, and dared to meet an unnecessary temptation. St. Paul would neither expose himself to a temptation, — nor in such things commit his character to the world: "We have sent," says he, speaking on the same subject, in another place, — "we have sent that brother who was chosen of the Churches to travel with us, with that bounty which was administered by us to the glory of the same Lord, and to show your readiness of mind, — taking care for this, that no man should blame us in our administration of this abundance, providing for things honest, not only in the sight of the Lord, but also in the sight of men," — that is, not resting in the consciousness of his own integrity, nor, on such a subject, in God's knowledge of it, — but careful to have it manifest in the public sight.

"At the time of his writing this Epistle to Corinth, St. Paul had formed an extensive plan for his future labors. During his stay of several years in Achaia, and at Ephesus, he had laid a sufficient foundation for the extension of the Gospel among the nations who used the Greek language, and he now wished to transfer his ministry to the West, — to visit Rome on his way to Spain, — and then to commence the publication of the Gospel at the extremity of Western Europe." * Previous, however, to putting this plan into execution, he had arranged to visit once more the Churches of Greece, with the twofold view of counterworking the disturbing influences which, from speculative philosophy on the one hand, and from Jewish superstitions on the other, had destroyed the Unity of the Gospel Spirit, and of furthering by his presence their benevolent inten-

* Neander.

tions for the afflicted Church at Jerusalem. It would appear, as we shall find when we come to the Second Epistle, that, in some previous message or Letter, he had promised the Corinthians, that on his way to Macedonia he would pass from Ephesus to Corinth, instead of taking the more direct course through Asia Minor, and that on his return from Macedonia he would come to Corinth again on his way to Palestine. The first part of this intention, however, he abandoned, through a tender reluctance to meet the Church immediately after a necessity had arisen for the severe censures of this Epistle, — and an extreme unwillingness that any personal intercourse should take place in a moment of irritation or estrangement. In such a moment the passions may precipitate the better nature into strife, — the fatal position may be taken from which there is no after retreating, — and the golden bridge of reconciliation be for ever broken down. It was certainly in the wisdon of Love that St. Paul avoided Corinth at such a time. This change of purpose, however, as we shall find in the Second Epistle, his enemies there attributed to the vacillating spirit of the man, and converted into a new pretext for disrespect. This alteration of plan he now announces. You will remember that this Epistle was written, not from Philippi, as the Postscript in our English Bibles affirms, but at Ephesus, in the year A. D. 56, and about the time of the Jewish Passover. "Now I will come unto you when I shall pass through Macedonia, for I do pass through Macedonia. And it may be that I shall abide, yea, and winter with you, that ye may bring me on my journey whithersoever I go. I shall not therefore (as I formerly intended) see ye now on my journey, — but I hope rather to abide with you a long time, if the Lord permit. But I will remain at Ephesus until Pentecost: for a great and effectual door is opened unto me, and there are many adversaries." The number, and the activity, of adversaries are no signs that a good cause is languishing, but rather the contrary. It is when you are suffered to live at peace, that you may fear you are exerting little influence in the world, that you are disturbing no cherished prejudice, alarming no established error. St. Paul connects the opening of the "great and effectual door" with desperate efforts on the part of the enemies of Truth and God for the preservation of their own Kingdom. The more widely the door of the Gospel was thrown open, and the Ephesians, deserting the Idol altars, crowded the strait gates of Evangelical Life, the more would those who were connected with the secular interests of the Established Religions be excited to active hostility. It was very shortly after this passage was written, that a violent popular outrage took place at Ephesus against St. Paul, — an unquestionable evidence of the success of his ministry. In the record, in the nineteenth chapter of the Acts, the progress of the Gospel, and the popular commotion against it, are brought into immediate juxtaposition: "So mightily grew the word of God and prevailed. After these things, Paul purposed in the spirit, when he had passed through Macedonia and Achaia, to go to Jerusalem, saying, After I have been there, I must also see Rome.

So he sent into Macedonia two of them that ministered unto him, Timotheus and Erastus; but he himself stayed in Asia for a season. And the same time there arose no small stir about that way. For a certain man named Demetrius, a silversmith, which made silver shrines for Diana, brought no small gain unto the craftsmen, — whom he called together with the workmen of like occupation, and said, 'Sirs, ye know that by this craft we have our wealth. Yet ye see and hear, that not alone at Ephesus, but almost throughout all Asia, this Paul hath persuaded and turned away much people, saying, that there are no gods which are made with hands; — so that there is not only danger that this our craft should be brought into contempt, but also that the temple of the great goddess Diana should be despised, and her magnificence should be destroyed, whom all Asia and the World worshippeth.' And when they heard these words, they were full of wrath, and cried out, saying, 'Great is Diana of the Ephesians.'" *

In this passage mention is made of Timothy being sent to the Churches in Macedonia, the Churches of Philippi and Thessalonica, — and in the tenth verse of this Chapter, without any notice of the Macedonian journey, we find an expectation on the part of St. Paul of his probable arrival at Corinth. This is one of those undesigned coincidences between independent writings, which afford the strongest moral proof of the authenticity of both, — the coincidence being of such a nature that it escapes

* Acts xix. 20-28.

rather than courts observation. St. Paul had expected Timothy to arrive in Corinth after this Epistle had been received, and so to be able to convey to him the impression it had produced. Nothing can be keener than the anxiety he manifests upon this subject. "I had no rest in my spirit," is his language. In this expectation of intelligence, however, he was disappointed, as Timothy, owing to some detention in Macedonia, was obliged to return to Ephesus without visiting Corinth at all. These circumstances are not without their interest, as they exhibit St. Paul subject to the casualties, the disappointments, the erroneous calculations, which disturb the arrangements of every life, and which discipline the spirit and the temper to be ever ready to abandon preconceived plans in order to make the best use of the unexpected exigencies that God may send. "That man appoints, but God disappoints," is a saying that is true only because man lingers with his own plans, and wants readiness of mind to follow God's beckonings, — else might he find in every case that God's disappointments are better than Man's appointments.

In this passage there is another expression, which Paley, in his admirable work on this description of evidence, has singled out as one of those undesigned coincidences which establish beyond dispute the genuineness and simplicity of a writer. "Now if Timothy come, see that he may be among you without fear, — for he worketh the work of the Lord, even as I myself do. Let no one therefore despise him." "Why *despise* him? This charge is not given concerning any other messenger whom St. Paul sent; and, in the different Epistles, many such messengers are mentioned. But turn to 1 Tim. iv. 12, and you will find that Timothy was a *young man*, — younger, probably, than those who were usually employed in the Christian mission, and that St. Paul, apprehending lest, on that account, he should be exposed to contempt, urges upon him the caution which is there inserted, — 'Let no man *despise* thy youth.'"

It is satisfactory to find from the twelfth verse that Apollos, who, probably not with his own consent, had been made the nominal Leader of one of the philosophical parties at Corinth which introduced speculative distinctions into the simplicity of the Gospel, had followed St. Paul to Ephesus, and was then acting in intimate union with him. There is no proof, indeed, that this eminent man, however inclined by education and mental peculiarities to the Oriental Philosophy, had ever sought to ingraft it on the spiritual elements of Christianity, — or to add it on to the Foundation, — the genuine acceptance by the heart of Jesus Christ as the moral Saviour and Guide to God. It would appear, indeed, that he left Corinth and followed St. Paul to Ephesus, because he was unwilling to be identified with any sectarian party in the Church, — and that he declined returning, even at the instigation of the Apostle, because he knew that the seeds of party division were still alive, and that his name and influence would be abused by those who ostentatiously, and factiously, preferred the speculative and rhetorical expositions of Religion which the Alexandrian had derived from his birth and education, to the unadorned moral preaching of the Power that was in the Life and Cross of Christ, by the Evangelical St. Paul. "As for our brother Apollos, I greatly entreated him to go to you with the brethren: but he was by no means willing to go at that time, — but he will go when he shall have a convenient season."

The thirteenth verse contains, in one sentence, an exhortation to the love and pursuit of those spiritual virtues, which their condition and their dangers most urgently required. Their condition, as we have seen, was one of *disunion*, growing out of a neglect of the simple principle of the Gospel Salvation, the acceptance of Jesus by the affections as the Image of God, the inspirer and pattern of the spiritual life in man. This simple love and imitation of the Lord Jesus, the source of unity and bond of peace, was deserted for every favorite tendency of superstition or philosophy that prejudice or education had introduced into the various minds, gathered out of every nation, that met at Corinth, — and the result was a struggle of conflicting Individualities, each claiming to stamp itself upon the Gospel, and to be essential to Christianity, instead of resorting to it as a common fountain of Life, — a fountain open to all who thirst for living water, whatever may be the diversity in outward form of their mental and national peculiarities. There was the *Grecian* type of mind, which would exalt *knowledge* above simple Trust in God and in his Christ, and would insist that every thing in Religion should be reduced to a scientific form; — there was the *Jewish* cast of spirit, imperfectly emancipated from days, and meats, and feasts; — there was the impetuous imitator of St. Paul, without fully comprehending his wise and tender spirit, who to show his freedom rushed into indecent excesses, sat down to meat in the Idol's temple to display his philosophic indifference to outward things, and tempted, by the rudeness of his liberty, the weak brother, for whom Christ died, to sin against his conscience; — there was the Christian woman whom the Gospel had elevated to the full dignity of human nature, in the first flush of excitement overstepping for a moment the modesty of nature; — and lastly, there was the natural man, unchastened by the Gospel, eager, with a *childish* vanity, for the most ostentatious display of spiritual Gifts, and more set on self-exaltation than on the edification of the Church. Among these, — the presumptuous, — the exalter of speculation above simple faith, — the childish rhapsodist who used his spiritual gifts for purposes of vanity, — the weak, the scrupulous, and the formalist, — the hard and proud sciolist, who would stand upon his abstract knowledge and concede nothing to the infirmity of a brother; — among these, how aptly are distributed the several clauses of the condensed exhortation, — "*Watch* ye, — stand fast in *the faith*, — behave like *men*, — be *strong*, — let all things among you be done in *Love!*"

St. Paul did not write his Epistles with his own hand. He dictated to an amanuensis, and authenticated the letter by a few words at the close in his own writing. This was rendered necessary by the appearance of forged Letters by those who wished to give currency, and the sanction of authoritative names, to their own favorite views, even in that early period in the Church, so falsely represented as pure. Of one of these forgeries in his own name, St. Paul complains in the Second Epistle to the Thessalonians. The autograph by which he authenticated his Letters, was generally some weighty sentence, suggested by the occasion and the thoughts he had been expressing, — with the Salutation of Christian affection. In the present case, it is the appropriate sentiment, going to the root of their divisions: "If any man love not the Lord Jesus Christ, — let him not belong to the Church"; — closing with the Syriac words, "*Maran-atha*, — the Lord is coming."

The distress occasioned by these words to some Unitarian commentators,* as if they contained a denunciation which the spirit of Christ would not justify, is entirely factitious, arising out of a false interpretation: "Let him be accursed: The Lord is coming." Yet would we rather be identified with those venerable men, who, believing it to be a denunciation, true to the spirit of Jesus, had the courage to condemn it even in an Apostle, — than with those dogmatic interpreters who also believe it to be a denunciation, but, false to the spirit of Jesus, seize upon it with a furious eagerness, — rejoice in it and justify it, — inflame by it their religious passions, — and defend by its authority a temper and a spirit which the Gospel never breathed. Better to belive Paul wrong, than

* See Belsham on the Epistles of St. Paul, at this place.

to believe Jesus intolerant,—but better still to find Paul and Jesus one in Wisdom and in Love. And this communion with the Catholic Spirit of the Lord, St. Paul claims for himself;—and with the expression of it closes his Epistle. "The grace of our Lord Jesus Christ be with you! *My* Love be with you all in Christ Jesus.—Amen."

THE SECOND EPISTLE TO THE CORINTHIANS.

PART I.

(CHAPS. I.–VII.)

ADMONITIONS,

AND EXPLANATIONS OF SPIRITUAL CHRISTIANITY,

ADDRESSED CHIEFLY

TO THAT PORTION OF THE CORINTHIAN CHURCH
WHOSE AFFECTIONS, BY HIS FIRST EPISTLE,
WERE REGAINED TO PAUL.

SECOND EPISTLE TO THE CORINTHIANS.*

PART I.

(CHAPTERS I.–VII.)

SECTION I.

ST. PAUL'S THANKFULNESS FOR AN EXPERIENCE OF TRIALS WHICH ENABLED HIM TO IMPART THE PEACE WHICH HE FOUND: FELLOWSHIP IN SUFFERING FOR A HOLY CAUSE SHOULD SHIELD FROM MISCONSTRUCTION: PAUL'S EXPLANATION OF HIS DEFERRED VISIT TO CORINTH.

CHAPS. I. 1–24 — II. 1–4.

I. 1. PAUL, by the will of God an Apostle of Jesus Christ,
and Timothy our brother, to the Church of God that
is in Corinth, along with all the Saints that are in all
2 Achaia, Grace and Peace be to you, from God our Father, and from the Lord Jesus Christ.

---

* Written from Macedonia about A. D. 57.

3 Blessed be the God and Father of our Lord Jesus
Christ, the Father of mercies, and the God of all con-
4 solation, who comforteth us in all our tribulation that we
may be able to comfort those who are in any trouble by
the comfort wherewith we ourselves are comforted by
5 God. For as the sufferings of Christ abound in us, so also
6 through Christ aboundeth our consolation. And if we
are afflicted, it is for your consolation and salvation; if
we are comforted, it is for your consolation, putting forth
its energy in the endurance of the same sufferings which
7 we also suffer. And our hope for you is steadfast, knowing that, as ye are partakers of the sufferings, so will ye be
8 of the consolation. For, brethren, we would not have you
ignorant of our affliction which befell us in Asia, that out
of measure we were pressed beyond our strength, so that
9 we despaired even of life. But we had the sentence
of death in ourselves, that we might not trust in ourselves,
10 but in that God who raiseth the dead: who from so great
a death delivered us, and doth deliver; in whom we have
11 placed our hope that he will yet deliver us; — ye also
working together for us in prayer, that the blessing upon
us out of many supplications may be acknowledged in
thanksgiving for us by many.

12 For our rejoicing is this, the testimony of our Conscience, that in simplicity and godly sincerity, not in fleshly wisdom, but in the grace of God, we have had our con-
versation in the world, and more especially towards you.
13 For we write to you no other things than those which ye
read and recognize [we have no ambiguous or disguised
14 meanings]: and I trust ye will recognize completely, as
in part ye have recognized us, — that we are your glory-
15 ing, as ye also ours in the day of the Lord Jesus. And
in this confidence I at first purposed to go to you that ye
16 might have a second benefit, both to pass through you

into Macedonia, and again to go to you from Macedonia,
17 and to be sent forward by you towards Judea. When I
purposed this, did I then practise any levity? Or in the
things that I purpose, do I purpose after a fleshly convenience, that with me there should be Yea yea, and
18 Nay nay? But God is faithful; because our word to
19 you was not made Yea and Nay. For the Son of God,
Jesus Christ, who was preached among you by us, by
me and Silvanus* and Timothy, was not made Nay and
20 Yea, but in him Yea has been, for all the promises of
God in him are Yea, and in him Amen, unto the glory
21 of God through us. And he who establisheth us with
22 you in Christ, and hath anointed us, is God; who hath
also sealed us, and given us the earnest of the spirit in
23 our hearts. And I call God as a witness for my soul,
24 that to spare you I came not yet to Corinth. Not that
we have dominion over your faith, but we are fellow-
helpers of your joy: for by faith ye stand.

II. 1. But I determined this with myself, that I would not
2 come again to you in grief. For if I grieve you, who
then is there to make me glad but he who is grieved by
3 me? And I have written to you this very thing, that in
coming I should not have grief from those in whom I
ought to rejoice, having confidence in you all that my joy
4 is the joy of you all. For out of much affliction and anguish of heart I wrote unto you with many tears, not that
ye should be grieved, but that ye might know the love
which I have more abundantly towards you.

About the year A. D. 56, and five years after his first introduction of the Gospel among them, St.

* Probably Silas; Acts xv. 40; xvi. 19; vii. 14.

Paul had occasion to write the former of his Epistles to the Corinthians. In that time the original impression both of the Preacher and his Doctrine was, no doubt, weakened. The local elements of character, temper, and philosophy had space to develop themselves within the bosom of the Church, — if not to the extent of destroying the Gospel principles, at least so far as to confuse and neutralize their power. In this strife of passion and prejudice, where the Greek, the Oriental, the Jew, and the natural Man unchastened by the Gospel, each gave way to his own predominating tendency, and palmed it on Christianity, St. Paul tried the effect of an argumentative and expostulatory Letter, restating the original principles of the Doctrine of Jesus, and exhibiting the spiritual Unity which might exist in the midst of the freest development of individual peculiarities, if only the heart was right, if only Love was present, and undue selfishness restrained. That Letter, as we have seen, was not harsh in tone, and much less was it authoritative or dictatorial. But it dealt with great evils, having their roots in unchastened passions; — and with such it is impossible to deal faithfully, and run no risk of offence. The Letter was tender, yet severe; for it was one of those cases where Truth itself is severity, and Tenderness is but a balm upon the wound.

The result of this argument and expostulation was a doubtful matter, — as in such cases it always is. It is impossible to interfere in the concerns of another's well-being, and especially if the assumption is that you deem yourself to be interfering from higher ground, without incurring the danger of aggravating the evil, by awakening the bitterness of some of the deepest passions that lurk in the self-love of man. St. Paul, than whom no man understood better the Rights of another's mind, and the irritabilities of Self-love, awaited at Ephesus in extreme anxiety for tidings of the reception, and effects, of the First Epistle to the Corinthians. This anxiety manifests itself in several characteristic particulars. In the first place, previous to the despatch of the Epistle, Timothy, who was then on a mission to the Churches of Macedonia, had directions to be at Corinth about the time of the Letter's arrival, that with the least possible delay he might report its effect upon the angry elements of that divided Church. This project failed, however, from some cause of detention of which we are not informed. Secondly, — no sooner was the failure of this channel of intelligence known to St. Paul, than he sent Titus,* an express messenger to Corinth, with directions that he should rejoin him at Troas. Thither he had fled from Ephesus, driven out by popular violence excited by the craftsmen whom the prevailing Idolatry employed; † — and there he awaited that information from Corinth which was to shape his future course. Not in inaction, however, though in the restlessness of spirit characteristic of moral anxiety, did he remain at Troas: he relieved his spirit by doing his Master's work, — and in his own striking language, "a great door was opened unto him

* This statement is only conjectural: it is Neander's view.

† Acts xix. 23.

by the Lord." Still Titus returned not, and Paul, impatient of delay, left the work that was prospering in his hands, and with troubled feelings crossed the northern part of the Ægean Sea into Macedonia, and at Philippi received at length from Titus the intelligence he had so eagerly looked for. It was, upon the whole, of a nature to allay his solicitudes. The former bonds of personal attachment and spiritual sentiment were drawn again with a fresh power, — and the larger and better part of the Church were awakened to deep shame for the abuses that had been suffered to live within their bosom. This anxiety for the result of his faithful and bold expostulation, — this tenderness of apprehension in a nature so lofty in its enthusiasm, and the relief it experienced when he heard of the better feelings excited among them, — is related by St. Paul himself in the seventh chapter of this Epistle, in a manner that needs no comment, and will bear no paraphrase: "When we had come into Macedonia, our flesh had no rest; we were troubled on every side; without were conflicts, within were fears. Nevertheless God, who comforteth those that are cast down, comforted us by the coming of Titus, and by the consolation wherewith he had been comforted in you, when he told us your earnest desire, your mourning, your fervent mind towards me, — so that I rejoiced the more. For if I grieved you by my Epistle, I do not repent; though indeed I did repent: — for I perceive that the same Epistle grieved you, but for a season. Now I rejoice, not that ye were grieved, but that ye sorrowed to repentance: for ye were grieved after a godly manner, so that ye have received no injury by us in any respect; — for godly sorrow worketh repentance to salvation, not to be repented of: but the sorrow of the world worketh death. Behold now this very sorrowing by you after a godly manner, what carefulness it wrought in you; yea, what clearing of yourselves; yea, what indignation; yea, what fear; yea, what vehement desire; yea, what zeal; yea, what vindication! In all things ye have shown yourselves to be now clear in this matter. — On this account we were comforted by reason of your comfort: yea, and we the more abundantly rejoiced for the joy of Titus, because his spirit was refreshed by you all. For in whatsoever I have gloried to him concerning you, I have not been put to shame; but as we spake all things *to* you in truth, even so our glorying *concerning* you to Titus is found to be a truth: and his tender affection is more abundant toward you, whilst he remembereth the obedience of you all, — how ye received him with fear and trembling. I rejoice that I have now confidence in you in all things."

This rejoicing, however, was not unmixed. Those more directly implicated in the dissensions and laxity of the Church were not humbled, but embittered by reproof; — and, galled by the submission of the majority, they set themselves to sow suspicions, and, by misinterpretation of words and actions, to undermine the influence of the Apostle. They said, "that he was powerful only in his Letters, but that his bodily presence was weak, and his speech contemptible"; — "that he was conscious of this weakness, and therefore was always threatening to come, but never came;—that from this consciousness arose the vacillation of purpose which led him to change his intention of an immediate visit to Corinth;—that thus doubtful of purpose and ambiguous in expression, if such was his *character*, such would be his *teachings*";—and finally, that the Christian affection and prudence which led him, in perfect simplicity of intention, to address himself to a spiritual sympathy in whatever connection it might be found, "was but a mixture of interest and artifice, making him all things to all men, not for *their* benefit, but for his own."

Under the influence of the mixed feelings produced by such intelligence, St. Paul wrote, from Macedonia, his Second Epistle to the Corinthians: and it breathes of this twofold sentiment,—of an affection, full and fervent, as if it would identify itself with the whole Church at Corinth,—and of a self-respect that vindicated his conduct and reputation, with a vehemence of spirit not disproportioned to the greatness of the outrage. It blends the utmost conciliation with a spirit that will abate nothing of personal Dignity and Rights. It is a mixture of conciliation and defence,—where the Defence is not the apology of conscious weakness, but the self-vindication of insulted strength.

It is remarkable how any earnest direction of the mind will color and shape the whole form of a communication, even in those parts and particulars of it which would seem to have the most remote connection with the strong purpose of the writer. This is the hidden source of that fine unity, which makes common natures sensible of the depth and power that belong to a genuine mind. You are never loose from the grasp of their strong purpose, even in those manifestations of themselves when it is not directly brought before you. The undertone of their moral feeling sounds out through all their varied voices, just as the gentlest ripple and murmur of the sea is still the play and whisper of a vast and awful Power. From such natures, the less earnest minds, who love to float, without any direct aim, on the stream and current of affairs, are apt to feel, not without antipathy, that there is no escape. Whether they urge their purpose directly, or seem to cast their nets more widely, you become sensible that the same powerful influences are hemming you in, and closing around you; and not unfrequently the injustice is committed of attributing to Art and deep-laid Design this moral Unity of bearing and impression, which is in fact nothing more than the unconscious betrayal of the ruling sentiment of an earnest mind. Art may teach those who have no earnestness of nature, how a semblance of Unity may be communicated to the productions of the mind; but the deeply moved soul cannot do otherwise than breathe, and speak, and act, in Unity of feeling,—and those whose feebler sympathies are strained by such sustained exertion, are not unapt to suspect that there is design and stratagem where there is only pure singleness of soul. Thus great Philanthropists are very apt to be called *Mannerists*, by those whose sympathies are soon exhausted and tired. Continued and constant purpose is soon voted to be a wearisome reiteration; — and the man whose Christian impulse and affection is as fresh to-morrow as to-day, — as ready to urge its claims anew, till all its objects are accomplished, — is selfishly dismissed as a man of *one* Idea. Such are the artifices, by which the colder protect themselves against the more earnest hearts. Their feebler moral nature gets no rest under these stronger souls. Such genuine minds are the tests how far the faith and spirit that are professed by a community are real and operating influences; and whilst, often, they create a saving shame and a new faithfulness in honest hearts, — they are, also, often maligned and violently repelled from the sympathies of those who have no thoroughness of nature, and who love nothing on earth so much as to feel no responsibilities, and to live at ease. Of such stimulating earnestness was the spirit, and mission, of St. Paul; —and it is the explanation of how one of such fulness of sympathies, so ready to adapt himself to any true element of the religious mind, had yet depreciators and personal enemies. We can well believe that, without designing it, he would be a thorn in the side of those partial receivers of a Principle, who professed to adopt the spiritual view of Salvation, the safety of the soul through moral union with the Christ of God, and yet nullified it by still continuing their reliance on the religion of Rite and of Observance; or of those who avowed the Christian doctrine of Mercy and Holiness, without feeling the daily impulses of a merciful and heavenly Nature, — and who, to use his own words, named the name of Jesus without departing from iniquity. His enemies at Corinth were of one or other of those classes who made some addition of philosophy, or of ceremony, to the doctrine of the Salvation of the soul by its spiritual union with God through the attraction of his Christ, — or who, professing to have died unto Sin, and to have risen to a new life with Christ, were still under a voluntary subjection to infirmity and evil passion.

But to return to that Unity of impression which, proceeding from the simplicity of an earnest nature, produces the effect of the most consummate Art, — we have an evidence of it, even in the forms of those thanksgivings to God which make the usual introductions of St. Paul's Epistles. In the first words, what the Prophets call "the burden" of the heart is unconsciously communicated. The purpose of the whole is hidden in the sentiment of the opening sentence. In his First Letter to the Corinthians, his object was to extinguish the feeling that there could be any essential difference in those whom a true discipleship in Christ made one, and accordingly his thanksgiving to God is for this fellowship of spirit: — "I thank my God always on your account, for the grace of God, — which hath been given you in Christ Jesus; that ye have been enriched in him, in every thing, in all utterance and all knowledge, — even as the testimony concerning Christ was confirmed among you: so that ye are deficient in no gift, — looking for the coming of our Lord Jesus Christ, — who will also establish you blameless unto the end. God is faithful, by whom ye have been called unto the fellowship of his Son Jesus Christ our Lord." In this Second Epistle, his object is to draw close the bonds of spiritual relationship between himself and the Corinthians, and to make it felt that the admonitions which had shamed some, and irritated others, were but the tender ligaments of this sacred connection; for that all self-love, or wounded self-esteem, must disappear in a spiritual friendship; — and accordingly, his thanksgiving to God is for that Christian experience which enabled him to enter with sympathy and understanding into the trials and consolations of another's mind: "Blessed be God, even the Father of our Lord Jesus Christ, the Father of mercies and the God of all consolations, who comforteth us in all our tribulation, that we may be able to comfort those who are in any trouble, by the consolation wherewith we ourselves are comforted in God." The world knows no connection of hearts so intimate as that which unites those who are suffering together for a holy cause. That supreme interest, exposed to peril, breaks down for the time all individual isolation, and gives to the most distant participator a brother's right of counsel, admonition, and reproof; — and the consolations that arise out of such noble trials are common property, not thoroughly enjoyed, as not righteously used, until they have been dispensed to fellow-sufferers who stand in need of their supports. St. Paul blesses God, that in a righteous cause he had sounded the depths of trial, that the peace of God which he had found there, the purest springs of living waters in the lowest depths, he might be able to communicate to others who had to tread the same ways of discipline. There is no secret of a blessed Life than this, — to be carried out of the poverty and weariness of self-regards in pursuance of great ends, and to feel that every ray of encouragement and light which God lets fall upon that Christian path, is an invitation from the Father of Mercies to share with his other children its joy and consolation. It is not that suffering is the best influence for character; — for happiness, and community in happiness, is the element in which our moral natures breathe most purely and most generously, — in which we are most devout, patient, and self-forgetting; — but then the happiness which produces such fruits must be derived from noble sources, — it must be the fragrance and incense of pure and heavenly sentiments, — it must arise to us, involuntarily, out of God's presence with fidelity in hardships, as the Peace that passeth understanding; and as there is no condition so productive of this blessedness, as the conquest of those difficulties that lie in the path of every lofty aim, it has hence arisen that sore trial and discipline have been so constantly associated with the well-being of Man. Yet is it not *suffering*, but the holy joy that arises in a faithful soul, the peace of dutiful affections, that constitutes its atmosphere of healthy and of saving sentiment. This indeed is the view which St. Paul here gives of the connection of sufferings with right and blessed states of the moral affections: — "for as the sufferings of Christ abound in us, so our consolation also aboundeth through Christ," — in proportion as the spirit of Christ, revived in us, by obliging us to take his path, exposes us to his sufferings, does it also fill us with the blessedness of those true affections to which God has enabled us to be faithful.

This fellowship St. Paul claims with the Corinthians, — and he claims also, though not in direct words, that it should extend to him their confidence in whatever part of his conduct and character he might for a moment be subject to a misconstruction. This indeed was the object for which he brought it forward. It was one of those indirect defences of the Heart, in which the evidence of the course and objects of a whole Life, the devotion and faithfulness of the long Past, — ought to make misunderstandings impossible, and to shame distrust. He had not lived to himself, — he had suffered in their behalf. But the benefit was mutual; — no man can do good to others without blessing himself, and he asked only that the spiritual advantages to *both*, wrought out by him, should bind them together in Christian confidence and love: "Whether we are afflicted, it has been for your salvation, for it has come to us in the ministry of the Gospel; — and if we are comforted, we have made you also participators in our consolations, for your own patient enduring of such sufferings, — both when they befall yourselves, and when they reach you through your sympathy with us."

Having thus alluded to his sufferings in their behalf as the foundation of an intimate spiritual relationship between them, with great tenderness and generosity of sentiment he proceeds to place that union on the grounds of an equality of service, by attributing his deliverance to their spiritual interest in him, and the influence of their prayers: — "We had the sentence of death in ourselves, and were but waiting for its execution, — but it was only that we might learn to trust in that God who raiseth the dead, who delivered us from so great a death, — you also working together for us in prayer, that the blessing which the intercessions of many obtained, the thanksgivings of many may acknowledge."

We must not do more than allude in passing to this subject, of the efficacy of the Prayer of intercession. It has its difficulties, if we assume to penetrate the philosophy of God's connections with Man; but perhaps not more so than the influence of strictly individual Prayer. A wise and holy heart will be as careful in asking blessings for itself as for others, not to substitute its own providence, or apprehension of what might be good, for the providence of God, — not to ask God to save us from the hours of His ordaining, in which our souls are troubled, — nor to let pass, without our drinking of it, the cup which His hand extends; — but with these restrictions, which apply to all filial applications to God, it is as natural, as irrepressible, a movement of the religious mind, to recommend others to the Heavenly help and love, as to recommend ourselves, — to set before us in our prayers those whom we cannot aid, in the spiritual light of God's almighty protection, — to comfort our human perturbations by bearing them on our hearts to Him, and leaving them with Him; — and both Faith and

Reason can perceive how blessings and consolations, the answers to such prayers, may belong to hearts thus spiritually united, which cannot be given to those who remember *self* only in their prayers, and do not feel daily that every human affection reposes in the faithfulness of our Father's Providence and Love. Who will say to what extent another's prayers, and spiritual interest in our welfare, might, through our relations with their hearts, affect our destinies, without implying any variableness in the purposes of God?

This intimate spiritual relationship between St. Paul and the Corinthians won for him an affectionate confidence from the larger and better part of the Church; — and as for that part of it which misunderstood and misinterpreted him, — it is a small thing for one who lives in the sight of God, and under the constant sense of Omniscient introspection, to be judged by man's judgment. No good man makes light of the opinion of another; — but the soul's peace depends not on human breath, and the deep fountains of our self-respect cannot be greatly troubled, when the clear waters lie open to the eye of God. "My rejoicing is this, the testimony of my conscience, that in simplicity and godly sincerity, not in carnal wisdom, but in the grace of God, we have had our intercourse with the world, and especially towards you." The worldly prudence and departure from simplicity attributed to him was, that, from some motives not creditable to his self-reliance and courage, he had shrunk from the fulfilment of an avowed intention, interpreted as a promise, of an immediate visit to

Corinth in its contentious condition. He meets the charge, as any man, however high, ought to meet such a charge, when it is openly made,—*first*, by an unequivocal assertion of his innocence; *secondly*, by giving the true explanation of the misrepresented conduct; and *lastly*, if his life and character entitle him to it, by a statement of such circumstances in relation to himself as ought to have protected him from any man's suspicion: "Having thus purposed, did I use any lightness? or do I, in the things that I purpose, follow worldly inclination and convenience, so that with me there should be yea, and nay? As God is faithful, my word toward you was not yea, and nay."

"Moreover, I call God for a witness upon my soul, that it was to spare you I came not as yet unto Corinth, — not that we claim any dominion over your faith, for in the faith Christ has made you free, but that we would be fellow-helpers of your joy." "I therefore determined that I would not come again to you to bring grief," — and "for that cause I wrote to you out of much affliction and anguish of heart with many tears, — not that ye should be grieved, but that ye might know the abundant love which I have for you."

"And lastly, the Master whom I serve, not without such evidences of faithfulness as sacrifice and suffering may give, — the Master whose own mission in the world was to be true, and to bear witness to the Truth, — in whom also the promises of his Father are so fulfilled that he is 'the Amen and true witness to God,' — and the God who has wrought through me, — and sealed my ministry by his own Power, and given me the earnest of his spirit, which through me ye also have received, ought to have been my sacred protection against the levity and injustice of evil thoughts."

"No man," said Jesus, "who shall do a miracle in my name, can lightly speak evil of me." *

"No man," implies St. Paul, "who has received a spiritual blessing at my hands, in whose service God has used me as His instrument, should lightly conceive evil of me."

---

* Mark ix. 39.

SECTION II.

ST. PAUL'S RESTORATION OF THE PENITENT SINNER. — THE SALVATION OF FORGIVENESS. — HIS THANKFULNESS THAT THE GOSPEL LIGHT HAD BROUGHT HEALING AND REPENTANCE, AND NOT AGGRAVATED SIN. — SIMPLE TRUTHFULNESS HIS ONLY COMPETENCY FOR A SAFE ADMINISTRATION OF GOD'S TRUTH. — LETTER AND SPIRIT.

CHAPS. II. 5 17—III. 1-18.

II. 5. BUT if a certain person hath caused grief, he hath
grieved not me, but in part you, that I may not press up-
6 on you all. Sufficient to such an one was that punish-
7 ment, from the majority; so that, now, ye ought rather
to forgive and comfort, lest such an one be swallowed up
8 by overmuch grief. Wherefore I beseech you to give
9 full force to your love towards him. For to this end also
I wrote, that I might know this proof of you, if ye are
10 obedient in all things. And to whom ye forgive any
thing, I forgive also: for if I have forgiven any thing, I
have forgiven it for your sakes, in the sight of Christ,
11 that we may not be overreached by Satan, for we are
not ignorant of his devices.

12 And when I came to Troas, to preach the Gospel of
13 Christ, and a door was opened to me in the Lord, I had
no rest in my spirit, on not finding Titus my brother, —
but taking my leave of them I went from thence into
Macedonia.

14 Now thanks be to God who always causeth us to triumph in Christ, and maketh manifest the odor of the
15 knowledge of Himself, through us, in every place! For
we are to God a sweet odor of Christ in those who are
16 saving, and in those who are losing themselves; in the
one the odor of death unto death, and in the other the
odor of life unto life. And who is adequate to these
17 things?. For we are not as the many who make a traffic
of the Word of God; but as out of sincerity, as from
God, before the face of God, we speak in Christ.

III. 1. Are we beginning again to recommend ourselves?
Or do we need, as do some, recommendatory letters to
2 you, or recommendatory letters from you? Ye yourselves are our Epistle, written in our hearts, known and
3 read by all men, manifestly shown to be the Epistle of
Christ, administered by us, written not with ink, but with
the spirit of the living God, not on tablets of stone, but on
4 the fleshly tablets of the heart. And we have this con-
5 fidence through Christ in God; not that we are adequate
of ourselves to reckon on any thing, as from ourselves,
6 but our adequacy is from God, — who hath made us competent ministers of the New Covenant, not of the letter,
but of the spirit; for the letter killeth, and the spirit mak-
7 eth alive. And if the administration of death, in the
letter, engraven on stones, was made in glory, so that
the children of Israel could not steadfastly look upon the
face of Moses for the glory of his countenance, a glory
8 that was to be done away, — how shall not the adminis-
9 tration of the spirit be more glorious? For if the administration of condemnation was glorious, much more
doth the administration of justification abound in glory.
10 For even that which was made glorious is not glorious in
11 this relation, because of the glory that excelleth. For if

that which is done away was with glory, much more
that which abideth is in glory.
12 Having then such Hope, we use great freedom of
13 speech; and not as Moses, who put a veil over his face,
that the children of Israel could not steadfastly look to
14 the end [the final object] of that which is abolished: but
their minds were blinded, for until this day remains the
same veil, in their reading of the Old Testament, not yet
15 lifted off because it is done away in Christ. But until
this day, when Moses is read, the veil lies upon their heart.
16 But when it shall turn to the Lord, the veil shall be taken
17 away. Now the Lord is that spirit, and where the spirit
18 of the Lord is, there is Liberty. And we all with un-
veiled face, beholding as in a glass the glory of the Lord,
are transfigured into the same image from glory to glory,
as from a Lord who is Spirit.

In the fifth chapter of his First Epistle, St. Paul had ordered a Corinthian convert who had formed an incestuous connection to be openly separated from the Church; both that the cause of Christianity should not suffer by the immorality of professors who had no practical fellowship with it,—and that the guilty individual, tainted perhaps by the rotten fruit of some unholy speculation on Morals, rather than a conscious violator of God's Laws, should be awakened to reflection and self-knowledge by this act of righteous discipline. The Kingdom of God on Earth, whose essence was Righteousness, and Peace, and Joy in a holy spirit, would be reduced to a level with the Kingdoms of the World, and have no characteristic excellence to sustain it on the

Earth, if *impurity* might show itself in connection with the profession of Christianity. Heathenism was then in possession of the World; Corinth was the head-quarters of its corruption; Christianity had just raised the standard of the Cross in connection with Righteousness, Temperance, and a Judgment to come,—the one witness for a holy God in the midst of an idolatrous licentiousness;—and it would be a monstrous and suicidal act to permit the standard-bearers of that consecrated Cross to be themselves partakers of the very impurity of manners and soul, against which it was the solitary protest on the Earth. At all times the professors of a righteous cause are charged with its destinies in the world,—but especially when the world is strong and adverse, and the righteous cause is but a ray of light that streaks the darkness. It was a matter of necessity that a man of Heathen heart and life presuming to lift the standard of Holiness with foul hands, should be disowned and excommunicated by the true disciples of the Cross. The language in which this act of excommunication is advised, we have already remarked upon in its place in the First Epistle, and its repetition now determines the Scriptural significance of a very important class of words:—"For I verily, though absent in the body, yet present in spirit, have judged him who hath so done this deed, that in the name of our Lord Jesus Christ ye do deliver up such an one unto Satan, for the extinction of the flesh, that the spirit may be saved in the day of the Lord Jesus." * The excom-

* 1 Cor. v. 3–5.

municated man was to have his lot among those with whom he assimilated in spirit and in life: he was to take his part with that Heathen World, which was then the Satan, or Adversary, of God and of his Christ. If, notwithstanding his guilt, — which might be the consequence of his Heathen training, or the foul fruit of some Antinomian theory, and not the work and evidence of a wicked heart, — he had imbibed any true affection, however faint, for the sentiments of the Gospel, he would not bear that severance from its communion, that identification with its enemies; he would sacrifice his passions to his higher leadings, rather than utterly fall away from Grace, — and, by the mortification of his sensual will, renew his broken bond with his Soul's Redeemer. And so it happened. With his Corinthian habit of mind, or through some Gnostic speculation, he had rather imperfectly conceived the Christian Law of purity, than hardened himself against it. His punishment brought contrition, and, as would appear from the terms applied to it, that overwhelming grief which attends the first thorough awakening of the heart to the knowledge of deep evil within itself. The Church which had administered the discipline of the Apostle, witnessing his penitence and despair, now became supplicants for his restoration, and St. Paul, — well aware that there are tides of agonizing and penitential feeling, which, "taken at the flood, lead on" to Christian sanctification and peace, but which, if suffered to ebb in neglect and bitterness, leave the heart harder and drier than before, — in the spirit of his Saviour, and of his Saviour's God, would not have those burning tears needlessly embittered, or that melted conscience chilled into obduracy by unforgivingness and scorn. So slight, indeed, are the allusions to the individual, that every thing of personal infliction is spared, which the delicacy of Christian mercy could suggest. "*Sufficient* to such an one is this punishment which he hath received from many; — so that now ye ought rather to forgive him, and comfort him, that such an one may not be swallowed up by overmuch sorrow. Wherefore I beseech you to give full force to your love for him. To whom ye forgive any thing, I forgive also; and indeed when we forgive, it is as in the spirit and person of Christ, lest Satan should get an advantage over us, — for we are not ignorant of his devices." To be unforgiving might be to lose the moment of grace and penitence, — to aid the Enemy of souls by a sanctimonious severity more akin to human pride than to God's holiness, — to stiffen anew the melted heart, — and to cast again upon the embrace of the world a spirit that would have abjured it for ever, if any holy bosom had been willing to receive it. And whoever speaks of this excommuication by St. Paul, let him tell the *whole* story, — the vindication of Christianity from all fellowship with impurity, and also its open fold for the return of penitence.

St. Paul takes occasion, as an additional sign of his spiritual solicitude for the Corinthian Church in this its unsound state, to mention his trepidation of mind as long as he was ignorant how his measures would be received, and the severity of discipline affect the conscience of the offender (verses 12, 13); — that so much was his heart with them, that signal success elsewhere in the work of his ministry — a great door opened by the Lord in Troas — could not shut out this leading anxiety of his mind; and then, in his most characteristic manner, he bursts into ardent thanksgiving, that, whether by instant success, or through temporary discouragement and later fruit, God's power and blessing had gone forth with his Gospel, and caused the knowledge of Himself, breathed from the lips of his Apostle, like a spiritual essence, to float upon the Gentile air. And constantly must the inspiration of that thought have been needed by the man who, alone in that age, stood fast by the spirit and truth of practical Christianity, — in other words, by the inward *temper* and *reality* of Religion; and who would not adulterate the simple Gospel to ward off from himself the persecution of the various parties who wished to mix up with that moral acceptance of Christ, which is the essence of Salvation, the ceremonies of the Jew, or the speculations of the Greek, or the extravagant pretensions of the independence of the soul on the body, the professed spiritualism and actual impurity, of the Mystic. In that age, when the practical Reason of Mankind had no voice in the world's worship, and the whole sphere of Religion was occupied by the two extremes of a sensual Superstition, relying for salvation upon external means, and serving God through fear, and of a mystical and air-drawn Philosophy, with no more application to real spiritual wants than a sick man's dreams, —

what must have been the moral courage of the intrepid Missionary of Christ who, at every step of his Apostolic way, had to brave the strong passions of the alarmed Fears of the one, and of the alarmed Pride of the other; — with the additional infliction, which no heart could feel more acutely than St. Paul's, that he was multiplying the responsibilities, and aggravating the condemnation, of those who wilfully kept to their darkness because their hearts were evil, — who might, comparatively, have had no sin had not light come into their world, but who had now no cloak for their sins! For a man cannot hear a new Truth, relating to his soul's health and peace, convincingly uttered, — or feel a movement of God's spirit within his own, and continue, in his Judge's sight, the same man that he was before. It is another talent for which God will reckon with him, — a new light upon the soul, or another shade upon that wilful darkness which is the dread sin against the Holy Ghost. Whoever sheds abroad upon the loaded atmosphere of the world the subtle and piercing essence of spiritual Truth, sends indeed the breath of life to some, but the odor of condemnation and death to others, and, — to weigh the moral solicitudes of such a service, — against the pure gain to those who are spiritually saved by receiving the good seed into the good heart, must be set the aggravated perishing of those who quench the spirit, and sin against knowledge. "And who is sufficient for these things?" The man who has trust in God that the TRUTH *must be spoken* whether it be for salvation or for condemnation, — whether it be an odor of life unto life in those who are saved thereby, or an odor of death unto death in those who wilfully perish;—the man who, in simple faith that God knows the workings of his spiritual Instruments, and Himself gives us as we are able to bear, abjures all *preparation* of the Truth, all qualified dispensing of Principle, as a matter too high for us, in any sense in which it is not immeasurably too low,—and which Omniscience alone can conduct in righteousness and wisdom;—the man who "will not corrupt the word of God, but must speak in Christ, as of sincerity, yea as of God, in the sight of God."

This expression of his confidence,—that God requires every Steward of his Truth simply to sow the good seed, and accepts him according to his faithfulness, and not according to the fruits,—but leaves the stony and barren, the volatile and worldly hearts to answer for themselves,—suggests to the Apostle's mind that this might be understood as a comparison of himself with the unworthy arts of some of the Party Leaders who were his enemies at Corinth, and be represented as breathing of that self-glory and commendation which, as we know, his Rivals alleged was not a little characteristic of his temper. He alludes to the canvassings for popularity, the recommendatory letters, and other arts of influence, employed by those who sought to subvert his authority with his own spiritual children: but *his* letter of commendation to them was within their own hearts on which he had engraved the Law of the spiritual Gospel,—and they were to the world the manifest signs of his Apostleship,—a letter of

Christ in his favor known and read by all men; "not written with ink, but with the spirit of the living God; not on tablets of stone, but on the fleshly tablets of the heart." This was his confidence, and this his title to claim the blessing of God on his Apostolic labors, that his sufficiency to meet the difficulties and perils of his calling was not in the skill with which he could adapt the simplicity of the Gospel to the theories or the passions of men, but in the sincerity with which he administered the unadulterated word, having trust in God through Christ, that this alone could work out the spiritual liberty of Mankind, their emancipation from the two great evils of the Mind, Superstition and Sin.

The fourth and fifth verses of the third chapter should be brought into immediate connection with the sixteenth verse of the second chapter, what intervenes being incidentally introduced: — "Who is sufficient for these things? Not he who would accommodate the Gospel to popular acceptance by mixtures of any kind, — but he who has trust in Christ, that, if brought home in simple power to the hearts of men, he is the saving spirit of the world: and our sufficiency is of God, and is summed up in this, — that we say nothing as from ourselves, but are ministers of the New Covenant, without alloy or addition, — not of the letter, but of the spirit, for the letter killeth, but the spirit giveth life." Even in prophetic times it was recognized as the characteristic of a better Covenant, that it would be a law of *Principle*, — that Letter it would have none, — that it would be a Spirit in the souls of men, lifting them into communion with the great Fountain Spirit, and doing the works of God from faith and love. Indeed it would be difficult to conceive a more powerful exposition of the spiritual principle of Christianity than is contained in the following passage of Jeremiah, not the most evangelical of the Prophets; and it shows how even then the purer mind must have felt the bondage of the Law, and sighed for that Law of the spirit of Life in Christ which introduced the glorious liberty of the Sons of God: — "Behold, the days come, saith the Lord, that I will make a new Covenant with the house of Israel, and with the house of Judah, — not according to the Covenant that I made with their fathers in the day that I took them by the hand to bring them out of the land of Egypt, which my Covenant they brake, although I was a husband unto them, saith the Lord: But this shall be the Covenant that I will make with the house of Israel: After those days, saith the Lord, I will put my Law in their inward parts, and write it in their hearts; and I will be their God, and they shall be my people. And they shall teach no more every man his neighbor, and every man his brother, saying, 'Know the Lord,' for they shall all know Me, from the least of them unto the greatest of them, saith the Lord; for I will forgive their iniquity, and I will remember their sin no more." * There could be no juster description of spiritual Christianity, — the Law of God written in the heart, — and the Spirit its own altar, its own sacri-

* Jer. xxxi. 31 - 34.

fice, its own priest. It is evident from the whole tone of this part of the Epistle, and the contrast it exhibits between the Old and the New Dispensation, that it was aimed at those Jewish obstructers of Gospel liberty, whose minds, wedded to Superstition, and enfeebled by Forms, had no understanding of what was meant by being "delivered from the Law that we should serve in newness of spirit, and not in the oldness of the Letter." The essential definition of a Christian man is, that he is one to whose affections, to whose Love and Faith, God and Christ are so dear and so manifest, that he is self-determined by his own spiritual nature in his choice of the Right, the Good, the Just, the True, the Immortal. He is not under the Law, but under the Spirit. His character is the gushing of an inward spring, — of a well of water springing up into everlasting life. There is no outward bondage upon his soul; in his service to God he knows no superstition, and in his service to Man he feels no pressure of external government. A divine affection rules him, and he would do the Right out of his own heart's love, self-determined, though there was no outward Law in the Universe, and no other witness for God than the voice of his own spirit. "The Letter killeth, but the Spirit giveth life." In how many senses does this hold true! Forms and institutions that grow not become obsolete, outgrown by the ever-growing mind; but the spirit which was embodied in these forms may find for itself diviner expression, and breathe its inspiration through nobler symbols. Such is Civilization. Its letter killeth, — chains down the Future beneath the Past; — but its spirit breaks the bond, and freely moulds the new forms of Life demanded by the developments of a progressive Humanity. Such is Religion. Its Letter is a bondage ever, and in time becomes a falsehood; — but its Spirit is undying and growing Truth, the eternal aliment of the Soul. What to the Jews was a full and adequate expression of their highest religious conceptions, would not be true to the more spiritual forms of Christian Thought: — but the spirit of the Old Testament rises again, with a transcendent purity, in the New, — and Christianity, having no Letter, can never become a bondage, for its Law, as written on the soul of Christ, is daily promulgated afresh from an inexhaustible spirit. "Except ye eat the flesh of the Son of Man, and drink his blood, ye have no life in you." In these words of our Lord the Letter killeth, and indeed is false, — but the Spirit opens to every soul the fountains of divine nourishment to which Jesus himself resorted; and accordingly he interprets this hard saying for the misapprehending Jew: "It is the spirit that quickeneth; the flesh profiteth nothing; the words that I speak unto you, they are spirit, and they are life." The most scrupulous exactness in the attempt to conform to an outward standard will only deaden the soul, if there are no consenting affections breathing from themselves the Righteousness of God: — and it is a proverb, that the closest observance of the letter of a Law is often the most effectual way to violate its spirit. Neither is it obedience, but the spirit in which it is rendered, the willing and the loving heart, that hallows Duty,—just as, in the daily intercourses of life, it is the affection that breathes and kindles through them which gives them all their value; for if it was absent, no value would be left to the offices of kindred and of home. Not to those alone who *pay* the service in the deadness of outward exactitude, but to those also who are doomed to the bitterness of so receiving it, the Letter killeth, and only the Spirit giveth life. And many are the services, or even faintest efforts at serving, ennobled by a spirit which this world does not limit, and all its riches could not duly reward; many a hired labor is performed with a love which the Universe could not purchase, and which only the Infinite Source of goodness has the power worthily to acknowledge and bless. The Letter, then, is the outward Law,—the Spirit is its Sentiment and Principle. The Type of the one is in the Commandments of Moses, written in letters, on stones: Thou shalt *not* do this; thou shalt *not* do that. The Type of the other is in the Law of the spirit of Life in Christ Jesus, written in Divine touches, and signatures, and impulses, on the Heart: "My Father worketh hitherto, and I work." And where the Spirit of the Lord is, there alone is this liberty of an unbound heart, acting, and feeling, out of the promptings of Faith, serving God through love, and having no will but His. He alone can, for he alone will, act like Christ, who has the sentiment and the soul of Christ. It is for the sake of these we must make a study of him, and hold continual converse with his life,—that, "beholding with open face the glory of the Lord," some of the divine rays may linger with us, so that "we may be changed into the same image, from glory to glory, as by a Lord who is Spirit."

In comparison with this Spiritual dispensation of Grace and Truth, the distinction of the Jewish Law was but as the temporary lustre that streamed from the face of Moses when he came down from the Mount, — a reflected and evanescent glory. And even that brightness, — the kindling of a soul that had just been elevated into communion with God, making the dark body the transparent medium of the inward light, — the dull-souled people demanded, in terror, to be veiled from their sight;* and whilst "Moses talked with the children of Israel, and gave them in commandment all that the Lord had spoken," he kept a veil upon his face. No unsuitable emblem, suggests St. Paul, of the figurative and unreal character of the Mosaic Dispensation, which revealed God only by symbols, and was but a shadow of good things to come, — the light of His glory streaming faintly through a veil of Forms. And still in St. Paul's time, and until this day, is it a custom with the Jews for the person who reads the Law in their Synagogues to put a veil upon his face. A fitting emblem, again suggests the Apostle, of the veil that is *upon their hearts*, so that, blinded by the outward forms, they could not see beyond the material letter, nor penetrate to the vital and everlasting spirit. Now, when Moses turned away from the people, and went in again before the Lord, he took the veil

* Exodus xxxiv. 29, *et seq.*

from his face; and so, when the Jew shall turn to Christ, the veil shall be taken away from his heart, and with open face he shall behold the glory of God, not struggling darkly though emblems, but embodied in the divine glory of His well-beloved Son. For the Lord, the divine and saving Christ, is the spirit and highest result of every Law, whatever may be its Letter. And where the spirit of the Lord is, *there is Liberty;* for whoever has penetrated to that spiritual Reality, to communion with the living mind of God's Son, and thence been lifted to God Himself, has got beyond all external veils in Religion, whether of words, or forms, or creeds, as Christ's spirit rent the Temple veil, and laid open to all the Holy of Holies; and whoever with open face gazes on that brightness of the Word made Flesh, of the Image of the Father, is "transfigured into the same image, from glory to glory, as by a Lord who is spiritual."

SECTION III.

SENSIBILITY TO HUMAN OPINION; ITS MORALITY. — PURE TRUTHFULNESS AND PURE LOVE, THE ONLY GUIDES THROUGH DANGER FOR AN APOSTLE OF CHRIST. — ST. PAUL'S SOLE RELIANCE ON HIS MANIFESTATION OF THE TRUTH. — CHRIST THE TRUTH: THE REAL IMAGE, NOT A FIGURATIVE EMBLEM, NOR AN ABSTRACT THEORY OF GOD. — THE POWER OF FAITH IN THIS TRUTH TO RENEW THE INNER MAN, AND TRANSFIGURE SUFFERING AND MORTALITY.

CHAP. IV. 1-18.

1 WHEREFORE, having this Ministry, as we have obtained
2 mercy, we faint not: but we have renounced the concealments of shame, not walking in craftiness, nor adulterating the word of God, but by manifestation of the Truth
commending ourselves to all consciences of men, in the
3 sight of God. And if our Gospel be veiled, it is veiled
4 to those who are losing themselves; among whom the god
of this world hath blinded the minds of the unbelieving,
so that the light of the Gospel of the glory of Christ, who
5 is the image of God, doth not shine clearly. For we
preach not ourselves, but Christ Jesus the Lord, and our-
6 selves your servants for Jesus' sake. For God, who commanded the light to shine out of darkness, hath shined in
our hearts, to give the light of the knowledge of the
glory of God, in the face of Jesus Christ.
7 But we have this treasure in earthen vessels, that the ex-

cellency of the power may be of God, and not of us.
8 We are pressed, but not reduced to straits; perplexed,
9 but not in despair; persecuted, but not deserted; cast
10 down, but not destroyed; always bearing about in the body
the killing of Jesus, that the life also of Jesus may be
11 made manifest in our body. For we while living are always delivered unto death for Jesus' sake, that the life
also of Jesus may be made manifest in our mortal flesh.
12 So that death works in us, but life in you. And having
13 the same spirit of Faith, according as it is written,
"I believed, and therefore have I spoken,"* we also be-
14 lieve, and therefore speak: knowing that he who raised
up the Lord Jesus, will raise us up also through Jesus,
15 and will present us together with you. For all things
are for your sakes, that the grace which hath abounded may, through the thanksgiving of many, redound to
16 the glory of God. Wherefore, we faint not; but even
if our outer man perish, yet the inner man is renewed
17 day by day. For our present light afflictions work for us,
18 ever exceedingly, an eternal weight of glory; while we
look not at the things which are seen, but at the things
which are not seen: — for the things which are seen are
temporal; but the things which are not seen are eternal.

THE love of popularity, a desire for approbation, when made a principle of *Action*, is perhaps the most corrupting and the most disappointing of all the affections of our Nature. It is corrupting, because it turns the regards of the mind in a selfish direction, defiles the motives by substituting the love of Praise for the love of *Praiseworthiness*, —

* Psalm cxvi. 10.

and destroys Truth and simplicity of Soul by introducing among the inward sources of Life temptations of a foreign and worldly character, that either interfere with the pure and natural movements of the mind, — or dishonor and deform them by bringing to their aid the alien supports of selfish ends. A man desiring, on any question, to see where Right and Principle would lead him, can no more bring his own accommodation and indulgence into the foreground of his thoughts without corrupting his moral sight, than a man can introduce the love of commendation into the consultations of his soul, without at once insulting and silencing the divine oracle of his spirit. The praise of God is the only Praise the love of which can influence a pure mind; for there only the two motives, the love of approbation, and a supreme regard for the highest Truth of the Conscience, cannot interfere. We do not say that it is the only Praise which, when it comes as a Reward, is pure or sweet, but that when regarded as a Motive, as one of the determining influences of the character, it is, for Adults, the only Praise that is safe and holy. And the desire for estimation is *disappointing*, as it is defiling. It is one of the retributions of God, that if the *rewards* of Virtues are suffered to occupy that place in the affections, which in a genuine and holy mind is given only to the Virtues themselves, the self-seeking becomes transparent, and the end is lost. Honor and Love must follow us: we must not follow them. If we seek first the Kingdom of God and His righteousness, these are some of the things which are "added unto us."

But if these secondary things become principal objects with us, not only will the Kingdom of God and His righteousness never be ours, but the very reputation or estimation to which we made these spiritual things subservient, will flee from us; — we have lost the charm of Grace and Truth; we are no more genuine; the hollow and selfish motive looks out through the eager and restless eyes; the unconsciousness, the freedom from all self-reference, which is the winning Power of Goodness, is brought into contrast with the determined self-seeking of that artificial mind, — and a character is contemplated with which no emotion of admiration or love can possibly coalesce.

Yet no man with Christian affections can be insensible to opinion, or set at defiance the approbation of those with whom his life has connections. To live in opposition to those upon whom all the influences of our characters are spent, is the next saddest thing to living in opposition to our own hearts. The worldly vanity that overrates estimation belongs indeed to a weak and low nature; — but there is something dark and malignant, almost terrible, in the inhuman pride that can stand aloof from sympathy, and find the regard of others not necessary to its peace. The commendation of our fellow-men, it would thus appear, must never enter into our motives of Action, and yet is necessary both to the happiest states of our hearts, and to the most useful workings of our characters. If we are to do good in the world, there must be a moral sympathy between ourselves and those whom we bless, — and yet, if we are to do good in the world, no sympathy but a sympathy with God must be permitted to influence or determine the spirit of our inward mind. These conditions can be reconciled, only as St. Paul reconciled them in his relations towards the Corinthians, by combining Holiness, or Truth of *Mind*, with a perfect disinterestedness of the *Affections*, — by seeking the Good of others, not their Love or Praise, — by desiring to be to them a source of blessedness for *their* sakes, not an object of interest for *his own*; — having confidence in God, that only by adherence to His Truth can any real blessing be communicated to Man, and having a generous faith in Man, that those who never accommodate themselves to Wrong, nor corrupt a Principle, will have their place of acknowledgment among the true benefactors of the World.

St. Paul had incurred the danger of losing the affections of the Corinthian Church. Their religious habits, and the make of their minds, demanded that he should permit them some other spiritual supports than the simplicity of the Gospel, — some other approach to God than that communion which spirit holds with spirit, — some other and more ostensible means of Salvation than the inward purification of the heart and life, — some outward way of ceremony which the Materialist might tread with certainty, and make sure of Heaven, — or some lofty and mystic Doctrine, conferring a privilege on the Speculatist to scale its heights by an intellectual path. In the midst of the animosities excited by the simple preaching of Jesus Christ the Saviour to the opposite tendencies of Greeks and Jews,—the one diverging from practical Religion in the direction of Superstition, and the other in the direction of Speculation,—St. Paul committed himself and his ministry to two great Principles: first, that he used no Instrument to open a way to their hearts but a manifestation of the Truth; and secondly, that no personal aim or selfish interest entered into his ministrations. The pure Truth of God, and a pure Love for those to whom he preached it, made the spiritual Trusts, in the strength of which he cast his bread upon the waters. In the first verse of this fourth chapter, the expression of the absolute confidence in which he commits himself to the simplicity of the Gospel, is perhaps obscured by the phrase "the hidden things of dishonesty," which imperfectly conveys the real meaning, namely, "that he had renounced all such concealments of the Truth as result from a want of moral courage." The sentiment, and indeed the emphatic word, are the same as occur in the Epistle to the Romans in a similar connection,—"I am not *ashamed* of the Gospel of Christ." "Seeing, then," says St. Paul, "that we have received such a ministry, as we have obtained mercy, we faint not amid discouragement,—but have renounced the concealments of false shame,—not using artifice and management, nor adulterating the word of God,—but by manifestation of the Truth, commending ourselves to every man's Conscience in the sight of God."

What was this *Truth*, the absolute possession of which the Apostle thus confidently claims? Is

St. Paul, after all, to be reckoned among the *Doctrinal* leaders, who hold that some abstract Truth is the salvation of Mankind, — and that its manifestation to every mind can be obstructed only by the corruption of the individual Will? Not so: — the Truth he here speaks of has no connections with the speculative knowledge, or the inferential views, which never can be entirely freed from the uncertainty that belongs to the fallibility of the intellectual faculty by which they are derived. *Truth*, in relation to Christianity, always means in Scripture *Spiritual Reality*, in opposition to the shadows, the symbols, the idols, in Lord Bacon's language, whether of the feelings or of the intellect, which Mankind had substituted for divine Realities within themselves, — for *Truth* in the inward parts. There are many spiritual *emblems* in the Universe, many types of God, many shadows of the Infinite, but there is only one thing that really represents Him, and that is, the soul and the life of *a good Man;* — all the rest are symbols, figures, material veils; but this is a similitude, a divine Reality, — a spirit partaking of His own nature, — not the emblem, but in some measure the Image of God. So also are there many modes of Worship, — the breathing rite, the emblematic ceremony, the temple service, the speculative approach and contemplation; but there is only one Worship that is *a Reality*, and that is, the reverence, and faith, and filial love that fill the soul of a good Man, — the sense of God's presence, in the power of His personal character, within the spirit of the worshipper. This was the sense which Christ attached to the word *Truth*, when he explained to the Woman of Samaria, who was inquiring of the modes of external worship, — whether on Zion or Gerizim was the service which God preferred: "God is a spirit, and not to be worshipped by emblems of any kind, but by *Realities* of the soul, in spirit and in *truth*." This was the sense which he attached to *Truth*, when he said, "I am the Way, the *Truth*, and the Life, — no man cometh to the Father but by me," — for he was the *Reality* of that union between God and Man, which is the new spiritual creation, in and for each of us, which Religion contemplates as her true, indeed her only work, — and by the realization of which within the individual soul, we can alone have access to our Father.

Now, emblematic, or speculative manifestations of God will be significant or not, according to the modes of conception, the habitual associations, or it may be the scholastic training, of the mind to which they are addressed. To the unsusceptible Imagination, or untrained Intellect, the Emblem may be a veil which no light shines through, and the speculative representation a cloud of words, which convey no living Truth, — and this attributable to no moral defects in the individual, but arising from the accidents of education. But the peculiarity of that manifestation of God which is here called *the Truth* is, that being not a dim emblem, nor an abstract speculation, but the very *reality* of divine things, the breathing Image of celestial Love, Blessedness, and Purity, it is a direct appeal to the spiritual nature, and cannot be rejected or unrecognized without implying the deadness and insensibility of the moral affections. The worst thing that can be said of the moral state of any heart is, that it does not know the signs of true Goodness, when it lives and speaks before it. As face answers to face in water, so does Goodness imprint an image on the pure and ready mirror of a good Heart; — and if there is no perception of its presence, there is no possible explanation but the absence of the assimilating affections, — that the soiled or worldly heart is not of a nature to seize and reflect the rays of spiritual beauty. If God gave us a revelation of Himself, conveyed, — not in shadowy types, which, as the emblematic forms of the material universe, are only figurative representations, — nor in abstract words, which express only intellectual conceptions, — but by the actual manifestation of His own character before us, — if He would withdraw the awful veil that conceals His presence, and take us into personal relations with Himself, — if He would afford us the opportunity of any real communication with His goodness, — if our Heavenly Father would but permit us *such* means of recognizing the tenderness of His regards as make known to us the unfailing love of earthly parents, — if we could know what, in relation to us, were the actual thoughts and counsels of our Father's mind, — if but for once the eye of God would look upon us, that we might see the Love that beams in it, — if but for once we could hear the voice in which Infinite Mercy would speak to us: — then, that would be a Revelation, unbelief in which would be an absolute impossibility, except on the supposition that the moral nature was utterly alienated from God, and there was no common spirit between them. Such a manifestation of the infinite and invisible Father is indeed impossible; — nevertheless the Revelation He has actually given us is *of this kind.* It is a Revelation not by emblems, but by Realities; the infinite God has given us *an Image* of Himself; he has projected all the spiritual features of His character upon the soul of Christ, so that he could say, "He that hath seen me hath seen the Father." We cannot see the Infinite, but we can see that perfect representation of Him on the scale of Humanity, which is the most direct outward appeal that the spirit of God can address to the embodied spirit of man. A spirit reflecting the moral features of God is the nearest approach to God Himself, — and a Revelation coming in this form could be rejected only by a heart that had deadened, or destroyed, its natural affinities with the Divine Realities. It is in this way that St. Paul speaks of Christianity, as of a living Image of God presented to the higher nature of man, so that, if that higher nature has any remaining life, it cannot avoid recognizing the Divine Reality. "If our Gospel is veiled," he says, "it is veiled to them that are destroying themselves, — to those unbelievers whose minds the god of this world hath blinded, so that the light of the glorious Gospel of Christ, who is the image of God, cannot shine unto them."

There are two facts involved in this Apostolic statement: first, that when not abused and defiled by worldliness, the soul of Man is naturally fitted to receive divine communications from God, to recognize His goodness, and know itself His child; — and secondly, that Jesus Christ, by his perfect representation of his Father's spirit, awakens all these higher susceptibilities, and acts as an instrument of divine attraction to draw the Soul into spiritual union with God.

The fullest and truest conception of Christianity would be obtained by developing the significance of that description of Christ, which represents him as the *Image* of God. An Image gives all the *proportions* of the original, though upon a smaller scale, — as when some boundless expanse of earth and sky is pictured, in every feature, on the smallest tissue of tender nerves within the eye. Thus when Christ is called the Image of God, it is meant that what God is on the scale of Infinity, — that Christ is, on the scale of Humanity. God possesses every moral attribute that characterized Jesus, and in the same relations to each other, — but in an infinitely greater and fuller degree. The moral features are the same, — only, in the one case, on the scale of created being, — in the other, on the scale of the eternal and immeasurable Mind. Thus, Christ's spirit of Mercy is the Image of God's Love; Christ's Holiness, of God's Holiness; Christ's active Goodness, of that Beneficence which worketh ever, and interrupts its loving constancy by no Sabbath pause; Christ's union of Sinlessness with compassion for Sin, the image of that Holy yet forgiving Father, whose arms are ever open to the wanderer, though he says to that holier child, who strays and wanders not, "Son, *thou* art ever with me, and all that I have is thine." The divine light diffused through the Universe, and in all the workings of Providence, was concentrated within the soul, and in the person, of Christ, that he might convey directly a representation of God to the soul of Man. "God, who commanded the light to shine out of darkness, hath shined into our hearts, to give the light of the knowledge of the glory of God in the face of Jesus Christ." If, then, we would know the moral character of God, we have only to look on the face of Jesus Christ, and then lift our thoughts and hearts to the Infinite Original. If Christ was merciful to man, — then God is infinitely merciful. If Christ was forgiving to the penitent, and had no difficulty in reconciling his personal Holiness with the throb of Mercy, — then God is infinitely compassionate, and his tenderness to the penitent is one form of his moral Perfection. If there was no unforgivingness in Christ, there can be no unforgivingness in God, — for the Image must be faithful to the Divine Original. Whatever moral feature, then, you find in Christ, ascribe it to God with an infinite fulness; — and whatever moral feature you do not find in Christ, ascribe it not to God at all.

Such was the Truth by the manifestation of which, in its simple purity, St. Paul commended himself to the affections and consciences of the Corinthians: it needed only that it should be preached without mixture of personal objects or regard to self, to bless and justify its Apostle. This is the link of transition, that leads him to speak of the sufferings which for their sakes he willingly encountered, in the preaching of this Gospel: "But we have this treasure in earthen vessels, that the excellency of the power may be of God, and not of us." The same faith in God, and love for Man, which had supported the Author and Finisher of this Truth himself, must also supply the inward strength of its persecuted Apostles, in the days of worldly conflicts, and of martyr zeal. Even the Lord Christ had this spiritual treasure in a frail and earthen vessel, so that the excellency of its power was only realized by a sustained, and sometimes struggling, faith in the invisible things of God. As Jesus mourned over in dejection, and upbraided the cities wherein most of his mighty works were done because they repented not, as though he must abandon that hard and thankless race, — and then, revived by trust in God, uttered with new and more fervent tenderness the appeal of undrooping Love, "Come unto me, all ye that labor and are heavy-laden, and I will give you rest"; as he sunk into trouble of soul under the contemplation of that awful weight of responsibility which was to press upon his bowed and suffering form, and in an hour when he would be alone in the world, only that his Father was with him, — and then rose into the light of the divine Purpose that had been clouded for a brief moment, — "Yet for this cause came I to this hour: Father, glorify thy name"; as the words of the remembered Psalm, learned in childhood's hour, fell, perhaps half unconsciously, from the trembling lips which agony had parted, — "My God, why hast thou forsaken me?" and then, to show that that spirit could not be forsaken, those lips closed for ever in strains of Faith, — "*It is finished:* Father, into thy hands I commend my spirit"; so, with all who would lead his life of Faith, and amid the outward forms and shows of things live true to the hidden spirit and secret purposes of God, the outward man perishes, and the outward life discourages, and the inner man of faith and spiritual endurance must be renewed from day to day, — and only through looking not to things which are seen, but to the things which are unseen, if they are pressed they are yet not in straits, — if they are perplexed, they are yet not in despair, — if they are persecuted, they are yet not forsaken, — if they are cast down, they are yet not destroyed, — and that if they bear about with them the suffering and the dying of the Lord Jesus, it is, that in his strength, and by God's blessing, the life also of the Lord Jesus may in some degree be worthily imitated, and represented in their mortal frame.

It is remarkable that in this passage St. Paul, speaking of the persecution and sufferings he endured for the sake of his children in the Faith, uses the very same sort of language which, when used by the same Apostle in reference to Christ, a speculative Orthodoxy interprets into the Doctrines of Atonement and Vicarious Death. He was "continually delivered up to death, that a divine life might be communicated to them"; "all his sufferings were for their sakes," — "and death worked in him that life might work in them"; — he was willing to meet affliction and death, if he could only thereby accomplish his mission, and impregnate them with Christian life, knowing that he who raised up the Lord Jesus would raise up him also, and present him together with those whom he had begotten in Christ." Then, at least, would his trust in the Truth, and the Love in which he administered it, be justified by God.

And the source of all this spiritual confidence, and the source too of all the strength that any spirit has, not in sufferings alone, but in prosperity's most favored hour, and amid the bloom and life of the most blessed affections, is derived from that inward eye which "looks through the things that are seen and temporal, to the things that are unseen and eternal." Affliction, — mental distress, — the pangs of pain and death; — these indeed may be seen and witnessed, — and dread and awful they are; yet when most lingering, they pass like a dream, and are among the things that are gone for ever; — but the unseen purpose of God into which the spirit entered abides for ever, a wreath of unfading glory for the now sainted head of Meekness and patient Trust. And does not Prosperity itself require us to enter into the unseen spirit and purpose of God as much as, perhaps even more than, Affliction, which brings its own warnings and spiritual suggestions with it? What, but this blindness to the unseen purpose of the spirit of God, turns many a life of outward blessings into the deepest miseries of a burdened existence, and takes away that inward peace, that life of the soul with God, without which we cannot drink of the springs of joy that gush up in our own dwellings, and follow us in our daily paths? And who that looks to the Seen, and not to the Unseen, would dare to encircle his heart with the wasting affections of a nature crushed before the moth, — with the perishable ties of mortal Love? No; — there is not one sacred hour of the Heart's intercourse with others, in which we are not looking to, and living upon, *the unseen.* The eye that looks on us is but the material organ of an unseen spirit's Love; — the familiar voice that speaks to us draws its tones from an unsearchable Heart whose life is hid with God; — the very hand that is clasped in ours has a pressure of tenderness that belongs not to flesh and blood, and is an impress from the *unseen Soul.* Blessed then be God, that they are the Things that are seen that are temporal, and the Things that are unseen that are everlasting!

SECTION IV.

THE TWO REDEMPTIONS; OF SOUL, AND OF BODY. — THE CHRISTIAN ON EARTH HAS OBTAINED THE ONE, AND LOOKS FOR THE OTHER. — THIS SPIRITUAL REDEMPTION MAKES SELF-GLORY A SELF-CONTRADICTION, FOR TO LIVE IN CHRIST IS TO BE DEAD TO SELF AS CHRIST WAS DEAD. — IN THIS LAW OF THE SPIRIT OF LIFE IN CHRIST JESUS, ST. PAUL FINDS PROTECTION FOR THE CORINTHIANS, AND A DEFENCE OF HIMSELF, AGAINST FALSE TEACHERS AND APOSTLES.

CHAPS. V.–VII. 1.

V. 1. For we know that if our earthly tent-house were
dissolved, we have a mansion from God, a house not
2 built with hands, eternal in the heavens. And therefore
we sigh, desiring to put on over us our house which is
3 from Heaven; if indeed, when putting it on, we shall not
4 be found disembodied. For we in this tabernacle do sigh,
being burdened, not that we desire to be unclothed, but
clothed upon, that mortality may be swallowed up by life.
5 Now he that hath wrought us for this selfsame end is
God, he who also hath given to us the pledge of His
6 spirit. Wherefore, always of good courage, and knowing
that when at home in the body we are absent from the
7 Lord, — for we walk by Faith, not by sight, — we are of
8 good courage, and are willing rather to be exiles from the
9 body, and to be at home with the Lord. Therefore also

we are zealous, whether at home or exiles, to be well
10 pleasing to him. For we must all appear before the
judgment-seat of Christ, that each may receive for the
things that he hath done in the body, whether good or
evil.
11 Knowing therefore the terror of the Lord, we persuade
men, and are made manifest to God, and I trust also are
12 made manifest in your consciences. For we are not
recommending again ourselves unto you, but are giving
to you an opportunity of glorying on our behalf, that ye
may have power against those who glory in appearance,
13 but not in heart. For if we are in an ecstasy, it is for
14 God; and if we are sober-minded, it is for you. For the
love of Christ constrains us, discerning this, that if one died
15 for all, then did they all die, and he died for all, that the
living should no longer live to themselves, but to him who
16 died for them, and was raised up. Wherefore we from
henceforth know no one after the flesh: though we have
even known Christ after the flesh, but now know we him
17 no longer. So that if any one be in Christ, he is a new
creature. The old things have passed away: lo, all
18 things have become new. But all things are from God,
who hath reconciled us to himself through Jesus Christ,
19 and given to us the ministry of reconciliation. So that
God was in Christ reconciling the world to himself, not
reckoning their trespasses to them, and having committed
20 unto us the doctrine of reconciliation. For Christ then
we are ambassadors, as though God did beseech you
through us; we in Christ's stead do entreat you, that ye
21 be reconciled to God. For he hath made him who knew
no sin, to be a sin-offering for us, that we might become
the justified of God in him.

VI. 1. We then as fellow-laborers also exhort you, that ye

2 receive not the grace of God in vain. For he says, "I
have heard thee in a time accepted, and in the day of
salvation have I succored thee." Behold, now is the ac-
3 cepted time, now is the day of salvation: Giving no offence in any thing that our ministry may not be blamed:
4 but in all things approving ourselves as ministers of God,
in much patience, in affliction, in necessities, in straits,
5 in blows, in imprisonments, in tumults, in labors, in
6 watchings, in fastings: in pureness, in knowledge, in
long-suffering, in kindness, in a holy spirit, in love un-
7 feigned, in the word of truth, in the power of God; by
8 the armor of righteousness on right hand and left, by
honor and dishonor, by good report and evil report; as
9 deceivers, and yet true; as unknown, and yet known; as
dying, and lo, we are alive; as chastened, yet not killed;
10 as grieved, yet always rejoicing; as poor, yet making
many rich; as having nothing, yet possessing all things.
11 O Corinthians, our mouth is opened unto you, our heart
12 has swelled. Ye are not straitened in us, but ye are
13 straitened in your own affections. Now as a recompense
for this, I speak as to my children, be ye also enlarged.
14 Become not uncongenially yoked with unbelievers: for
what is there common to Righteousness and Sin? or what
15 communion hath Light with Darkness? and what concord
hath Christ with Belial? or what part hath a believer with
16 an infidel? and what agreement hath the temple of God
with idols? For ye are the temple of the living God, as
God hath said,—"I will dwell in them, and will walk
with them, and I shall be their God, and they shall be my
17 people." Wherefore, "Come out from the midst of them,
and be ye separated, saith the Lord, and touch not the
18 unclean thing, and I will receive you; and will be a
Father unto you, and ye shall be sons and daughters unto
me, saith the Lord Almighty."

VII. 1. Having then these promises, beloved, let us cleanse ourselves from all impurity of flesh and spirit, perfecting holiness in the fear of God.

In explanation of the peculiar form of St. Paul's language, in the commencement of the fifth chapter, we must refer to those conceptions of the Second Coming of Christ to which it is adapted, — and which, in the fifteenth chapter of the former Epistle, we have already found shaping his representations of the immediate applications of the Doctrine of Immortality. In that chapter are distinctly expressed the two ideas which are prominent here, — that some who were then living might be found alive at the coming of the Lord, and the end of the World; and the idea of two bodies, our present one, adapted to the conditions of our Earthly state, and another, to be the imperishable organ of a purely Spiritual Nature. The external change which qualified for entering into the Kingdom of God in Heaven, was wrought by Death, in the laying aside the corruptible, and putting on the incorruptible body: "Flesh and blood cannot inherit the Kingdom of God, neither doth corruption inherit incorruption," and therefore, says the Apostle, "*we must all be changed*," — in order that what is mortal in our constitution should be adapted to the conditions of an immortal existence. Upon the faithful dead this change would be of the nature of a Resurrection, in the form of that celestial body of which our present terrestrial body is the seed; when that which is sown in weakness shall be raised in Power, and that which is sown in dishonor shall be raised in Glory. Upon those found alive at the Coming of the Lord, the change would be of the nature of a transfiguration, — the mortal garment would be made immortal without passing through the transition state of death, — or, as St. Paul expresses it in our present context, "without being unclothed, they would be clothed upon, and mortality swallowed up of life." So near, in the apprehension of the times, was the Day of the Lord, that "all might *not die*, nevertheless all must be *changed;* — in a moment, in the twinkling of an eye, at the last trump, the dead should be raised incorruptible, and the living transfigured."* The parallel between the two passages holds in every part, though the form of expression is varied. What in the former is the *animal* Body, is here "*the earthly tent-house*," the frail and slight Tabernacle that belongs to our pilgrim days; — translated in our version, without the least regard to English idiom, and almost unintelligibly, "the earthly house of this tabernacle." What in the former is the spiritual Body, is here a building of God, a house not made with hands, not produced according to the earthly course of human formation, but according to laws of our Nature we have not yet ascended to, celestial and everlasting. What in the former is represented by "the mortal putting on instant immortality," and by "Death being swallowed up in Victory," is here the investiture of the incorruptible garments, without experience of the

* 1 Cor. xv. 51, 52.

disembodied state, so "that mortality is swallowed up by Life." The metaphor of "Death being swallowed up in Victory," and of "Mortality swallowed up by Life," is founded on the conception that there are three states for man, — Mortal Life, Death, Immortal Life; — but that, in the case of those found alive at the coming of the Son of Man, the change would be so immediate that Death in the usual sense could not be said to exist at all, so that nothing would intervene between Mortal Life and Immortality.

With this explanation, we will now translate freely the first four verses of the fifth chapter, bearing in mind the connection in which St. Paul introduces them, namely, "that he was devoted to the ministry of spiritual Christianity, that Truth which God had caused to shine into his heart by giving him the light of the knowledge of His glory in the face of Jesus Christ, — and that, though as yet we had this treasure in earthen vessels, and could realize it only by struggling Faith, yet, after the example of Christ himself, through all present discouragement, mortal weakness, suffering, and death, the spirit of Life might show itself triumphant, for, though the outward man perished, the inward man might be renewed day by day, — provided we look not to the things which are seen, but to the things which are unseen; for the things which are seen are but for a season, and the things which are unseen are everlasting." "For we know," proceeds the Apostle, "that if our earthly *tent*-house was dissolved, we have a *mansion* built by God, a house not made with hands, celestial and imperishable. And whilst in this our earthly tent, our sighings are directed towards our immortal Body, earnestly desiring to put on our house which is from Heaven, yet upon this condition, that we should be clothed with our spiritual Body, without first meeting the nakedness of Death; for we who are in this tent sigh, being burdened, not that we desire to be disembodied and unclothed by Death, but at once to be clothed over by our great Change, that Mortality may be swallowed up by Life."

There are two *Redemptions* spoken of by St. Paul: first, a redemption on earth, the "*spiritual Mind*," which is life and peace, the release from sin and from dead works of superstition to serve the living God, — *the Soul's* redemption; — and secondly, the Body's redemption, — deliverance from all "the ills that flesh is heir to," — that manifestation of the Sons of God for which the persecuted Church waited, and sighed, in suffering and bondage. In the fifth verse, the first of these Redemptions is called the pledge and promise of the second. The spiritually redeemed should have faith in God that He will complete what He has commenced: and the emancipated soul sustain, in hope and courage, the brief conditions of the earthly state: "Now he who must work in us this great external change is God; and as an assurance of that coming glory and release, He has given us the earnest of the spirit": that is, He that hath taken the spirit into filial relations with Himself will complete, in all things, the glorious liberty of his sons, — and the *heart* that is made inwardly free by the Truth as it is in Christ, must never sink, in faithlessness or fear, beneath the burdens of mortality. St. Paul has repeated the whole sentiment of this argument in his Epistle to the Romans. I shall recite the passage from the eighteenth verse of the eighth chapter. It speaks of the two Redemptions; — of the first being to Faith the earnest of the second, — and, to those who faint not, but are strengthened from the Life within, of the momentary affliction working out the everlasting glory: — "For I account the sufferings of this present time not worthy to be compared with the glory which shall hereafter be revealed in us. For the earnest longing of the earthly creature waiteth for the manifestation of the Sons of God, for we were made subject to frailty, in hope that we shall be delivered from the bondage of corruption into the glorious liberty of the Sons of God. For we know that every creature groaneth and travaileth in pain together until now, and even *we who have the first fruits of the Spirit*, even we ourselves sigh within ourselves, looking for our adoption, to wit, *the redemption of our Body*."

And the spirit which Christ had made free, waiting for the redemption of the Body, could no more be subject to the ordinary temptations of human good or human evil. Neither fear nor flattery, neither Death nor Life, could now make the influences, or direct the path, of a mind that, having buried its earthly affections, and risen together with Christ to a diviner hope, was hourly expecting the second coming of the Son of Man, to judge the world in Righteousness. Might not *he*, without suspicion of self-commendation, cast off the imputation of interest or ambition, who, being new-born in Christ, had entombed his *past* existence, come out from it as clear as though his soul had never breathed but in Christian air, knew no man any longer after the flesh, but only in his spiritual relations, and taking the Gospel of the Kingdom as his mission in Life and his confidence in Death, had cast in his lot with that crucified and risen Master whose ambassador he was? If he lived, though to meet toil and exile and all the forms of moral persecution, still it was in his Master's service and after the similitude of his Master's Life;—and if he died, though it should be the martyr's fate, it was still, after the similitude of his Master's death, to pass to life eternal, and redeemed, both in flesh and spirit, to join for ever the emancipated Sons of God. If for such a mind there could be any seduction from the pure service of the Gospel, Death might offer it, but Life could not;—yet, whatever the desire of Nature to walk by sight in glory, rather than by faith in toil, to be absent from the body and present with Christ,—one care only could press upon that heart, whether absent or present, living or dying, to be the Lord's. "Wherefore," says St. Paul, casting off, by the force of the spiritual argument, whatever imputations his enemies might affix to the motives of his ministry,—"Wherefore, we are always of good courage, knowing that while we are present in the body we are absent from the Lord; for here we are walking by faith, not by sight,—and only this one thing we strive for, that, whether present or absent, we may be his accepted, — for we must all appear before the judgment-seat of Christ, that every one may receive for the things done in the body, according to that he hath done, whether it be good or bad."

Such was his defence against those who attributed the peculiar character of his Ministry, especially its spiritual Liberty, — its abrogation of all religious service but that which flows from the inward Law of the Heart, — to the common motives of human fear or favor. God had called him to that work, — and woe unto him, if he preached not the Gospel! A necessity was laid upon him, — and no fear could contend with the fear of quenching the Spirit that spoke to him the divine command. The Truth that makes free was not of his making; — it had come to him direct from God, carried by a divine force into his alien heart, as the lightning opens the bosom of the night, — and his commission was, not to tamper with it, nor seek its present triumph by adapting it to man's weakness or expectations, but *to proclaim* it, and *to trust* it. What human influence could struggle in that heart which *believed* that God had so charged it, — and that but a day, or an hour, was between it and the judgment-seat of Christ! "Knowing, therefore, the terror of the Lord, we would persuade men; to God we are manifest, — and we would hope also that we are manifest to your consciences."

It was necessary at this point, considering the style of imputation employed by his opponents, for St. Paul to remind the Corinthians, that all this self-defence did not proceed from any personal interest, but was required lest the representations of his enemies, who were also the enemies of the severe simplicity of Gospel Liberty, should have an undue influence with men weak in the spiritual faith, and who in their unconfirmed state might be entangled again in the yoke of bondage, and "hindered from obeying the Truth." It was not for his own glory, but to strengthen *them* against those who wished to lead them captive again in the train of forsaken superstitions, that he sought to establish their confidence in his Ministry, — not that *he* might be honored, but that *they* might stand free: — "For we are not recommending ourselves again unto you, but we are giving *you* occasion to glory on our account, — that ye may have wherewith to answer those who would glory for appearances, and not for realities of the soul."

The passage from the thirteenth verse to the close of the fifth chapter is intended to show, that whatever might be any man's desire for personal distinction, whatever interested motives might have sway with him, yet that all self-glory in relation to Christianity was an impossibility, and a self-contradiction. No man could appropriate to himself that gift of God, or could arrogate any share in that glory which had flowed from the divine Mercy and Truth alone. No man, without violating its spirit, and showing that he had no part in it, could make the Gospel of grace and forgiveness minister to the pride of self. If St. Paul could thus show that the very essence of Christianity extinguished those selfish aims, the imputation of which was weakening his influence at Corinth, he might afterwards speak freely of those circumstances in his Apostolic relations towards them which, by giving him a claim upon their confidence, and confirming his authority, should enable him to frustrate the attempts of those who would mislead them from the Truth. Accordingly, he here speaks of the impossibility of personal glory being grafted on the divine beneficence of Christianity, — and, that suspicion being removed, in the next chapter he proceeds to state those circumstances which, by accrediting both his Apostleship and his disinterestedness, ought so to establish his influence as to enable him to preserve his own converts in the uncorrupted simplicity of the spiritual Gospel. The passage (ver. 13–21), to which we now proceed, is one of the battle-grounds of doctrinal controversy; — but it must receive its explanation from the connection in which it occurs. We shall regard it solely in that relation.

St. Paul averts from himself the charge of ambition in connection with his ministry of the Gospel, on two grounds: — first, that no man could make it a ground of personal glory, for it was no man's boon, but the gift of God to all, — all alike require it, — it found all needy and made them whole; and secondly, that it was the very essence of Christianity, that no man should live to himself, or seek his own. If its Apostle was ever transported beyond himself, it was not for his own glory, — but for the glory of God: or, if he became all things to all men, that by wisdom and prudence he might win them to Christ, it was not for his own sake, but for the sake of the weak brother for whom Christ died. For the love of Christ held back his Apostle from any course not dictated by that divine Love;—for he thus judged, that if one died for all,—then all had died,—died, as he had died, to a selfish life, else they were none of his;—because he died for all, that all should be dead to their past existence, and live no longer unto themselves, but unto him who died and rose for them. So that the Christian must no longer consider any man in his worldly aspects, or with a regard to persons;—he must know him no more after the flesh, but in his spiritual relations, in which all men are alike, and vainglory is excluded. Nay, though he had once viewed Christ after the flesh, in his Earthly and Jewish relations, and connected carnal, and national, hopes with the Hebrew Messiah, now must he know him so no more;—for these old, exclusive views have passed away,—the Christ had died to abolish all spiritual distinctions among mankind, national and individual,—by Death he had disrobed himself of all partial affinities, and all things were become new;—the Jewish Messiah had fulfilled the Law, and passing into the Heavens out of the sphere of Jewish peculiarities had become the Saviour of the World;—and now no man could graft self-glory on Christianity, either on personal or on national grounds, for *all* were alike related to the spiritual Christ, and *all* were of God, who was reconciling the world unto Himself through his one Mediator, not imputing their past trespasses to those who, through spiritual faith, had become new creatures in him. In this universal kingdom and glory, St. Paul claimed but an elder brother's place in relation to those who had not yet received it; and besought them, as in Christ's stead, the elder Brother of Mankind, to be reconciled to God; for He had broken down the partition-wall between Jew and Gentile; — there was no more of legal disqualification, or ceremonial fitness. As the sin-offering under the Law cleansed away the ritual impurity which Priest or People had unknowingly contracted, and restored their lost consecration, — so, in this sense, was Christ a lamb without spot or blemish, as the sin-offering of the World, for with him was abolished for ever the Righteousness of ordinances, and all men were placed in purely spiritual relations to their God, — their true and inward bond with the Father of their souls being now the Righteousness of God that flows from Faith, — out of a filial and a trusting Heart.

You will recollect that the sin-offerings of the Law never removed moral guilt, but only some ritual offence, which, under a ceremonial Religion, disqualified for worship. You will remember also that it was from such ritual disqualifications, *and such alone*, that the death of Jesus, with whom the Law of ordinances was abolished, redeemed for ever the whole world, who were no longer under the Law but under the Spirit. That this is the whole extent of the sacrificial efficacy figuratively applied to the death of Christ, is distinctly stated in the Epistle to the Hebrews, at the fifteenth verse of the ninth chapter: "He is the Mediator of the *new* Covenant, that by means of death, *for the redemption of the transgressions that were under the first Covenant*, they who are called might receive the promise of the everlasting inheritance."

And when we bear in mind the connection in which the death of Christ is here introduced, it will be evident that the only idea in the mind of the Apostle was the abolition of religious distinctions, and the union of all men in spiritual Liberty; so that none could find the sources of personal importance in that Gospel whose first principle it was, that, dying to the Law of self and sin, they should live no more unto themselves, but the Life of him who died in Love, and now liveth unto God.

(Ch. VI.) But though that Gospel extinguished the selfish and ambitious sentiment, still its Apostle, as an ambassador for Christ, had a commission from God to urge it home upon the hearts of all people, —and a claim to be esteemed very highly, in love, for his work's sake. That he sought no glory for himself, was no reason why his just influence and authority should be weakened amongst those who evidently had not strength to stand alone in the liberty wherewith Christ had made them free,—and who, not grown up in spiritual things to the stature of the Apostle, were open to the seductions of the false teachers who dispensed some Jewish or Heathen notions, accommodated to the frailty of these babes in Christ. To such he did not hesitate "to magnify his office," if, by impressing them with his just claims on their gratitude and confidence, he could persuade them to receive the Truth of Christ in the spiritual form he had administered it to them, and so preserve them from the moral dangers incident to men who, not having their stability within themselves, depended for their safe guidance upon the soundness of those to whom their trust was given. It was right, therefore, that, as one "put in trust with the Gospel," he should exhort them not to receive the grace of God in vain; — that, for those who would become new creatures, casting behind them their former feebleness of outward dependence, "*now* was the accepted time, *now* was the day of Salvation"; — and that, against the influence of unspiritual advisers tampering with their new-born and feeble faith, he should confirm his own authority by setting forth every plea that justly entitled him to a power over their hearts. It was with this view that he drew up that noble statement of his labors in the Gospel, as one who used no undue means with those whom he regarded as his children in the Faith, — "seeking to give no offence in any thing, that the ministry might not be blamed, but approving himself to God, in patience, in affliction, in imprisonments, in watchings, — by pureness, by long-suffering, by love unfeigned, by the word of Truth, by the power of God upon the convinced heart, — by the armor of righteousness on the right hand and on the left, offensive and defensive; through honor and dishonor, — through evil report and good report, — treated as a deceiver, and yet true, — as obscure, and yet having a name that would never perish, — grieved, yet rejoicing, — poor, yet making many rich, — having nothing, yet possessing all things."

When the fountains of the heart are once broken up, thoughts pour forth which at all other moments would be restrained: whatever is in the soul is then borne out on the torrent of the affections. St. Paul had not intended to make this personal appeal,—but it came:—"Our tongue is loosed, O Corinthians, for our heart is burst. Be not straitened towards us, as our heart is not straitened towards you: we speak to you, as our spiritual children, and as our recompense we ask only that you would open to us your bosoms,—turn away from seducers,—hold no more communion with unrighteousness,—and, as temples of the living God, cleanse the soul from idols,—accepting the overture of God, 'I will be their God, and they shall be my people.' Come out from among them,—touch not the unclean thing, and 'I will receive you, and will be a Father unto you, and ye shall be unto me as sons and daughters, saith the Lord Almighty.'"

Throughout this Section, I have sought no present applications, nor transferred a word or a thought from the relations between St. Paul and the Corinthians to our own business and bosoms. But as the Gospel never dies, its warnings and its promises are never out of season. Notwithstanding Paul's expectation, the End is not yet: but to those whose hearts Death hath rent, and whom Mortality makes to feel that, as they walk this Earth they are treading on their graves, never can come amiss the warning voice,—"*Now* is the accepted time, *now* is the day of Salvation";—and to the feeble and lapsing

Faith of a nature tempted and frail as ours, never can be unneeded the word of exhortation, to "receive not the grace of God *in vain*," and if we have a heavenly Hope, "to cleanse ourselves from all disqualifying sins of flesh and spirit, perfecting holiness in the fear of God." (Ch. VII. 1.)

SECTION V.

THE LAW OF MORAL INFLUENCE. — PAUL'S INTENSE THANKFULNESS THAT HIS REMONSTRANCE WITH THEIR SINS HAD NOT SPIRITUALLY INJURED THE CORINTHIANS. — THE DOCTRINE OF CONTRITION. — THE SORROW THAT IS ROOTED IN THE WORLD; AND THE SORROW THAT IS ROOTED IN GOD.

CHAP. VII. 2-16.

2 Receive us; we have wronged no one, we have corrupted no one, we have taken advantage of no one.
3 I speak not to condemn you, for I have already said,
that ye are in our hearts, to die together and to live to-
4 gether. Great is my freedom of speech towards you;
great is my glorying for you: I am filled with consolation; I exceedingly abound in joy under all our affliction.
5 For when we came into Macedonia our flesh had no rest,
but on all sides we were troubled: without were fightings,
6 within were fears. But God, who comforteth those who
are cast down, comforted us by the coming of Titus;
7 and not by his coming only, but also by the comfort
wherewith he was comforted by you, when he told us of
your desire, your mourning, your zealous affection for
8 me, — so that I rejoiced the more. Because if I pained
you by the Epistle, I do not repent, even if I did repent,
for I see that same Letter, though but for a season, has

9 pained you. Now I rejoice, not that ye were pained, but
that ye were pained unto repentance, for ye were pained
after a godly manner, so that in nothing have ye received
10 injury from us. For godly sorrow worketh a renewal of
the soul unto Salvation, that has not to be repented of;
11 but the sorrow of the world worketh death. For, behold,
this selfsame thing, that ye were pained after a godly
manner, what carefulness it wrought in you, yea what de-
fending, yea what discontent, yea what fear, yea what desire, yea what zeal, yea what vindication! Altogether ye
12 have proved yourselves clear in this matter. If then I
so wrote to you, I did it not on account of him that did
the wrong, nor on account of him who was wronged, but
that the care which we have towards you, for your own
sakes, might be made manifest in the sight of God.
13 Wherefore we were comforted in your comfort, and rather we more abundantly rejoiced in the joy of Titus, be-
14 cause his spirit was refreshed by you all. So that if I
have boasted to him any thing on your behalf, I am not
ashamed, but as I have said all things to you in Truth, so
also my boasting of you to Titus has become Truth.
15 And his tenderness is more abundant towards you, whilst
he remembereth the obedience of you all, how ye re-
16 ceived him with fear and trembling. I rejoice that altogether I have confidence in you.

THERE are in this Chapter some of the inconsistencies of feeling that belong to a generous nature, when its affections are brought into intimate relations with those who are not altogether worthy of its love. It speaks out of the fulness and richness of its own heart; it takes no grudging measure of what *they* may be worthy to inspire, but pours out upon them a love and confidence that come from inward springs. Yet as such natures are genuine, as well as generous, the bare and unadorned truth will at times be forced upon them, the barrenness of the hearts on which they have shed their light and warmth will lie exposed in all their bleakness and poverty, — and there will be alternations in the bosom, of gushing affections, and chilling experiences of the unworthiness of their objects. In a strong and noble heart the generous affections, whether deserved or undeserved, will always regain their sway, and must at last create in others the characters they have presupposed.

Such changes are not properly inconsistencies; they are not shifting and capricious feelings in relation to the same objects, but the just and natural emotions of the same heart, according as its own strong trusts, and tender longings, and ardent sympathies, are in sole possession of its thoughts, — or the painful images of barren and unanswering natures are filling the mind, and pressing too distinctly upon fainting hopes. We have here St. Paul, at one moment pleading with the Corinthians for their confidence and love, — and in the next, rejoicing in his *possession* of them; — at one moment asking for his place in their affections, stating his claims in the spirit of one who was doubtful of his position, — and in the next, glorying in their obedience, and expressing an assurance that they would justify his most confiding hopes. His claim indeed upon their moral love was one which the infirm side of human nature is slow to acknowledge, even where it is maintained with the wisdom of the serpent, and the harmlessness of the dove. He had been simply true in his spiritual treatment of their case; — he had not helped them to disguise or cover their sins; he had made no compromise with their pernicious doctrines; nor hesitated to disturb their habits, and their ease, by clear exposure of the dangerous laxity of their associations and their friendships. He had even touched the unsound spot, placed his hand upon the sinner among them, and demanded the separation of the diseased member; — he had singled out the superstitions, and speculations, that were disturbing the moral power of the Law of Liberty, and he had required their renunciation of the very world in which they lived, since they could not breathe in it safely, — "Come out from among them, and be ye separate, and touch not the unclean thing," — rather than that evil communications should corrupt good principles, and their yet feeble Faith inhale some polluting influences from the surrounding habits of an idolatrous life. He had suffered no evil thing to cleave to them without laying his hand upon it, and now with a clear conscience, as one who had dealt honestly with their souls, he could stand before God, and advance the highest claims which one human being can have upon another, — spiritual faithfulness, — sacredness preserved, and sympathy not violated, — fidelity to all moral interests, as the first Duty and the only Love: — "Receive us: we have wronged no man, we have corrupted no man, — we have taken advantage of no man."

What other benefits, kindnesses, compliances, or unmoral self-sacrifices and reluctant yieldings of a gentle nature, unwilling to give pain and unaccustomed to oppose, — will compare their weight of Love with a service of this kind, with that noble Truth which breathes a higher sentiment through the weakness of the affections, — which has the strength to resist evil, — which holds that it has no life when it ceases to be sacred, and that its highest function towards any other heart is to be a pure, full, and unsuspected witness in whatever relates to the interests or the perils of the moral principle. For no support, when we are right, can be derived from those who are ready to yield to us even when we are wrong. Those who cover our sins cannot sustain our virtues. Those who are ready to soothe us with their indulgence and soft flatteries, when we are weak and erring, have lost the privilege to hold us up, when we must stand alone against unmerited reproach, and follow our own conscience against the world. Those who nurse our weakness abdicate the power of ministering to our strength. And so, simple compliance yields every thing that is worth keeping or living for; for to have the opinions and the sympathies of another entirely at your command, unable to resist the spell of your influence, is just to lose all the moral uses of that mind, inasmuch as it is impossible to draw from it any independent support. And hence the holy necessity of Sympathy being kept in strict subordination to inviolable Truth.

There is no lack of Kindness in the world; the instincts of Humanity are gentle and tender; what is wanted is that these instincts should become honored and sacred, — that the Heart in its nearest relations should ally itself with the calmest fidelity to convictions of Duty, — that no other part of our Nature should have the power of compromising our holiness, our individual sense of Right. It is in the closest intercourses of life that temptation to this unfaithfulness abounds, — sometimes from natural partiality, leading to weakness and blindness; sometimes for the sake of peace; sometimes through the fear of giving pain; and sometimes from the prevailing influence of a stronger mind, ungenerously used; and then there are two seducers, the tempter and the yielder. For it is treasonable to Love, as to Duty, when our communion with others is suffered to break our fellowship with God, — when that which the Heart permits condemns the Conscience, — when the interest that another has with us, or the power of persuasion that another has over us, leads us away from strict union with ourselves, and so dethrones the moral Principle which is the light and guide of the Affections. These are the unconscientious connections and intercourses that "*corrupt*" the heart of Life. When the mere tendency to assimilation, the immediate sympathies, are stronger than the moral Principle, the elements of highest influence are all cast away, and the most intimate connections are the most actively engaged in weakening the character. As parental Love degrades itself to a mere instinct, except when it manifests its tenderness through the guidance of sentiments of the most unyielding sacredness, — so our moral connection with others becomes low and selfish whenever, either in our inward or our outward Life, it interferes with the simplicity and truth of the individual mind. Indeed, only weak or selfish affections could thus consent to live; the generous and self-devoting ones would never expect either to receive or to confer good, if by any compromise they quenched or dishonored the light of God and Truth within themselves.

Not that it is necessary that we should become Censors of one another, — or that there should be even a show of interference with our moral Liberty. To deem it a Duty to press our notions of Right upon all around us is often, even where we are most right, only a mischievous activity that betrays a very superficial sense of the deep and individual sources from which moral acts must spring, if they are to have the least value in themselves, — or to be of any genuine efficacy in elevating the character. In the equal intercourses of life, it is no part of our social responsibility that the more enlightened Conscience should insist upon making a direct conveyance of its superior knowledge to the less instructed, or that the honest and faithful Conscience should demand an account from every lapsed and faithless one. It is enough that we are clear, unambiguous, uncompromising, in our own words and lives, — that by manifestation of the Truth we commend ourselves to every man's Conscience in the sight of God, — and that, if any man sins or tampers with conviction, *we* have not made his fall easy to him, or helped to conceal the Light that condemns him. Of course there are cases when our Duty goes far beyond this, — when more is demanded of us than open and consistent Example, — when every bond of sacredness requires that we should come into direct collision with the evil thing, lay our hand on our brother's shoulder and search his very heart, — remonstrate, entreat, persuade, warn, and rebuke, with a manly and a holy freedom: but the general moral action of Society is not of this nature, and is mainly carried on by each man being simply true to himself, without any thought of exerting an influence on the sentiments of other men's hearts, or the directions of other men's lives. And this is the purest and the most effectual exertion of moral Power, because it acts simply through the maintenance of its own sincerity, and without offence to those personal jealousies which resent direct appeals. Rarely indeed would the necessity for direct interference be found to arise, if Society and Individuals made their convictions respected by never participating in their violation. Without any public man assuming the position of a Censor, or contracting the reputation of a Purist, public Honor might be maintained inviolate, if Public Assemblies encountered every exhibition of the Corruption of the times with a cold and forbidding sternness, whose severe, though unuttered, repulse Dishonor would be forced to understand. If the principled, without any assumption, were simply true to themselves, the unprincipled would quickly find their standing. The mere negative action of every man of Honor, in his cold withdrawal from Dishonor, simply refusing every species of association with it, would preserve at a high standard the purity of Public Opinion, by far the most important of our earthly Tribunals. And it is not the corrupt alone who are the corrupters, but even the personally pure, so long as they withhold at least this negative counteraction, a decided manifestation of the absence of all sympathy or coöperation with any public man stained with corruption. Again, in private or domestic life, or in the common intercourses of Society, without any one being required to take upon himself the invidious office of direct reproof, how effectually might social offences be subdued, and graver corruption made to know itself and its place, if the Truth and Sincerity of every individual heart deliberately refused to lend the slightest cover to the wrong, — if the inward sympathies of the Conscience were regarded as better guides than the false courtesies of usage, — if no man's levity or folly received the patronage of insincere smiles, and no man's coarseness or profligacy could show themselves in intimate communication and friendship with gentle and honorable minds. The law of Christian Purity requires no man to be a Reprover of his Brethren, but it does require every man to make manifest his own Conscience, to hold himself apart from every association with evil; and if this is not done, — not offensively, but *unequivocally*, — the sounder part of Society cannot say that it "has corrupted no man," — for it has borne with corruption, and smiled upon it, and taken it by the hand, and kept its company, and God may charge the guilt upon those who have done nothing to abate the evil, even as he declared that he would require the souls of those who died in their sins at the hands of the Prophets who raised no warning voice; for now all are commissioned Prophets, charged to reveal the holiest Light that is in them, that God may be glorified.

It is evident, indeed, that when St. Paul says of himself, that "he corrupted no man," he was not supposing that any one had charged him with the direct introduction of vicious influences: — he was contemplating that Corruption which he might have promoted, by withholding the Light, which he had the power of directing against it. And in this sense, the real corrupters of Society may be, not the corrupt, but those who have held back the righteous leaven, the salt that has lost its savor, the innocent who have not even the moral courage to show what they think of the effrontery of Impurity, — the serious, who yet timidly succumb before some loud-voiced scoffer, — the heart trembling all over with religious sensibilities, that yet suffers itself through false shame to be beaten down into outward and practical acquiescence by some rude and worldly nature. Such unmanifested, and acquiescent, Consciences must not plead, that they have been "wronged," and "corrupted," and "taken advantage of," by the stronger and coarser natures: they are the wrongdoers and corrupters, for they have sinned against Light, and refused their Mission.

And the mind that administers a moral influence, simply because it must be true to itself and show its

Love in union with its Holiness, whilst it sustains the sacred character that belongs to all pure affections, clothes that sacredness with the mightiest powers of persuasion. For moral influence breathes a different spirit, and works totally different effects, when it is felt that it comes necessarily from the Truth and Consistency of the mind that imparts it, — and when it is suspected that it is an intended lesson, purposely designed to awaken or instruct a defective Conscience. These arrows of influence should be stripped of their barbs, and strike without being aimed. They should be seen to come down upon us from calm heights, from a fixed sacredness that cannot alter, — and without disturbance of the passions. When the Heart preserves all its tenderness, and the Conscience all its sacredness, and the moral act is one of simple Truth and Love, there is hope that the personal influence, because perfectly pure, will be perfectly effective. No sooner does St. Paul find himself placing his claims upon the Corinthians on grounds that might imply something of a moral separation between them, than he adds the assurance that the Affections were not disturbed, and that the very freedom with which he had spoken manifested a love towards them that, by betraying no higher interest, might be able to justify itself in the sight of God: "I speak not this to condemn you, — for I have said before, that ye are in our hearts, to die together and to live together." And, like every noble nature, he dealt even with their wrong in that spirit of confidence which exalts rather than depresses, and lifts above the evil in the same moment that it is exposing its existence: "Great is my freedom of speech towards you, — great is my confidence in you: I am filled with comfort, I exceedingly abound in joy under all our tribulation." Again, at the twelfth verse, he affirms with something even of the exaggeration of a right Principle, that it was not their wrong-doing, nor any sentiment of his mind in relation to the evil merely, but his love for them, and his desire for such a union of the affections with them as God could approve, that had led to his freedom of remonstrance: — "If, therefore, I so wrote unto you, I did it not for his cause that had done the wrong, nor on account of him that had suffered the wrong, — but rather that our earnest affection might be manifested for you, as if God were to be its witness."

We have also the picture of his own sufferings, whilst the effects of that remonstrance were yet in doubt, — all the symptoms of a sensitive mind that can consent to give pain even to the guilty only because the highest Truth and the highest Love require it, — the inward suspense and fear, — the outward restlessness and change of scene until the anxiety was removed, — the hurried sending of one messenger after another, — the deep thankfulness when the assurance came, that he had touched and purified the evil, without wounding or embittering the heart.* There is a remarkable expression in the ninth verse, showing the sense that St. Paul entertained of the injurious, and even corrupting, effects that might at-

---

* See page 261.

tend moral interferences not conceived in the purest spirit:—"Now I rejoice, not that ye were grieved, but that ye sorrowed to repentance: for ye were grieved after a godly manner, so that *ye have received no damage from me in any respect.*" No wonder that, with that tender respect for Humanity, his pure and healing influences excited no hostile and counteracting passions, and stirred only that spiritual sorrow which renews the heart: "The Sorrow that has relation to God worketh a renewal of the soul unto Salvation, never to be repented of,—but the Sorrow that has relations only to the World worketh death."

Here is the whole spiritual philosophy of Contrition in a few pregnant words;—its uses and abuses marked with a distinctness in the separating line, of which moral subjects rarely admit, and which only a master's hand can draw. The Sorrow that brings the heart into relations with God, is his healing messenger, drawing closer our communion with the Source of our being, and leading to that Repentance, which is only another name for a new and diviner Life;—whilst the Sorrow that does not bring the heart into healing and strengthening relations with God, but settles on the worldly aspects of our Grief, calls no angel Emotion to unbar our prison doors, but leaves us to ourselves in that hour of woe and weakness,—alone with our humiliation, our darkness, our anguish, and our sin. The Sorrows which the same Affliction awakens may be so absolutely different in kind, as to have nothing moral in common. It may be the godly Sorrow that restores spiritual Life: it may be the Sorrow whose eye is on the World, that sinks in moral Death.

The sorrow of Conscience: Is it affected most by our altered relations to the World, or by a new view of our relations to God? Does it arise from a sense of outward evils entailed upon us, or from a sense of *what we are within?* Is it only the burning shame of exposure,—the agony of disgrace,—remorse for the forfeiture of reputation,—and self-contempt for all the folly that has involved us in this social humiliation and loss;—or is it the deep sense of inward unworthiness, the consciousness of an abused, dishonored, injured Nature,—a grief of the spirit for its own weakness, unfaithfulness, self-abandonment to evil? In the one case, it is a sorrow that reunites the soul to God,—in the other, that leaves it with the World.

Again, the sorrow of Adversity: Does it look to the worldly, or to the spiritual aspects of a changed condition? Is it for the loss of outward prosperity, honors, influence, position,—or does it regard an abridged power of moral action and spiritual culture? Does it brood over the external circumstances, as cause and consequence, or does it lift itself up to see the hand and will of God, as its ordaining Source? In the one case, it is a Sorrow that worketh abjectness and prostration of spirit; in the other, that leads to an experimental knowledge of the divinest Truths,—that "a man's life consisteth not in the abundance of the things that he possesseth,"—that "man lives not by bread alone, but by every word that proceedeth out of the mouth of God."

Again, the sorrow of Bereavement: Is it selfishness, or tenderness? Is it anguish, or is it love? Does it centre on the outward and worldly change, and the personal loss? Is it the rebellion, or the devotion of the heart? Is it too feeble and earthly to be constant, in all outward change, and to draw living emotions and support from an unseen being? Or, does it contemplate the spiritual facts, and fill the lonely heart with the images of Heaven, and breathe its air? In the one case, it is the Sorrow of the World that leaves "the dead to bury their dead"; — in the other, it is a divine Affection, drawn from the Source of Love and Goodness who has given us the earnest of His spirit, and sanctified by the faith "that there are no dead, for that all live unto God."

And the signs of a Sorrow derived from a sense of our true relations to God are, that it is a Sorrow that has Fruits; it is not remorse, but Repentance, — not despair and dull death, but new Life; it belongs to a changed heart abjuring its former self, and "working carefulness, fear, struggle, vehement desire, unsparing self-punishment, and retribution."

And whoever would awaken these saving emotions in a lapsed Nature, must treat it with the Apostle's reverence, and approach it with the generous Trust that inspires the sense of Power. To some of us there may appear a tone of exaggeration in St. Paul's address to these unconfirmed penitents: "I rejoice that I have now confidence in you in all things"; — but this is the spirit that reaches a heart that has any thing noble in it, and produces new effort and watchfulness, rather than unjustifiable Self-Reliance.

And there can be no spiritual healing without *some* Self-Reliance; and the best part of Salvation has regard not so much to the height of our attainments as to the soundness of the Heart, the trust we can now repose in our honest desire for Reformation.

And thus, not spiritual healing, but corruption dark and stern, may be occasioned even by the Truth, if unaccompanied by the Love that awakens some saving emotions in the Heart. And thus a man may sin, most deeply, in uttering even merited rebukes; he may administer moral lessons of unquestionable Truth with a poisonous effect; and, by the rudeness and hardness of his touch, turn even the germs of new life in the soul into deadly roots of bitterness. And thus, in all parts of Character, Christianity requires us to act with the presence of *all* our forces, with a union of contrasted qualities. And to be equal to the divine work of moral healing upon Earth, one must be in the spirit of the Master, full of grace as of truth, — with something of the blended Goodness and Severity of God himself, — so as to speak the Truth in Love, to yield no Principle, yet lose no Sympathy, — to "corrupt no man," by Speech or Silence, and yet stir no emotion less sanctifying and gentle than "the godly Sorrow that leadeth to Repentance."

PART II.

(CHAPS. VIII.–IX.)

ST. PAUL URGES THE CORINTHIAN CHURCH TO DISCHARGE THE FULL DUTIES OF BROTHERLY LOVE TOWARDS THEIR AFFLICTED BRETHREN OF JERUSALEM. THE LAW OF GIVING.

PART II.

ST. PAUL URGES THE CORINTHIAN CHURCH TO DISCHARGE THE FULL DUTIES OF BROTHERLY LOVE TOWARDS THEIR AFFLICTED BRETHREN OF JERUSALEM. — THE LAW OF GIVING.

CHAPS. VIII., IX.

VIII. 1. Now, brethren, we make known to you the grace
2 of God given in the Churches of Macedonia, — that in a
great trial of affliction the overflowing of their joy, and
from its depth their poverty, abounded in the riches of
3 their single-mindedness. For according to their power, I
bear witness, and beyond their power, they were willing of
4 themselves, — praying us with much entreaty for this
5 favor and fellowship in the assistance of the saints; and
not according as we expected, but first they gave them-
6 selves to God, and to us by the will of God. So that we
desired Titus, that as he had begun, so also he would
7 finish among you, this work of grace also. And as ye
abound in all things, in faith, in word, in knowledge, and
in all zeal, and in your love towards us, that so also ye
8 may abound in this grace. I speak not by commandment,
but on account of the zeal of others, and to prove the
9 genuineness of your love. For ye know the grace of
our Lord Jesus Christ, how for your sakes he became

poor, being rich, that ye by his poverty might be rich.
10 And herein I give my advice, for this is expedient for
you who have begun before not only to do, but also to
11 be in forwardness, a year ago. Now, therefore, perfect
the doing of it, that as there was a readiness to will, so
also there may be a completion of it, out of that which ye
12 have. For if there be first a willing mind, a man is accepted according to that he hath, and not according to
13 that he hath not. Not, indeed, that there should be a re-
14 mission to others, and a burden on you, but that by way
of equality, now in this time, your abundance should
supply their want, that their abundance likewise should
be a supply for your want, — that there may be an
15 equality. As it is written, " He that gathered much had
nothing over, and he that had gathered little had no lack."
16 But thanks be to God who put this same earnest care for
17 you into the heart of Titus: that indeed he accepted the
exhortation, and being more zealous, of his own accord
18 he went unto you. And we have sent with him the
Brother whose praise in the Gospel is throughout all the
19 Churches: and not that only, but who was also chosen
by the churches to be our fellow-traveller with that grace,
administered by us to the glory of the Lord himself, and
20 as a proof of our readiness. Taking care for this, that
no one should blame us in this abundance which is ad-
21 ministered by us: Providing for things honest not only in
22 the sight of the Lord, but also in the sight of men. And
we have sent with them our brother whom we have often
proved in many things, and now much more zealous, be-
23 cause of this great confidence in you. Now, with regard
to Titus, he is my fellow, and my fellow-worker towards
you; — and the brethren, — they are the Apostles of the
24 Churches, the glory of Christ. Wherefore show to them,
in the face of the Churches, the demonstration of your
love, and of our boasting on your account.

IX. 1. But indeed it is superfluous for me to write to you
2 concerning this ministering to the saints. For I know
the forwardness of your minds, for which I boast of you
to the Macedonians, that Achaia was ready a year ago,
3 and your zeal has stirred up very many. Yet I have
sent the brethren, that our boasting of you in this matter
should not be made vain, — that ye may be in readiness,
4 as I said ye were. Lest if the Macedonians should come
with me, and find you unprepared, we, not to say ye, should
5 be put to shame for this same confidence. Therefore, I
thought it necessary to exhort the brethren, that they
should go before unto you, and prepare beforehand this
your blessing already declared, so that the same should
6 be ready as a blessing, and not as an extortion. And this
I say, He that soweth sparingly shall also reap sparingly,
and he that soweth bountifully shall reap also bountifully.
7 Let each man give according as he purposeth in his
heart, not regrettingly, nor constrainedly, for God loveth
8 a cheerful giver. And God is able to make all grace redound towards you, that in all things, having all suffi-
9 ciency, ye may abound to every good work. As it is
written, "He hath dispersed abroad; he hath given to
10 the poor: his righteousness remaineth for ever." Now
he that supplieth seed to the sower will also supply bread
for you, and multiply your seed sown, and increase the
11 fruits of your righteousness: Being enriched in all things
to all ingenuousness, which worketh through us thanks-
12 giving to God. For the ministration of this service is not
only supplying the wants of the saints, but also abounds
13 in many thanksgivings to God. Through the experience
of this ministration they glorify God for the submission
of your confession of the Gospel of Christ, and for the
sincerity of your fellowship with them and with all men,
14 whilst they also earnestly long after you, in their prayer

for you, on account of the exceeding grace of God in
15 you. Now thanks be to God for his unspeakable gift.

We obtain the richest Lessons in moral Wisdom, whenever a great Mind applies itself to determine the *permanent Principles* that are involved in some pressing, practical occasion. We then get the Ideal of Duty, but clear, definite, and of commanding obligation, because exhibited in immediate connection with actual affairs. It is like Christ's sketch from Life in answer to the question, "But who is my neighbor?" — and with no escape from the closing appeal, which seems to proceed out of the circumstances like the voice of Righteousness itself: "Go thou, and do likewise." — In the eighth and ninth chapters, St. Paul sets forth the spiritual *Laws* of Christian Liberality; the Principles of Action which must direct, preserve, and ripen its impulses, that they may bear their best fruit. The special occasion was the sympathy of the Gentile Churches with the Poverty and peculiar afflictions of the Parent Church at Jerusalem, — the source of their own spiritual riches, — and the Duties of that Sympathy.

A year before, when St. Paul was closing his First Epistle to the Corinthians, he had commended to their charitable care the poorer brethren at Jerusalem, and given directions as to the manner in which their Benefaction should accumulate. On the first day of each week, a contribution, proportionate to the prosperity which God had given, was to be laid apart. — Jerusalem must have stood out before the imagination of a converted Heathen as the City of God, venerable in holiness and privilege, — and to provide for its necessities a pious duty, a dear service, — such as in all ages the strong hands and hearts of the world have regarded the office of ministering to the wants of those, from whose supposed sacredness and devotedness of life has been derived the knowledge of spiritual and eternal things, — the Sages, Priests, and Prophets of Mankind. More venerable than Delphi to the Greek, might well appear Zion to the converted Gentile; and even an enthusiasm of Charity and Self-Devotion be nothing more than natural to those thus brought into living relations with that "Oracle of God," when told that "the Saints" of the Mystic City, the brethren and disciples of the Lord, their own Teachers and Fathers in the Faith, were in poverty and persecution. From the beginning, this connection had existed between the mother and the daughter Churches. When Paul and Barnabas went up to Jerusalem from Antioch to consult on Christian Union and Gentile Liberty, they were charged, as a sign of the Brotherhood of the Churches, that they should remember the Poor.*

The zeal of the Corinthians in this service of Brotherhood, St. Paul now instigates by the example of the liberality of the Macedonian Churches, Philippi, Thessalonica, and Berea. He had sent forward Titus, and other representatives of the Churches, to take charge of the practical details; and in

* Gal. ii. 10.

these two Chapters he unfolds and enforces the duty and the principles of Christian sympathy between Church and Church, nation and nation, man and man, as members of one spiritual Family. He hints at the comparative poverty of Macedonia, and then records, as an example, their eminent generosity. The merit of this was increased by their great and recent sufferings on account of their profession of Christianity: "In a great trial of affliction their spiritual joy, and out of its depths their poverty still overflowed and brought forth the riches of *Single-mindedness*." This benevolent spirit St. Paul calls the "grace of God, bestowed on the Churches of Macedonia," the fruit of His most signal favor and presence in their hearts. So is every good disposition, the best and greatest of His gifts. This is the true Christian sentiment: "Not unto us, O Lord, not unto us, but unto *Thy* name give glory, for Thy goodness and Thy truth's sake!"—We are most richly blessed by God when He puts it into our hearts to do and to wish Good; a blessing infinitely greater than the *means* of doing so with which He has endowed us. We have already received more at God's hands in the *disposition* to give, than any brother can in the external gift that we communicate.

1. The source of this disposition in the Macedonians is indicated in that word, in the second verse, so unhappily translated "liberality."—In their "*Single-mindedness*," they adopted the doctrines and principles of the Gospel as realities of the Heart,—they entered into the spirit of Christian Union and Broth-

erhood, — in the Apostles' language, they "gave themselves to the Lord." We are not now discussing the Political Economy of Alms, but the actual effects Christian principles would produce on hearts possessed by the Gospel sentiment, if they believed that *Brethren* were in destitution.

St. Paul calls every motive into play, by stating that he would not wish the Corinthians to be inferior to any other Church in such gifts: and we may provoke one another to good works. He hints also, that, as they made no slight pretensions to other distinctions, they should not be deficient in this the crowning gift. (VIII. 7.) Yet he takes not away the grace of their benevolence by spoiling its spontaneous character; he only fans the flame that was self-kindled, by the warming breath of sympathy with the active goodness of others. He tells them that he had himself made use of their own readiness in order to kindle the flame in Macedonia, — that their zeal had stirred up many, — and that he had even boasted of their promptitude, so that his own credit was now involved in the zealous completion of their liberality. (IX. 2 – 5.)

2. (VIII. 8, 9.) He affirms the principle that their zeal in this cause would test the degree of reality in which they had embraced the doctrine of Jesus, who identified himself with all mankind, and *therefore* became poor and rejected of men, as the Universal Saviour, when he might have been rich and accepted as the Jewish Messiah. Beautiful argument for Christian Mercy, when addressed to Gentile Churches! That *they* should now identify them-

selves with the Jewish Christians, and, in the sentiment of their spiritual brotherhood, forget their Nationality, — even as Christ had divested himself of Jewish glory, that he might identify himself with Humankind. "Ye know the grace of our Lord Jesus Christ, that though he was rich, for *your* sakes he became poor, that ye by his poverty might be rich." These words have no relation to a preëxistent state. He was rich as God's Christ; and if he had consented to be the Jewish Messiah, — if he had followed the suggestion of the Tempter, — from the pinnacle of the Temple looked down upon the Jewish world as his Messianic realm, and descended among them as the expected Deliverer, — would have had a Monarch's place; and his poverty, and rejection in this world, were the consequences of his faithful purpose to be the spiritual Saviour of Mankind. You will observe that St. Paul, writing to Gentiles, says, — "It was for *your* sakes he became Poor." And it is always in this connection with *Gentile* Redemption, that mention is made of the Humiliation of our Lord. He was rejected of the Jew for the Gentile's sake. He would not sit upon that narrow, theocratic Throne. He would not be the Son of David; he must be the Son of Man, and the Son of God.

3. (Verses 10, 11.) He states it as a Rule, and Principle of Love, that we should complete, and accomplish without hazardous delay, the merciful projects of the Heart. What the impulse of Mercy prompts to be done, can with no safety, and with no faithfulness, be put off: — "You have been in

forwardness a year ago, and now it is expedient for you, that *you perfect* the doing of it." Many a charitable design comes to nothing, — many a kind feeling and purpose bears no fruit. The heart urges, and gives its ready pledge; — but something interposes, and its counsels come to naught; and that they may not come to naught, the good deed should be put in train, and if possible be perfected whilst yet the heart is warm. How many right designs, and brotherly projects, has delay ruined! There is no wilful insincerity; — but we have delayed, — and meanwhile the feeling has cooled, and other interests have intervened. Sufficient for each day is the *good* thereof, equally as the evil. We must do at once, and with our might, the merciful deed that our hand findeth to do, — else it will never be done, for the hand will find other tasks, and the arrears fall through. And every unconsummated good feeling, every unfulfilled purpose that His spirit has prompted, shall one day charge us as faithless and recreant before God. "Now therefore finish the *doing of it*, that, as there was a readiness to *will*, so there may be a *performance* also out of that which ye have."

4. (Ver. 12.) For the *willing* mind which accomplishes what it can, is that which God accepts. It is not the *material* part, but the *spiritual* part, of Charity that God regards. Do what you can, — give what you have. Only stop not with feelings; — carry your Charity into deeds; do and give what costs you something; — if nothing else, contribute your honest sympathy with another's Joy, — your unaffected tears for another's Grief. If Charity

was accepted only according to its external gifts, the Poor would be deprived of this peculiar grace. But the Poorest, according to the Beatitude, may have as much of the Joy of beneficence, of the Kingdom of Heaven, in their spirit, as the richest and the greatest; for it is the sincerity of the working sentiment that is accepted and blessed, and small service and offering from *them* is often more than the wealthiest have *the power* to give. Indeed, so far as wealth is the instrument of Charity, where it exists in great abundance it takes from the power of making sacrifices, except in those cases, unhappily not rare, when the Wealthy are blighted and blinded by narrow-heartedness and the fear of Poverty, and then they lose the power, by losing the will: — but the Poor take their gifts out of their own comforts, often out of their own necessities; — "they give their mites, even all that they have." If the Poor tend a sick friend or neighbor, they take it from their rest, and add it to their already excessive toil, whilst the rich man sends hired care, and never feels the sacrifice. If they take an orphan child, as they often do, into their narrow homes, it is to share their poverty and make it poorer, to feel the daily pressure of another's maintenance at their scanty board, whilst the rich man, who does such deeds, *contributes* to its support, and is unhampered by its existence in purse, privacy, or comfort. And they are the Poor who mainly nourish the Poor. The rich man's bounty falls, occasionally, in overflowing abundance, like a sudden shower; but the sympathy of the Poor for one another is the ever-falling dew. And in this is the Promise fulfilled: "Blessed are the Poor, in spirit, for theirs is the Kingdom of Heaven." God makes all men equal in the opportunities of the divinest joys.

> "Man is dear to man: the poorest poor
> Long for some moments, in a weary life,
> When they can know, and feel, that they have been
> Themselves the fathers, and the dealers out
> Of some small blessings; — have been kind to such
> As needed kindness; for this single cause,
> That we have, all of us, ONE HUMAN HEART."

5. (Ver. 13–15.) Again, St. Paul urges no extravagance of Charity. He states that there is no obligation on any one to reduce himself to destitution, that others may live at ease; — but that still it is the mission of Christian Principle and Love to tend to that Equality, which the physical Laws of the Universe do not produce: "I mean not that others be eased and ye burdened: but that, by way of equality, your abundance may at this time be a supply for their want, and their abundance also may at another time be a supply for your want; so that there may be equality, as it is written, 'He that gathered much had nothing over, and he that gathered little had no lack.'" We are often tempted to say, when we look upon the inequality of human condition, Is God impartial? Is He an equal Father? — Is the Gospel Doctrine true? But we should rather ask, Have *we* acted as the children of that equal Father? Are the marks of His Spirit upon us? Have we recognized our Brotherhood? God's object in this life is not, by material distributions and measurements, to exhibit His own Paternal

Character in unclouded Light, but to educate our spiritual Nature, and to train to perfect action our filial and fraternal Love. Christian men ought to adjust what, for this very purpose, God has left unequal. The means are given, and nothing is wanting but the Brother's Heart: and if the Brother's Heart *is* wanting, shall we charge the inequality upon the Universal Father? He has given enough for all, but His children must care for each other, and be the stewards and distributors of His Bounty. If God produced the works and results of Love and Wisdom by His own acts of power, where would be the Education of the human Soul? If God daily dropped our rations out of Heaven, what would become of human energy, — what of human self-denial and love? Our souls are trained and perfected through our bodily conditions. He spreads the feast over the all-nourishing Earth,— but Brother must distribute to Brother, or teach him to collect his portion for himself. As He cast the Manna on the Desert, and though some gathered more, and some less, according to their opportunity, yet, when Distribution was made, enough was found for all,— so with that unfailing Manna which His bounteous hand spreads around us every day. Some gather more, — some less, — some *none*, according to opportunity, talents, health, advantages, natural or acquired: all these are *His* gifts, — and shall the spiritual Grace alone be wanting that would lead all, by help or instigation, to the attainment of their share?

It is not by material impartialities and uniformities that God shows Himself in intimate paternal connections with Man: — it is by giving us of His own spirit that this is most fully manifested, by imparting the ruling principles of His own Nature; — and the obscure and destitute in whom the Heart of Love is warm, is more God's Child, is more favored, and *partially* treated, by God, than the prosperous, or the great, who are not united to Him by this kindred bond, by this true affinity of Nature and Beatitude.

This, then, is the quality, the gift and grace of God, that we should strive first to equalize. If we could give something of a right Heart, all other givings would follow in their course. And this is the great moral mission of social and individual Man, in the infinite variety of their aptitudes and situations, — each to his work, with his own weapons. Some are to equalize God's gifts by warring with the oppression, the monopoly, the injustice, that restrain and confine His natural Bounty. Others are to equalize God's gifts, not by warring with the wrongdoer, for which they may have no fitness or faculty, but by sympathy with the wronged, by the tender spirit of Mercy, repairing in a measure by individual Beneficence the evils of Society. Some are to equalize God's gifts by extending Education, awakening the self-reverencing Mind, giving to it the spiritual armor that is mighty to pull down iniquity, and all sense of degradation. Some are to equalize God's gifts by spreading the Gospel, by preaching Christ to the Poor,— exalting the Valleys and making low the Hills, that the Glory of the Lord may be revealed, and all Flesh see it together from those spiritual heights that command a vision of our Immortality. And some are to equalize God's gifts, by showing how deeply this spirit has penetrated to their own hearts; by exhibiting in their own demeanor, in all the intercourses of Life, the example of a Christian estimation of our Brethren, of the Honor due to all men. In all these ways is the blessed Mission of Humanity carried on; — and if all work, in their own spheres and aptitudes, there will be realized all the Equality that spiritual man is concerned to see. The very Child does something to equalize God's gifts, when it reawakens the fading sense of youth and buoyant happiness in older hearts; or when, at a later age, by obedience and respect, and careful love, it compensates the toils, and lightens the load of life, — even as the Mother is equalizing the gifts of God when sheltering the helplessness of infancy, or dropping gentle wisdom into its unstored heart. Woman is equalizing the gifts of God by interweaving with manly life gentle thoughtfulness, domestic holiness, a tender refinement, and ideal grace; and Man is but acknowledging the debt, and contributing to equality, when sharing with her the products of his Strength, his Patience, his Genius, or his Toil. To each man has God given some peculiar gift, for the enriching of all the rest. And it is the Christian sentiment alone, the sense of spiritual relations, that directs all these *Gifts* to the centre of the common Good, that unites these various Missions for one End, and brings together, for purposes of equalization, the poor and the rich, the young and the old, the strong and the weak, the sound-hearted and the broken-hearted, the captive and the free.

6. (VIII. 16-24.) St. Paul carefully divests himself of all personal interest in the Bounty of the Churches. He associates *others* with himself, both in its collection and in its distribution, and he refuses to undertake the responsibility without inspection and control. Here is a great example: here is the rarest of unions, — the mixture of Prudence and Enthusiasm. This should be a Principle with all men in matters of Trust. We should put our Integrity into safe Custody. No man should lay himself open to a possible temptation of unknown power, — or feed the evil spirit of suspicion and calumny by rash and inconsiderate self-exposure. A *moral Principle* in practical affairs is here indicated, and should be religiously observed.* — The Brother whose praise was in all the Churches, and who was appointed to travel with St. Paul, is generally supposed to be St. Luke; but his Gospel, which is made the grounds of the supposition, was not written at this time. It is impossible to know who the two companions of Titus were, but there is no more probable conjecture than that they were Luke and Apollos.

7. (IX. 6.) Another principle of Charity stated in this argument is, that the Law of Love is the same as the Law of Labor. As is the sowing, so is the reaping. This Law is mentioned not to give life to the sentiment, which cannot be *created* by *such* calculations, — but to lead it on to a practical accomplishment, — to prevent it perishing in mere *feeling*.

* See pp. 243, 244.

He that soweth sparingly shall reap sparingly, — and he that soweth bountifully shall reap bountifully. He reaps the blessings of a satisfied benevolence, — the new strength given to the sentiment itself, — the harvest of healthy, happy, remunerating sympathies that spring up whenever Benevolence is carried into all available Action, — the cheerful views of Life, and the blessed connections which the Heart whose love works outwardly holds even with the sorrows that it heals. Contrast with this the sickly feebleness, the discontent, and miseries, of inoperative Benevolence, of the voluptuaries of feeling, — when the Heart is not justified and blessed by the Conscience: how helpless in itself, how morbid, wearying, and offensive to others, this sentimental sympathy! In sympathies, as in moral trials and difficulties, there is no blessing from God, except upon the Doer of the work. Christ's Picture of the Judgment is drawn from the contrasted harvests to be gathered by those who sow their sympathies in the furrows of human wants and woes, and by those who kill them by Self-love, or fastidiously preserve them in a Napkin. "Then shall the King say unto them on his right hand, Come, ye blessed of my Father, and inherit the Kingdom prepared for you; for I was an hungered and ye gave me meat, — I was thirsty and ye gave me drink, — I was a stranger and ye took me in, — naked and ye clothed me, — I was sick and ye visited me, — I was in prison and ye came unto me. Then shall the righteous answer him, saying, Lord, when saw we thee an hungered and fed thee? or thirsty and gave thee drink? — when saw we thee a stranger and took thee in? or naked and clothed thee? — or when saw we thee sick or in prison, and came unto thee? And the King shall answer, Verily, I say unto you, Inasmuch as ye have done it unto one of the least of these my brethren, ye have done it unto me. Then shall they, on the left hand, answer him, saying, Lord, when saw we thee an hungered, or athirst, or a stranger, or naked, or sick, or in prison, and did not minister unto thee? Then shall he answer them, Verily, I say unto you, Inasmuch as ye did it not to one of the least of these, ye *did it not to me*."

St. Paul even refers to the temporal blessing which by natural and beautiful consequence is often shed on free and abounding Love, — increasing its basket and its store, so that the generous hand is refilled by God. He quotes a single verse of the 112th Psalm, — the whole of which is to the same purport: "He hath scattered his blessings; he hath given to the poor; his goodness shall endure for ever, — his horn shall be exalted with honor."

8. Another Rule and Principle of Christian Charity, stated in the seventh verse of the ninth chapter, is, that in these interests the Heart is our Counsellor: "Let every one give as he purposeth in *his heart*." The instincts of the Heart are to be reverently regarded, — and its dictates to be submitted to no revisal, except that of its wiser, purer, and more conscientious *self*. The Heart to the Christian, is what Genius is to the Intellectual world. It is the inspiration of the Man, — his highest utterance, — the very blossoming of our moral Nature, when it is cul-

tivated, and carefully guarded from external stain and injury. Prudence, Self-interest, calculations of lower Expediency, have no right to revise or reverse its Dictates. Only a higher, wider, and more far-seeing Benevolence should control instinctive Benevolence. Only *the Wisdom* of Love should modify or guide its impulse; and no faculty but that of Conscience is qualified to give a direction to the Heart.

If we give under any guidance or revision but that of Love itself, we give grudgingly, — and God loves a cheerful giver, — it is the only thing in our work of Charity that He does love, — for what in His sight is the outward gift!

9. (11 – 15.) And lastly, it is declared to be one of the operations, and beatitudes, of practical Mercy, that it causeth thanksgiving to God; — by our means it makes the wretched feel that God cares for them; — it introduces them into His family, and gives them at once Brethren and a Father. In this respect, reversing the sentiment of the Psalm, our Goodness extends to God, as well as to the saints that be upon the Earth.

St. Paul trusted that the influence of Gentile Liberality, in this respect, would heal the one great division of the Early Church, — that it would reconcile the Jewish Christian to his Gentile Brother, — inasmuch as it would show *experimentally* the blessed fruits that the spirit of the Gospel could produce and ripen, independently of ritual and ceremonial relations: — "By the experience of this ministration, they will glorify God for the subjection which ye profess unto the Gospel of Christ, and for the sincerity of your fellowship with them and with all men; earnestly longing also after you, in their prayer for you, on account of the exceeding grace of God in you." And thus should all religious divisions be healed, — and thus only can they be healed, — by that unquestionable evidence which the life of Love can give, that through all varieties of form one spirit breathes, — that under all outward differences beats the Brother's heart; — and so the excellent bond of Charity take the place of all less universal less spiritual, less essential, affinities between Man and Man, — between Man and God.

Now "Thanks be to God," says St. Paul, contemplating this its wide and blessed operation, "for his unspeakable Gift!" — for this Christian sentiment that makes a human Brotherhood, — a Universal Church, — identifying general with individual good. There is no unity, no equality, no principle of lasting peace among men, except this. It is that vital Love which, existing in God Himself, gave birth to the Universe, — which redeemed it and created it anew in Christianity, — and which, in proportion as it spreads through human hearts, becomes the bond and blessing of the world. To have it, and extend it from heart to heart, is our Christian Mission.

"A new Commandment give I unto you, that ye love one another." "Herein is my Father glorified, that ye bear much fruit: so shall ye be my disciples."

PART III.

(CHAPS. X. – XIII.)

ST. PAUL'S CLOSING VINDICATION

OF HIS

APOSTOLIC CHARACTER AND AUTHORITY

AGAINST HIS DETRACTORS AT CORINTH.

PART III.

(CHAPTERS X.–XIII.)

SECTION I.

ST. PAUL'S OPPONENTS.—HIS PERSONAL INFIRMITIES.—HIS APOSTLESHIP DENIED: ITS WARRANTS.—HIS DISINTERESTEDNESS MISCONSTRUED.—SELF-COMMENDATION: ITS FOLLY, AND ITS JUSTIFICATION.

CHAPS. X., XI.

X. 1. Now I, Paul, who in presence am lowly among you,
2 but when absent am bold towards you, beseech you by
the meekness and gentleness of Christ; I entreat you that,
when present, I may not be bold with that confidence
wherewith I reckon to be bold against those who reckon
3 of us as if we walked according to the flesh. For walk-
4 ing in the flesh, we do not war according to the flesh: for
the weapons of our warfare are not carnal, but mighty
5 through God to the pulling down of strongholds: casting
down imaginations, and every high thing that exalteth itself against the knowledge of God, and bringing into cap-
6 tivity every thought to the obedience of Christ; and being
ready to avenge all disobedience, when your obedience is
completed.

7 Consider the things that are before your face. If any
one trust in himself that he is Christ's, let him of himself
think this again, that as he is Christ's, so also are we.
8 For if I should boast somewhat more of our power, which
the Lord hath given us for your edification, and not for
9 your destruction, I should not be put to shame: that I
10 may not seem as if I would terrify you by Letters. For
his Letters, they say, are weighty and powerful, but his
11 bodily presence is weak, and his speech of no account. Let
such an one reckon on this, that such as we are in word
by Letters when absent, such also are we, when present,
12 in deed: For we dare not to rank, nor to compare, ourselves
with some that commend themselves; but they, measuring themselves by themselves, and comparing themselves
13 with themselves, are not wise. But we will not glory of
things beyond our measure, but according to the measure
of the line which God hath determined for us, to reach
14 even unto you. For we stretch not beyond ourselves as if
not reaching unto you, for even as far as you have we
15 come, first, with the Gospel of Christ. Not boasting of
things beyond our measure, in other men's labors, but
having a hope, when your faith is increased among you,
16 to be enlarged according to our measure beyond you, so
as to preach the Gospel beyond your limits, and not to
boast in another man's line, of things made ready for us.
17 But he that glorieth, let him glory in the Lord. For not
18 he that commendeth himself is approved, but he whom
the Lord commends.

XI. 1. Would that ye would bear with me a little in this
2 foolishness; yea, do bear with me! For I am jealous
over you with a godly jealousy, for I espoused you to
one husband, to present you as a chaste virgin to Christ.
3 But I fear, lest by any means, as the serpent beguiled

Eve through his subtilty, that so your minds should be
4 corrupted from the simplicity that is in Christ. For if
he who cometh preacheth another Jesus whom we have
not preached, or if ye receive another spirit which ye
did not receive from us, or another Gospel which ye
5 have not obtained, ye might well bear with him. But I
reckon myself in nothing behind the very chief of the
6 Apostles: for though I am rude in speech, yet not so in
knowledge; but altogether have we been made manifest
7 in all things among you. Or have I committed an offence in humbling myself that ye might be exalted, because I have preached to you the Gospel of God as a
8 free gift. I spoiled other churches, taking their pay for
9 your services; and when present with you and in want,
I was chargeable to no one: for the brethren who came
from Macedonia supplied my wants, and in every respect I have kept myself from being a burden to you,
10 and will so keep myself. It is the truth of Christ in me,
that this boasting of mine shall not be stopped in the
11 regions of Achaia. Wherefore? Because I love you
12 not? God knoweth. But I do this, and will do it, that
I may cut away occasion from them who desire an occasion, — that in that in which they glory they may be
13 found even as we. For such are false Apostles, deceitful workers, transforming themselves into the Apostles of
14 Christ. And no wonder, for Satan himself is transformed
15 into an angel of light. Therefore it is no great thing, if
his ministers also are transformed as ministers of righteousness, — whose end shall be according to their works.
16 — I say again, let no one think me foolish; but even if
so, then even as a fool receive me, that I too may boast
17 myself a little. That which I speak in this confidence
of boasting, I speak not after the Lord, but as it were
18 in foolishness. Since many glory after the flesh, I will

19 glory also. For, wise yourselves, ye endure the foolish
20 sweetly. For ye endure it, if any one bring you into
bondage, if any one make a prey of you, if any one
plunder you, if any one exalt himself, if any one smite
21 you on the face. I speak with reference to reproach, as
that we had been weak. But in what any one is bold,
22 in foolishness I speak, in that I am bold also. Are they
Hebrews? So am I. Are they Israelites? So am I.
23 Are they of the seed of Abraham? So am I. Are
they ministers of Christ? I am more so; I speak as
one foolish: in labors more abundant; in blows beyond
24 measure: in prisons more frequent; in deaths oft. From
the Jews five times received I forty stripes save one.
25 Thrice was I beaten with rods; once was I stoned;
thrice I suffered shipwreck; a night and a day I passed
26 in the deep. In journeyings often, in perils of rivers, in
perils of robbers, in perils of mine own people, in perils
of the Heathen, in perils in cities, in perils in the wilderness, in perils in the sea, in perils among false brethren.
27 In weariness and painfulness, in watchings often, in hunger and thirst, in fastings often, in cold and nakedness.
28 Besides these outward things, there is that pressure upon
29 me daily, — the care of all the Churches. Who is
weak, and I not weak? Who is offended, and I burn
30 not? If I must boast, I will boast of the things that
31 concern my infirmities. The God and Father of our
Lord Jesus Christ, He, the blessed for ever, knoweth that
32 I lie not. In Damascus, the Ethnarch of Aretas the
King guarded the city of the Damascenes, desirous to
33 apprehend me. And through a window, in a basket, was
I let down by the wall, and escaped his hands.

If we peruse this Epistle, as we always ought to do, on the same principle on which we should read an ordinary Letter, it is impossible not to be struck, not only with the abruptness of the transition, but with the whole change of tone and manner, from the commencement of the Tenth Chapter. From the warm language of undoubting confidence recommending a work of charity and Love, in which it is all along assumed that their willing hearts, full of Christian sentiment, would require little urging from colder obligation and principle to move them to free and generous action, the writer passes, on the instant, into a different region of feeling; adopts the guarded manner of elaborate self-defence, of wounded and disappointed affections, vindicating their claims; and a style at times so severe, that the commentators, in a somewhat faulty spirit of criticism, — the natural man in them exulting in the Apostle's pungency, — call our attention to it as the perfection of bitter irony. Hence it has been maintained that these Chapters cannot form the genuine continuation of the Epistle: but as there is no doubt that they are St. Paul's, a theory has been suggested to account for their existence in their present place. It is highly unnatural, it is said, that after the effusion of tenderness, the gush of affection, which is expressed in the chapters immediately preceding, St. Paul should so abruptly resume the tone of reproach and self-assertion in which the remainder of the Epistle is written. It is supposed to be more probable, that this latter portion had been written before the arrival of Titus from Corinth. After that arrival, and the account it brought of their zeal, penitence, and affection, St. Paul, it is argued, felt as very sensitive people do, when having complained of those they love they find that the affection which they feared was on the decline is as warm towards them as ever. Paul appears to be at a loss to find words expressive enough of his kindness to the Corinthians. "His heart is enlarged," he wishes to embrace them all, to inclose them in that heart which had ached a short time before, and manifested its pain and disappointment in words of expostulation. How could the tone of complaint, and even of threatening, be thus suddenly resumed? How could such an affectionate writer allow the Epistle to end so coldly, and with such self-reference, as it does at present? Hence it is conjectured, that from Chapter Ten to the close had been in preparation when Titus arrived with the intelligence that the Corinthian Church, notwithstanding its errors and credulity, was, in the main, still sound in heart and mind; — that then Paul laid it aside, as not in harmony with the revulsion of feeling thus produced, — but that the reverence with which those near him looked on his writings, did not allow them to destroy this fragment; that having been originally intended for the Corinthians, it was afterwards inserted at the end of the copies of the Letter which was actually sent, as an Appendix; — and finally, that the ancient copyists, not being very exact about marks of distinction between different parts of a composition, and not knowing under what title to give this fragment, united it, as a component part, with the Second Epistle to the Corinthians.

Ingenious as this statement unquestionably is, it is pure conjecture; nor is the difficulty so great, the order of thought and feeling so inexplicable, as to oblige us to have recourse to an hypothesis so entirely arbitrary. St. Paul, in these chapters, is in fact addressing himself to persons totally different from those with whom his tones of expostulation had melted into tenderness, and his wounded sympathies into the overflowing warmth of recovered confidence. It is certainly in the moment when the heart has *regained* a friend,—warmed anew into the confidingness of a love over which some chill of distrust had passed,—that we are least capable of measured restraint in the expression of the affections, and totally incapable of barbing our words with severe and lacerating truth. But there is a third Party concerned in these Epistles, *remaining* in hostile relation to St. Paul,—professing neither affection for his Person, nor respect for his Authority,—a faction of rival Teachers, not raw converts thoughtlessly misled, but artful and designing misleaders,—and a residue of the Church, to whom the mixture of dross and clay with which these Teachers adulterated the Gospel, proved more acceptable than the pure and uncompromising form of Spiritual Christianity. It is to these two parties, the false Apostles, as they are here called, and their abettors, who with the spiritual nature of Christianity wished to conjoin the carnal dependence of Judaism, its spirit of reliance on outward qualifications, that these chapters are addressed. We might, for the purpose of illustration, conceive of a disaffected Province, in which simple and unlettered men, with vague and crude notions of the fundamental principles of Society, and of their own Duties and Rights as members of a Community, — exposed on all sides to the tempting Logic of convenience, had been led to the very brink of the practical assertion of false theories, destructive of the very existence of Civilization. Now such a Community, even when trembling on the verge of such evil, it is possible that a paternal Government by the exhibition of a generous sympathy with the sources of temptation, by the ready removal of all known causes of just offence, by instruction and persuasion, by salutary measures of conciliation and prevention, might win over, out of all the elements of disorder, to a sound mind, an enlightened conscience, and a well-affected heart, — and yet totally fail of producing any such impression on the leaders and instigators of the movement, — on men not honestly misled by false Doctrines, but cunningly pursuing selfish purposes, working their own ends out of popular ignorance, credulity, and ruin. The utmost mildness might be due to one of these parties, and the utmost severity to the other, — and if we supposed the rightful and legitimate Authority to issue an address of Remonstrance and Persuasion, to the tempted and the misled, it might most properly speak only of forbearance, forgiveness, and even strong confidence in their healthier and better mind, — whilst to the tempters and prime movers, baffled, but not penitent, it spoke only of the vindication of its outraged Law, and in the threatenings of its Power. The Ecclesiastical condition we are considering was exactly parallel to this state of things. St. Paul was the rightful Authority, the legitimate Apostle; — there was a disaffected Church which he had won over by his meekness, earnestness, and love, to the simplicity that is in Christ; and there was a residue of factions and interested partisans, upon whom these mild measures produced no effect, and to whose evil and unthwarted influences the Church could not be left exposed. There is a limit to the degree in which the evilly disposed ought to be treated with forbearing gentleness, and that limit arises out of the necessity of protecting the peace and virtue which they have the power to corrupt and disturb. It was a party of this description, whatever may have been their number, of which we are not informed, who kept alive the flames of religious animosity and personal pretensions. They professed to teach a more legitimate Gospel, which was in fact a compound of Christianity, Judaism, and speculative Philosophy, — and to be in their own Persons clothed with an Apostolic Authority more genuine than St. Paul's. The peace of the Church, the claim upon him of those who adhered to his person and authority, required that these pretensions should be discomfited and their evil source exposed. It is therefore after lavishing the persuasive resources of his Christian mind and spirit upon those who were open to conviction, that he closes with this address to those whose element was strife, and warns them that their Power for evil must be destroyed.

Against the Church he would direct no severity; he would employ only the meekness and gentleness of Christ; he would not even come to them whilst the shadow of misunderstanding lay between them;—but when Love and admonition had done all that moral instruments can effect,—then must it be shown that his forbearance had not its source in weakness; and the incorrigible, whom Persuasion could not render penitent, a just Authority must render *powerless.* This is the mingled sentiment of the sixth verse, the desire to reserve all exercise of *Power* until Moral influences had gained over all those with whom there was any chance of their being effectual: "We shall be ready to avenge all disobedience, when your obedience shall be complete." What was the nature of the Power to be employed, and of the Punishment threatened, is open to conjecture, and the subject is usually dismissed by saying, that the supernatural energy of the Apostle would be called in to make clear his own superiority, and punish the offenders. But these are the methods of triumph which the passionate and unspiritual mind is always eager to see adopted; and it would be as impossible to prove that they were ever contemplated by St. Paul, as that this would be a justifiable employment of such gifts, or at all suitable to the exigency of the case. St. Paul himself speaks of very different instruments as the weapons of his warfare; but Miracles are the ready means by which those, whose dependence is on an external and sensible Revelation, are impatient to have every difficulty cut. Yet Christ's treatment of the Pharisees, that piercing flash of indignant Truth into the most secret bosom of craft and pretension, that terrible self-revealing to which no answer was possible or was attempted, might have been enough to show, without Miracle, the natural ascendency of such spirits, and the power of unsparing exposure, whenever it chooses to exert it, which Truth has over Falsehood, Light over Darkness, Good over Evil. To that perfect Being who exhibited every phase of Power, this prerogative of Light and Purity of soul could never be his loved or favorite exercise; but still, that the representation of spiritual energy might be complete, we have that one example of the meekest of beings, by the force of Truth, withering selfishness and falsehood, as by fire from Heaven. In the conflict with Darkness and Evil, Light and Goodness require no weapons, but those which their own essence supplies, and for him who can utter the " Word of God," "it is quick and powerful, sharper than any two-edged sword, piercing even to the dividing asunder of flesh and spirit, a discerner of the intents and thoughts of the heart." Accordingly, in the passage before us, speaking of the instruments to be directed against the devices of the enemies of the pure Gospel, St. Paul says, with no apprehension of their insufficiency, " The weapons of our warfare are not carnal, but mighty, through God, to the pulling down of strongholds, — overturning imaginations and every high thing that exalteth itself against the knowledge of God, — and bringing into captivity every thought to the obedience of Christ." We can readily conceive, without having recourse to Miracle, what overwhelming exposure an Apostolic Mind could make of the false, selfish, and carnal spirit cloaked in Religion. And such a mind, we religiously believe, is ripening for our own day, and will have its Mission from God, and its Prophet-tongue unloosed, when the fulness of time is come.

We have in these chapters strange glimpses opened to us of the kind of difficulties and embarrassments which a Preacher of pure Spirituality in Religion, of the simplicity that is in Christ, encountered in those days; and if they do not well accord with that traditional halo with which we have surrounded the person and authority of an Apostle, they may bring us nearer to the reality of things, and show us the patient and struggling means, in the midst of low and discomfiting circumstances, by which, in every age, Truth and Principle must be contented, slowly, and as they can, to advance their standard. We are apt to imagine an Apostle as one, before whose heavenly and inspired Eloquence, Doubt and Obduracy vanished; and in the presence of whose sainted Authority, every resisting tendency was reverèntly silent. Nothing could be farther from the truth than this unexamined remnant of our childish thought, and *that*, not from any deficiency of Power or Holiness in the first Preachers of the Gospel, but because Evil and Error are real and stubborn Forces, and yield not without a conflict. We shall attempt to make distinct, from the slight traces here recorded, the nature and spirit of that opposition, which obliged St. Paul to have recourse to two expedients, which, except with reference to the exposure of such evils, he tells us, the spirit of Christianity did not permit, — to threaten, and to boast, — to vindicate his own claims as an Apostle on the love and submission of the Church, against those who denied them.

1. There was something, we know not what, in the person and demeanor of Paul, which his enemies at Corinth did not scruple to place in humiliating contrast with the loftiness and energy of his intellectual character. This indeed is the lowest weapon of vulgar minds: but such was the fact, — and we must remember that this was facilitated by the natural tendencies of the Greek Mind, which made a Worship of the Beautiful; and whose highest accomplishment, in their social relations, was a faultless Eloquence. It would appear that these personal characteristics, whatever they were, threw a certain air of feebleness over his actual presence and address, so that it was not difficult to contrast, mockingly, the fire and energy of the Writer, with the weakness and unimposingness of the Speaker. If this was so, we shall never be able to rectify our associations in this matter: nor is a severe reduction of our impressions to historic reality on such a point worth the labor it would cost; for who could readily mould his mind to the habitual remembrance that Paul at Athens, that Paul before Agrippa, that Paul before the Council of his Nation, was feeble and ineffective in form and utterance. Such, however, is the relation of physical Powers to the effect of Oratory, that this is possible; and if we sought a case in point, we might remember that Burke, who possessed a mind the richest in the gifts of Eloquence that the

world has ever seen, and who, moreover, had most of the external advantages that aid these powers, through some infelicity of Delivery, rarely could command the attention of an Audience, for the very Speeches that every one was eager to read. It may be true, therefore, which indeed could hardly be affirmed unless it was true, and which Paul does not concern himself to deny, "that though his Epistles were weighty and powerful, his bodily presence was weak, and his speech contemptible." The use that was made of this circumstance, was an attempt to reduce the boldness of his writing to the insignificance of his personal address, to represent it as mere boasting, — distant thunder, which when it came near would sink into a murmur. This, which gives its point to the first verse, is obscured by the word "base," which does not convey the proper image: "Now I, Paul, who when present among you, am of poor and mean appearance, but when absent am bold towards you, beseech you not to cause it to come to pass, that when present I should be bold towards you with that confidence, with which I must be bold against those who represent me as actuated by a worldly and carnal spirit, walking according to the flesh." There is a tradition in the Church respecting the personal appearance of St. Paul in conformity with these notices, mentioned by Chrysostom, and I believe even by earlier writers; but it would be impossible to determine whether this was history, or merely of the nature of a myth, framed into correspondence with the supposed sense of these passages.

2. It was objected to St. Paul, that, as he had no

personal intercourse with Christ, he could not possess the requisite qualifications of an Apostle, and that his Authority was not legitimately derived, but rested on grounds of his own stating. To this he replies by an appeal to the signs of his Apostleship, which were afforded by the successful labors of his Preaching and his Life. The actual conversion of a large part of the Heathen world to Christianity through his means, was a claim to be recognized as a Minister of Christ, which they who used the objection could not advance upon their own behalf. They had done nothing but commend *themselves*, — they had come to the scene of another man's labors, and on the very field which he had won from Idolatry and fertilized with living waters, sought to calumniate his name. I shall give the spirit of the argument from the seventh verse to the end of the chapter, which is scarcely intelligible in our Translation: "Consider that which lies before your eyes, — that which I have done in your Church, which owes to me even its origin. If we are bold in word, we are also earnest in work; for we are not of those who are content with a simple commendation of themselves, having no deeds to praise them; for they, taking an inward measurement of themselves, not according to their outward performances, but according to their self-appreciation, are not wise; but *we* will not boast beyond the measure of what *we have done*, but only within that sphere of action which God has assigned to us, and which has brought the Gospel even unto you; — nor in reaching you have we overstepped the lands that lay along the line of our Apostolic progress, but have to come to you in the regular succession of our course, and we have hope that you will not detain us longer on our way, — that when your faith is strengthened you will suffer us to pass on, in our glorious Mission to the regions that lie beyond you; for as our works and not ourselves must praise us, we have not entered into other men's labors, nor, like you false Apostles, sought glory in another's sphere, from things which *his* toil had made ready to their hands. But let him who would glory, glory in his Lord's work done, — for it is not he who commendeth himself that is approved, but he whom his Master commendeth."

3. What might least be expected, it was imputed to some consciousness of an usurped office that he preached the Gospel of God freely, and refused to derive from it the support for which he was dependent on the liberality of other Churches; "Have I committed an offence in humbling myself that ye might be exalted, because I have preached to you the Gospel of God without cost? I spoiled other Churches, taking wages from *them* that I might minister to you; and, when I was present with you and wanted, I was chargeable to no man, for the brethren who came from Macedonia supplied my want, and in every respeet I have kept myself from being burdensome unto you, and so will keep myself." This peculiar course St. Paul may originally have been led to adopt in relation to Corinth from the noted worldliness and venality of that city, and from the crowd of Sophists and Rhetoricians who, under the name of public Teachers, had become a proverb

of pretension and corruption; and it would appear, from the twelfth verse of the eleventh chapter, that he thought his example in this matter necessary to shame and restrain the charge of an inordinate thirst of gain, from those whom he calls the false Apostles: "What I have done, that I will continue to do, that I may cut off occasion from those who seek occasion, — that in that wherein they boast, they may be found even as we."

Against such opposition, amidst such low contention, had St. Paul to maintain his way; and it belongs to the inherent greatness of his character, that though we read these things, no association with them attaches to his image in our thoughts. The circumstances, however mean and limiting, which magnanimity conquers, fall away from around the noble spirit, and show it only in the meekness and loftiness of its Power. No life can be low where great ends are followed; and the spirit that will not work its Mission within the trammel of Circumstance will never be a true servant of that Master who came to found a Kingdom of Heaven upon Earth, and who had to associate with him in the work men of another spirit than his own, and even the traitor who sold away his life.

It is evident that the self-commendations of these men must have had their effect, else would St. Paul never have exposed the counterfeit by bringing his own merits into contrast; — but as there might be a time when a patriot would have to speak of what he had done without reward, in order to shame some official plunderer on pretence of service, so if the

Corinthians, as is stated in the twentieth verse, "bore it patiently when such men brought them into bondage, made a prey of them, took their goods, lorded it over them," it was full time to hear the boasting of one who had truly served them, and sought nothing in return. Such boasting, indeed, Paul repeatedly says, is in itself utterly foolish; but it might do good, if it exposed those who boasted without a cause. How tender is the reproach addressed to the Church whom St. Paul won to the Truth, and whom such men for a moment could deceive! "I am jealous over you, with a zeal for God, for I have espoused you to one husband, and thought to present you as a chaste Virgin to Christ. But I fear lest as the serpent beguiled Eve, that your minds may be corrupted from the simplicity that is in Christ. If, indeed, they that intruded themselves among you preached another Jesus whom I had not preached, or enriched you with a spirit and a Gospel which you had not received from us, then might you have reason to have given them the hearts that were ours, — but we are in no respect inferior to the chief of the Apostles, and this has been made thoroughly manifest among you all."

And then, he recounts his sufferings, indignities, and humiliations as the world and his enemies would think, but the true honors of him who gloried in some share of his Master's Cross, and thanked God that he was found worthy to suffer shame for his name. We know nothing finer in sentiment, or eloquence, than that passage, — "If I must boast, I will boast of my infirmities." To boast of degrading sufferings, of stonings, stripes, and bonds, of fastings, cold, and nakedness, — this was a glory in which his traducers would not seek to rival him. To suffer, that others may rejoice, — to be poor, that others may be truly rich, — to watch and guard, and open our own bosoms to the world, that others may have peace and blessing and the life of Life, — this is the captivity which Christ leads captive, the servitude which God exalts into that Greatness which belongs to those whom He has anointed with His own Spirit.

SECTION II.

ST. PAUL'S QUALIFICATIONS NOT FROM HIMSELF, BUT OF GOD'S GRACE. — HIS VISIONS AND REVELATIONS. — THE ACCOMPANIMENT OF THE CHASTENING THORN IN THE FLESH. — HIS CLAIMS UPON THE LOVE AND OBEDIENCE OF THE CORINTHIAN CHURCH. — HIS PRAYER THAT THEIR RESTORATION TO A CHRISTIAN MIND MAY REDUCE THEIR APOSTLE TO THE LEVEL OF THEIR BROTHER. — EXHORTATION AND BENEDICTION.

CHAPS. XII., XIII.

XII. 1. Boasting, indeed, is not expedient for me: I will
2 come then to visions and revelations of the Lord. I
knew a man in Christ, fourteen years ago, — whether in
the body, I know not; or out of the body, I know not;
God knows, — who was caught up to the third heaven.
3 And I knew such a man, — whether in the body, or out
4 of the body, I know not; God knows, — how that he was
caught up into paradise, and heard unspeakable words
5 which it is not permitted to any man to utter. For such
an one will I glory: but for myself I will not glory, un-
6 less of mine infirmities. For though I should desire to
glory, I shall not be a fool, for I will speak the truth;
but I forbear, lest any one should account me above that
which he sees me, or what he heareth of me.
7 And that I should not be too much exalted through the

abundance of these revelations, there was given to me a
thorn in the flesh, an angel of Satan to buffet me, that I
8 should not be too much exalted. For this thing I besought the Lord thrice, that it might depart from me.
9 And he said unto me, "My grace is sufficient for thee:
for my strength is made perfect in weakness." Most
gladly, therefore, will I rather boast in my infirmities,
10 that the power of Christ may tabernacle with me. Wherefore I am well pleased in infirmities, in reproaches, in
necessities, in persecutions, in straits for Christ's sake;
11 for when I am weak, then am I strong. I have become
a fool: ye have forced me to it; for I ought to have been
commended by you, for I am nothing behind the chief of
12 the Apostles, though I am nothing. Verily the signs of
an Apostle have been wrought among you in all persever-
13 ance, in signs, and wonders, and mighty deeds. For
what is there wherein ye were inferior to the other
Churches, unless it be that I myself was not burdensome
14 to you? Forgive me this wrong. And now I hold myself in readiness for this third time to come unto you,
and I will not be burdensome to you; for I seek not yours,
but you; for the children ought not to lay up for the pa-
15 rents, but the parents for the children. But I will very
gladly spend, and be spent, for your souls, even though
16 the more abundantly I love you, the less I be loved. But
be it so, I did not burden you; nevertheless, being crafty,
17 I caught you with guile? Did I make a gain of you, by
18 any of those whom I sent unto you? I desired Titus, and
with him I sent a brother. Did Titus make a gain of
you? Walked we not in the same spirit? Walked we
19 not in the same steps? Again, think ye that we excuse
ourselves unto you? Before the face of God, in Christ
we speak all these things, beloved, for your edification.
20 For I fear lest when I come I may not find you such as I

would, and that I may be found by you such as ye would
not: lest there be strifes, envyings, wraths, cabals, back-
21 bitings, whisperings, swellings, tumults. Lest when I come
again my God may humble me among you, and I shall
mourn for many of those who have sinned before, and
have not repented of the uncleanness, and fornication, and
lasciviousness, which they have committed.

XIII. 1. THIS is the third time I am coming to you: by the
mouth of two or three witnesses shall every word be es-
2 tablished. I told you before, and forewarn this second
time, as if I was present, though I am absent, those who
have heretofore sinned, and all others, that if I so come
3 again, I will not spare: since ye seek a proof of Christ
speaking in me, who towards you is not weak, but is
4 mighty among you. For though he was crucified in
weakness, he yet liveth by the power of God. And we
also are weak in him, yet shall we live with him towards
5 you, by the power of God. Try yourselves whether ye
be in the faith: prove your own selves. Or, know ye
not of yourselves whether Jesus Christ is in you? If
6 not, ye are without proof. But I trust ye shall know that
7 we are not unproved. Now I pray to God that ye do no
evil; not that we may appear approved, but that ye
should do that which is right, though we may be unproved.
8 For we can do nothing against the truth; but for the
9 truth. For we are glad when we are weak, and ye are
10 strong, — and even this we wish, your restoration. Wherefore I write these things, when absent, that when present
I may not act severely, according to the power which the
Lord hath given me for edification, not for destruction.
11 Finally, brethren, farewell. Be reconciled; be of good
comfort; be of one mind; live in peace; and the God
12 of love and peace shall be with you. Greet one another
13 with an holy kiss. All the saints salute you.

14 The grace of the Lord Jesus Christ, and the love of God, and the fellowship of the Holy Spirit, be with you all!

True greatness and simplicity of mind, are in nothing more apparent than in their occasional violations of the conventional Moralities of life. They know when to overstep that network of artificial manners and restraints, by which the lower minds sometimes attempt to place them in a false position. And this they do by having the courage to be true, — by showing outwardly what they are feeling inwardly, — by having the sincerity to *speak* what every body knows must be passing in their thoughts. Self-commendation is one of the gravest offences against conventional Morals. It belongs to the class of odious *Manners*, of which Society is often more intolerant than it is of absolute *Vices*. This is one of the cases in which evil suppresses evil, not by eradicating, but by forcing it into concealment. It is for the most part our own Self-Esteem, that makes us so determined to suppress the exhibitions of it in others; for to none is it so little offensive, as to those men of large Nature, of calm and self-relying hearts, who are completely free from it themselves. There is an *irritation* excited by the display of Self-Esteem, which too plainly shows that our Vanity is encroached upon by the Vanity of another; and that the universal suppression of this folly in good Society is rather a compact of decorum, an agreement to avoid mutual offence, than any proof of a prevailing humility or self-forgetfulness. And the minds that are most consumed by Self-Love, are those which adopt the most self-depreciating language, for they well know that this is the only means to extort the flattery of Society. Society, which resents Self-commendation, is, in fact, propitiated by the opposite exhibition of Self-depreciation; and so there is often an ostentatious sacrifice of Self-praise, as the means of evoking that other Praise which is infinitely sweeter. It has often been observed, that nothing is more dangerous than to take at their word those who are in the habit of depreciating themselves; — the Mask is instantly taken off, the tone altered, and the object of the feigned humility exposed. Every one knows, indeed, that some expression of self-disparagement is the common trick by which to direct attention to one's self, and draw forth the very dregs of commendation from the most reluctant lips; — but there are certain refined modes of laying this snare, which by deceiving the common observer are eminently successful, — and even self-deceive the wily heart that practises them. The vainer minds turn to account the conventional rule which prohibits the display of Self-Esteem, by such large sacrifices to the letter of this Propriety, by such open exhibitions of the opposite extreme, that notwithstanding their violations of its spirit, Society is flattered by the seeming concession and takes up their praise; whilst the truly modest minds, elevated far above Self-Esteem by the very nature of their pursuits, by the character of their desires, unconsciously observe these conventional Laws, yet can on occasion set them aside with a manly simplicity, whenever any interest higher than

Self-Love requires that *the Truth* should be spoken, even though it must assume the painful form of Self-Commendation. It may happen as it did at Corinth, that Truths, Facts, Influences, of the last importance in their moral action on mankind, may be staked on the personal reputation of an Individual, and may be obscured and discredited by the successful machinations of an Impostor. Would St. Paul have been deserving of praise for his humility, and not rather of the gravest condemnation for sacrificing the perilled interests of Christianity to a conventional propriety, if through the small fear of speaking the Truth about himself, of being charged with self-glory, he had abandoned the Corinthians, and the cause of the free Gospel at Corinth, to the unworthy arts of those who traduced his character that they might preach another Gospel? As he had nothing of that false humility which seeks praise by Self-depreciation, he had nothing of that slavish subjection to social fear which would forbid him to speak the Truth respecting himself, when the influence of evil men was to be restrained. And it is the privilege of Simplicity, of Singleness of mind, should occasion arise, to speak of itself without offence, — of its labors, services, and the interests in which it has spent its strength. A vain, self-seeking man cannot speak of himself with weight and effect in any circumstances. A man of small mind will not comprehend the magnanimity of speaking of one's self with the same openness as of an indifferent person, if any good cause, or noble interest, is perilled on his personal credit. As it is Meekness, and not fiery passion, whose resistance to wrong is the most impressive, and Gentleness that wears the glory of the loftiest Courage, so it is only the utmost simplicity and singleness of purpose that can gracefully break through conventional restraints, and speak of itself, when need is, with a just self-respect. The occasion, indeed, must be one *that requires* such an effort; but if so, this mingled humility in relation to self, and loftiness of bearing in relation to any confided trust, is only one example of those contrasted functions, which real greatness of Mind always knows how to reconcile. He who loves the Truth must bear any thing for Christ's sake and the Gospel's, even the pain of vindicating his personal credit, though a generous spirit would more willingly bear its cross.

At Corinth, men attached to material views of Religion, to the superstitions and the machinery of worship, had opposed themselves to the simplicity of the Gospel Salvation as Paul preached it; and to seduce his converts, they did not hesitate to undermine his reputation, and even to deny his Apostolical Authority. We have seen, in the last Section, how he adopts Boasting as a strange work; as in itself an utter folly, and only justifiable by the absolute necessity of exposing false pretensions in connection with pernicious purposes; and how at last,—in the true spirit of Christianity, that Greatness consists in Service, that the greatest Benefactor of his race is the greatest of Men, — he reposes on his infirmities, his humiliations, his indignities, his persecutions, as his highest honors, — confident that in this kind of glory, the spirit of the World, and of the World's philosophy, would enter into no rivalry with the Apostle of the Crucified.

In the Chapters now before us, in the continued contrast between himself and those who wished to seduce the Corinthians from the Simplicity that is in Christ, he rests on those distinctions which, as not flowing from personal qualifications, exclude all Self-glory; which were conferred upon him by Divine favor, and were not the fruits of his own natural powers, — on those visions and revelations of the Lord which had impressed a new direction on his life, and which, he here tells us, still blessed and sustained his Christian course, — and on the infirmities which, offered to the great work with a true devotion, Divine Grace made sufficient for its purposes, — the weakness wherein, as in Gethsemane's trembling and tears, God perfects His strength, — the degradations, "the necessities and distresses for Christ's sake," the obscure, dishonored life, the utter poverty of the Instrument, by which the living Word, the spirit of the Gospel, a heavenly Energy, worked out its glorious triumphs on the Earth. So much indeed does he shrink from self-exaltation, that he marks these visions and revelations as not belonging to his own individuality; and speaks of himself, as of another person in whose distinctions he had no intrinsic participation: "I knew a man in Christ, who (whether in the body I cannot tell, or whether out of the body I cannot tell, God knoweth) was caught up to the third heaven. Concerning such an one I will glory; yet of myself I will not glory, save in my infirmities." "By the figurative expressions here employed, St. Paul seems merely to indicate the nearness in which his spirit found itself to God." * To be carried into Heaven, to be in the bosom of the Father, is the Jewish expression to denote the possession of a divine communication; and the local presence of God they called the third Heavens, beneath which were the starry Heavens, and lower still the aërial Heavens, the region of the atmosphere and clouds. Thus it is said of Moses, "There arose not a prophet since in Israel like unto Moses, whom the Lord knew face to face"; † — and Christ says of himself and of his own communications with God, — whilst yet, in bodily presence, he was standing on the Earth and speaking to his Disciples, — "And no man hath ascended up to Heaven, but he that came down from Heaven, even the Son of man, *which is* in Heaven." It is evident from this, that by being in Heaven was meant, not a local translation, but a state of intimate communication with God.

It is remarkable that though St. Paul mentions "these visions and revelations" as evidences *to himself* of Divine Favor, and, *to his own spirit*, undoubted signs of his Apostleship; yet, except so far as they had outward fruits and *wrought in Power*, he was aware that they could not be adduced to other minds as Proofs of any thing; he was aware of the futility, as an argument, — of the danger, as an instrument of deception with credulous minds, of appealing to secret experiences as the grounds of spir-

* Billroth. † Deut. xxxiv. 10.

itual distinction. This would be to claim a glory which lay out of the reach of observation, — and which therefore with no modesty or justice could be urged on another's belief. St. Paul's claim to such communications was indeed supported by all the properties that could win personal confidence; but he does not on this account found pretensions to higher spiritual distinctions than he manifests in word and deed. He would make his claim to the secret influence of Divine Grace strictly commensurate with its outward works. The rapt elevations of the spirit are rarely asserted with such a calm suppression of the wildness of enthusiasm, of the extravagance of the Mystic who demands general belief in visions which he acknowledges no eye has witnessed but his own. The sixth verse, taken into connection with what precedes, presents the rarest combination of frames of mind, — a confidence in ecstatic visions with the clearest discrimination of their relations to others, with no desire to convert a secret experience into an argument or a claim, except so far as it could be manifested by undoubted signs: "I might indeed glory in such things, and speak only the truth, but I forbear, lest any one should think concerning me, above that which he *seeth me to be, or that which he heareth from me.*"

As a further reason for the suppression of spiritual Pride in himself, St. Paul mentions, that these visions and revelations were not only free gifts of God, to which he had no intrinsic claim, but, as if purposely to check self-exaltation, they were accompanied by, or at least coexisted with, some personal infirmity, some source of humiliation in the work of his Apostleship, which plainly manifested that the Divine treasure was in an earthern vessel, and that the excellency of the Power was of God, and not of him. What was this "thorn in the flesh," this instrument of the Tempter to prove him, we are not informed; — and on such points we would allow no license to idle conjecture. But though we cannot specify it, the connection seems to identify it with that defect or weakness, whatever it was, mentioned in the last Section, which threw an air of feebleness over his personal ministrations, and enabled his enemies to represent him as "in bodily presence weak, and in speech contemptible." We might naturally suppose that the treatment he received at Corinth, and his anxiety for their restoration to the Truth, was the "thorn in the flesh," a pain of spirit sharper than a wound; but the prayer to God that it might depart from him, with the answer, that through the very instrumentality of weakness, if grace was sought, a Divine Power would act, exclude this interpretation, and limit it as something personal to St. Paul. Otherwise he could not say, "Since grace is sufficient for even me, and God's strength made perfect in my weakness, most gladly therefore will I glory in these infirmities, that the power of Christ may rest upon me." It was after the weakness of that Prayer, thrice renewed, "O my Father, if it be possible, let this cup pass from me," that heavenly grace strengthened the filial spirit, which ever closed its supplication with the divine sentiment, "Nevertheless, not my will, but thine, be done." It was through his humiliation that God wrought his exaltation. Amid the insults of the Judgment Hall he is most divinely great. The mocking crown of thorns has become an everlasting crown of glory. A suffering and rejected Saviour rules the world. Spiritual greatness made the Cross a Throne. It was this power of Christ that the Apostle prayed might rest upon him, that when he was weak, then might he know strength.

At the eleventh verse there is a sentiment expressed, which has a very general application to the social relations of our ordinary life: "I am become a fool in glorying; *ye have compelled me*, for I ought to have been commended by you, since I am in nothing inferior to the very chiefest Apostles, though I am nothing." It is as if he had said, "The invidious necessity of urging my own claims as a Representative of Christ you have imposed upon me; you compel me to manifest myself, that I may shield you from impostors." And so it is in Life, often only to evil issues: we "*compel*" the self-regarding elements of character into dangerous activity; — we excite by mere friction the latent sparks of self-esteem. Our own tone and manner often provoke the social evils that we most dislike. Self-assertion, — when it has not St. Paul's excuse, that higher interests demand it, — will yet break out under injustice, indifference, or careless scorn. We show ourselves insensible to Affection, and when we "*compel*" it, unhappily indeed and unwisely for itself, to assert its claim, we forget that the exaction is only the retribution of our own conduct, and that, in some way or other, we must pay our debt to every human being, — and that in the debts of Kindness, as in every other obligation of life, instant acknowledgment is the only smooth and honest clearance. We do cold and scanty justice, and the Self-Love that consideration and gentle courtesy would have extinguished, is aggravated by resentment, or quickened into open arrogance. We check what we deem vanity or presumption by hard and insulting resistance, and it burns out against us with ungovernable violence. How many a Parent suppresses the affection and loving confidence of a child by an over-anxiety to acquire it, — by seeming to exact that which must be free and spontaneous, — by encumbering with self-consciousness the natural spring of the heart, — "compelling" it, by the most beautiful Law of its nature, to shrink into concealment and reserve! How many a Parent stimulates immoderate self-esteem by injudicious efforts to destroy it, by provoking a jealous self-observation, and fixing a dangerous degree of attention on the wounds and mortifications of the most irritable class of our feelings! There are some minds that act as conductors to every selfish and fiery spark that lurks in human character, so that no evil is latent in their presence; and others that come in contact with no noxious element, and by the unaffected spirit of a just respect and concession, awaken only the better and happier parts of character, and take away all nourishment from the spirit of self-assertion. Nothing is more common than to find the same man, in one Society or under one treatment, sensible, temperate, and modest, — in another Society or under another treatment, irritable, swollen, and overbearing. And though no offence can *be excused* because of such provocations, it may be *accounted* for, — and it may be avoided, and "Woe unto him by whom the offence cometh." It is the spirit of Justice and Generosity in ourselves,— of true respect for every social and individual Right, which awakens all the answering Virtues in other minds, and "*compels*" Self-Love itself to die out in presence of the Meekness of wisdom. The Presumption that will resist Rebuke will utterly change its character before a truly courteous spirit, — and it would be well to remember that every time an evil tendency is touched, it is confirmed. And an evil spirit cannot be conquered by an evil spirit. Satan will not cast out Satan. The offences that provoke Anger, Anger will not cure. Our own form of Self-Love will not extinguish the Self-Love of another. This is the divine prerogative of the spirit of Goodness. We can only overcome Evil with Good.

The remainder of the Epistle is occupied by St. Paul's entreaty to the Corinthians that all opposition between them — all conflicting pretensions, whatever could give occasion to the humiliation of either — should disappear, — that *they* should return to a Christian simplicity and purity of Life, and that *he* should have no more occasion to speak of Authority or Reproof, but of brotherly Intercourse and Love. Twice had he altered a purpose of meeting them in person, that such close intercourse might not be embittered by the necessary severity of moral disapproval; but this forbearance could no longer be exercised lest its motive should be misconstrued, and the consciousness of weakness which his Opponents attributed to him, gain credence among them. Yet, disappointed as he had been, wounded in affection, slighted in Authority, most gladly would he forfeit all opportunity of proving that the Power of Christ was with him, by any manifestation on their part that the Spirit of Christ *was in them.* To those who, in contumacy and unbelief, *sought a proof* that Christ spoke in him, his weakness and humiliation, like that of his Crucified Master, would not prevent the Power of God being manifested through him, to the confusion of his Enemies: "For as he who was crucified in weakness, yet liveth by the power of God, — so we who have a fellowship in his weakness, shall also live to manifest the *power* of God towards you." "Try *yourselves*, whether ye be in the faith; prove your own selves. Know ye not your own selves whether Jesus Christ is in you? Are ye in this respect destitute of proof? But I trust you will know that I am not without proof that the power of Christ is with me. Yet I pray to God that I may be called to no exercise of authority against you; — I pray, not that *I* may triumph, but that *you* may do that which is good, even though, through your penitence and restoration, my Authority should have no outward vindication. We shall rejoice that in this respect we remain as weak and unavenged, if you will be strong; for this only we pray for, *even your Restoration.* Finally, Brethren, farewell: be perfect; encourage and sustain each other; be of one mind; live in peace; — and the God of Love and Peace shall be with you."

We have now examined in detail the two Epistles to the Corinthians. They are the liveliest Pictures we possess of the first action of Christianity on the Religion and Philosophy of the Grecian mind. They exhibit, principally, the doctrines of spiritual Freedom; of the direct intercourse of each soul with God without the aid of System, Ritual, or Priesthood; of the moral Salvation of *oneness* of heart and will with God, through the influence and attraction of His Christ: — and in their antagonist aspects, they are mainly opposed to asceticism; to superstitious observances; to violations of unity of spirit; and to the admixture of speculative tenets with the simple acceptance of Christ as the Law of Life, the Image of the Father, and the First-born of many brethren to the holy Power and glorious Liberty of a Son of God. It is impossible, I think, to read these two Epistles, and doubt that they sprung out of real circumstances, — that they are the intense strivings of an earnest and generous Mind with an existing condition of things. They are not Epistles that one who wished to do honor to Christianity would have forged. They exhibit no marvellous triumphs; — they detail freely the humiliations of its Apostle; — they show him meeting suspicions and charges, which many a man, with not more virtue, but with less love, would deem himself exonerated from noticing; they show the patience and perseverance with which the divine Charity that seeketh not its own can contend for Holiness and Truth, against their natural enemies. The authenticity of these Epistles is unquestioned by any man, whether believer or unbeliever; and so far as Christianity can be established by these Epistles, *it is established.*

And if, in the last place, and for a moment, we refer to the confirmations which these Epistles afford of that Gospel of the Kingdom, which reveals in God a Father, — in Christ His holy human child, what all the Brethren of that Master are called to be, — and in the human Soul, to use another Apostle's words, "a partaker of the divine Nature," a spirit capable of being taken into communion with the Father of Spirits, — we do so, because, standing against the general faith of Christendom, we are required by every Law of humility to lose no opportunity of examining whether the decisive testimony is with us or against us. The Father, — the Christ, — the spirit of God in every soul, willing, if we will permit it, to draw us more and more towards him who had that Spirit without measure, — is not this the substance of Christianity, the Gospel lesson of God and of Religion?

Had we to state our Faith, it should be in the Baptismal formula: "The Father, — the Son, — the Holy Spirit" in Man, to unite him with God the Source, and with Christ the Perfection of his Nature; — or, it should be in the Benediction which closes this Epistle: "The grace of the Lord Jesus Christ, and the love of God, and the fellowship of the Holy Spirit, be with you all!" Amen.

THE END.

www.ingramcontent.com/pod-product-compliance
Lightning Source LLC
LaVergne TN
LVHW020100110826
845151LV00001B/35

* 9 7 8 1 4 2 5 5 4 5 0 5 5 *